Other Kaplan Books for College-Bound Students

College Admissions and Financial Aid

Parent's Guide to College Admissions
Straight Talk on Paying for College: Lowering the Cost of Higher Education
The Unofficial, Unbiased Guide to the 328 Most Interesting Colleges

Test Preparation

ACT
AP Biology
AP Calculus AB: An Apex Learning Guide
AP Chemistry: An Apex Learning Guide
AP English Language & Composition: An Apex Learning Guide
AP English Literature & Composition
AP Macroeconomics/Microeconomics: An Apex Learning Guide
AP Physics B: An Apex Learning Guide
AP Psychology
AP Statistics: An Apex Learning Guide
AP U.S. Government & Politics: An Apex Learning Guide
AP U.S. History: An Apex Learning Guide
AP World History
Domina el SAT: Preparate para tomar el examen para ingresar a la universidad
Frankenstein: A Kaplan SAT Score-Raising Classic
PSAT
Ring of McAllister: A Score-Raising Mystery Featuring 1,046 Must-Know SAT Vocabulary Words
SAT
SAT 1600
SAT Math Mania
SAT Math Workbook
SAT Vocab Velocity
SAT Verbal Workbook
SAT Vocabulary Flashcards Flip-O-Matic
SAT II: Biology E/M
SAT II: Chemistry
SAT II: Literature
SAT II: Mathematics Levels IC and IIC
SAT II: Physics
SAT II: Spanish
SAT II: U.S. History
SAT II: World History
What Smart Girls Know About the SAT

SAT® II
WRITING

2004–2005 Edition

By the Staff of Kaplan, Inc.

Simon & Schuster

New York · London · Sydney · Toronto

Kaplan Books
Published by Simon & Schuster
1230 Avenue of the Americas
New York, New York 10020

For bulk sales to schools, colleges, and universities, please contact Order Department, Simon & Schuster, 100 Front Street, Riverside, NJ 08075. Phone: (800) 223-2336. Fax: (800) 943-9831.

Contributing Editor: Jon Zeitlin
Project Editor: Déa E. Alessandro
Cover Design: Cheung Tai
Interior Page Layout: Renée Mitchell
Production Manager: Michael Shevlin
Managing Editor: Déa E. Alessandro

Manufactured in the United States of America.
Published simultaneously in Canada.

March 2004
10 9 8 7 6 5 4 3 2 1

ISBN 0-7432-5196-2
ISSN 1087-7916

CONTENTS

HOW TO USE THIS BOOK

For more than 50 years, Kaplan has prepared students to take SATs. Our team of researchers and editors knows more about SAT preparation than anyone else, and you'll find their accumulated experience and knowledge in this book. As you work your way through the chapters, we'll show you precisely what knowledge and skills you'll need in order to do your very best on the Writing Test. You'll discover the most effective way to tackle each part of the test, and you'll reinforce your studies with ample practice drills. At the back of the book you'll find five full-length, in-format tests with answer keys and detailed explanations. We'll even help you estimate what your results might have been on the actual SAT II: Writing Subject Test. In addition, the Ready, Set, Go! section contains helpful tips on beating test stress while you're preparing for the test and pulling off a victory on test day.

The Best Prep

Kaplan's five practice tests give you a great prep experience for the SAT II: Writing Test. Try using the first practice test as a diagnostic and the rest to gauge your improvement.

Get Ready to Prep

If possible, work your way through this book bit by bit over the course of a few weeks. Cramming the week before the test is not a good idea; you probably won't absorb much information, and it's sure to make you more anxious.

If you find that your anxiety about the test is interfering with your ability to study, start off by reading the Stress Management chapter in this book. It provides many practical tips to help you stay calm and centered. Use these tips before, during and after the test.

The Basics

The first thing you need to do is find out what's on the SAT II: Writing Test. The section of this book called "The Basics" will provide you with background information about the Subject Tests and what they're used for. It will also explain the structure of the SAT II: Writing Test, show samples of each question type, and give the ground rules for the essay section.

Time to Time It

The best way to take our practice tests is with time limits. If you simulate true test conditions while you prep, you'll be better prepared for the real thing.

Kaplan's Five Practice Tests

Use the first of our five practice tests as a "diagnostic." Take it under timed conditions—that is, spend the first 20 minutes on the essay section and the last 40 minutes on the multiple-choice section. Read through all of the explanations closely, even for the questions that you got right. Following these steps will allow you to assess confidently your strengths and weaknesses. Take the second, third, and fourth practice tests when you feel ready for them. We suggest saving the final practice test for a dress rehearsal the week before test day.

The SAT II: Writing Question Types

This book is set up to let you focus on particular Writing Test question types. Your performance on the diagnostic test will give you an idea of which question types are easy for you and which are harder. Budget your study time accordingly. Spend a lot of time with the chapters dealing with question types that you found challenging. But don't neglect your strengths—after all, you want them to remain strengths right up to test day. Read through each chapter and do each drill carefully—at least once. Don't worry about timing too much as you progress through the book. It's more important to get the knowledge and skills down first.

Kaplan's Writing Clinic

Many students particularly dread the essay section of the Writing Test. But you don't need to worry. We've boiled down the skills you need for the essay into Principles of Good Writing. In the Writing Clinic chapter, we'll show you ways to start writing better—right now.

Before the Test

A day or two before the test, be sure to review Chapter 9: The Final Countdown. It includes essential "how-to" tips that will help you get the upper hand on test day. Then, relax! Read a book or watch a movie. And most important, get a good night's sleep. How you approach the days leading up to the test really does matter!

On the morning of the test, eat a light breakfast (nothing too heavy to make you sleepy!) and quickly review a few questions if you feel like it (just enough to get you focused). Walk into the test center with confidence—you're ready for the challenge!

Other Test-Prep Resources

While this book contains everything that you need to prepare for the Writing Test, the College Board has released some test questions that you might want to tackle. *Taking the SAT II: Subject Tests* has some sample questions. More important, *The Official Guide to SAT II: Subject Tests* has a full-length, in-format test. Try working on this test under testlike conditions.

A Special Note for

International Students

If you are an international student considering attending an American university, you are not alone. Over 582,000 international students pursued academic degrees at the undergraduate, graduate, or professional school level at U.S. universities during the 2001–2002 academic year, according to the Institute of International Education's Open Doors report. Almost 50 percent of these students were studying for a bachelor's or first university degree. This number of international students pursuing higher education in the United States is expected to continue to grow. Business, management, engineering, and the physical and life sciences are particularly popular majors for students coming to the United States from other countries.

If you are not a U.S. citizen and you are interested in attending college or university in the United States, here is what you'll need to get started.

- If English is not your first language, you'll probably need to take the TOEFL® (Test of English as a Foreign Language) or provide some other evidence that you are proficient in English. Colleges and universities in the United States will differ on what they consider to be an acceptable TOEFL score. A minimum TOEFL score of 213 (550 on the paper-based TOEFL) or better is often required by more prestigious and competitive institutions. Because American undergraduate programs require all students to take a certain number of general education courses, all students—even math and computer science students—need to be able to communicate well in spoken and written English.

- You may also need to take the SAT® or the ACT®. Many undergraduate institutions in the United States require both the SAT and TOEFL of international students.

- There are over 3,400 accredited colleges and universities in the United States, so selecting the correct undergraduate school can be a confusing task for anyone. You will need to get help from a good advisor or at least a good college guide that gives you detailed information on the different schools available. Since admission to many undergraduate programs is quite competitive, you may want to select three or four colleges and complete applications for each school.

- You should begin the application process at least a year in advance. An increasing number of schools accept applications year round. In any case, find out the application deadlines and plan accordingly. Although September (the fall semester) is the traditional time to begin university study in the United States, you can begin your studies at many schools in January (the spring semester).

- In addition, you will need to obtain an I-20 Certificate of Eligibility from the school you plan to attend if you intend to apply for an F-1 Student Visa to study in the United States.

*Kaplan English Programs**

If you need more help with the complex process of university admissions, assistance preparing for the SAT, ACT, or TOEFL, or help building your English language skills in general, you may be interested in Kaplan's programs for international students.

Kaplan English Programs were designed to help students and professionals from outside the United States meet their educational and career goals. At locations throughout the United States, international students take advantage of Kaplan's programs to help them improve their academic and conversational English skills, raise their scores on the TOEFL, SAT, ACT, and other standardized exams, and gain admission to the schools of their choice. Our staff and instructors give international students the individualized attention they need to succeed. Here is a brief description of some of Kaplan's programs for international students:

General Intensive English

Kaplan's General Intensive English classes are designed to help you improve your skills in all areas of English and to increase your fluency in spoken and written English. Classes are available for beginning to advanced students, and the average class size is 12 students.

TOEFL and Academic English

This course provides you with the skills you need to improve your TOEFL score and succeed in an American university or graduate program. It includes advanced reading, writing, listening, grammar, and conversational English. You will also receive training for the TOEFL using Kaplan's exclusive computer-based practice materials.

SAT Test Preparation Course

The SAT is an important admission criterion for American colleges and universities. A high score can help you stand out from other applicants. This course includes the skills you need to succeed on each section of the SAT, as well as access to Kaplan's exclusive practice materials.

Other Kaplan Programs

Since 1938, more than 3 million students have come to Kaplan to advance their studies, prepare for entry to American universities, and further their careers. In addition to the above programs, Kaplan offers courses to prepare for the ACT®, GMAT®, GRE®, MCAT®, DAT®, USMLE®, NCLEX®, and other standardized exams at locations throughout the United States.

Applying to Kaplan English Programs

To get more information, or to apply for admission to any of Kaplan's programs for international students and professionals, contact us at:

Kaplan English Programs
700 South Flower, Suite 2900
Los Angeles, CA 90017, USA
Phone (if calling from within the United States): 800-818-9128
Phone (if calling from outside the United States): 213-452-5800
Fax: 213-892-1364
Website: www.kaplanenglish.com
Email: world@kaplan.com

FREE Services for International Students

Kaplan now offers international students many services online—*free of charge!*
Students may assess their TOEFL skills and gain valuable feedback on their English
language proficiency in just a few hours with Kaplan's TOEFL Skills Assessment.
Log onto www.kaplanenglish.com today.

---

*Kaplan is authorized under federal law to enroll nonimmigrant alien students. Kaplan is accredited by ACCET (Accrediting Council for Continuing Education and Training).

SECTION ONE:
The Basics

CHAPTER 1

ABOUT THE SAT II: SUBJECT TESTS

You're serious about going to the college of your choice. You wouldn't have opened this book otherwise. You've made a wise decision, because this book can help you to achieve your college admissions goal. It'll show you how to score your best on the SAT II: Writing Test. But before you begin to prepare for the Writing Test, you need some general information about the SAT IIs and how this book will help you prep. That's what this chapter is about.

Common Questions about the SAT IIs

Before you dive into the specifics of the content of the SAT II: Writing Test, check out the following FAQs (frequently asked questions) about SAT II Subject Tests in general. The information here is accurate at the time of publication but it's a good idea to check the test information on the College Board Web site at www.collegeboard.com.

What are the SAT IIs?

Known until recently as the College Board Achievement Tests, the SAT IIs focus on specific disciplines in five general subject areas: English, History, Mathematics, Sciences, and Languages. Each Subject test lasts one hour and consists almost entirely of multiple-choice questions, except for the Writing Test, which has a 20-minute essay section and a 40-minute multiple-choice section.

How Do the SAT IIs Differ from the SAT I?

SAT I is largely a test of verbal and math skills. True, you need to know some vocabulary and some formulas for SAT I; but it's designed to measure how well you read and think rather than what you know. SAT IIs are very different. They're designed to measure what you know about specific disciplines. Sure, critical reading and thinking skills play a part on these tests; but their main purpose is to determine exactly what you know about writing, math, history, chemistry, and so on.

"What Does That Spell?"

Originally, *SAT* stood for *Scholastic Aptitude Test*. When the test changed a few years ago, the official name was changed to *Scholastic Assessment Test*. In 1997, the test makers announced that *SAT* no longer stands for anything, officially.

Well, What Do You Know?

The SAT IIs are intended to find out what you know about specific subjects.

Double Duty

Colleges use your SAT II scores in both admissions and placement decisions.

Call the College

Many colleges require you to take certain SAT II: Subject Tests. Check with all of the schools you're interested in applying to before deciding on which tests to take.

The Writing Test's designed to determine how familiar you are with the rules of standard written English. Don't worry, you don't ever have to explain the rules. But you must apply them: to your own writing (in the essay section) and to others' writing (in the multiple-choice section).

How Do Colleges Use the SAT IIs?

Many people will tell you that the SATs (I and II alike) measure only your ability to perform on standardized exams—that they measure neither your reading and thinking skills nor your level of knowledge. Maybe they're right. But these people don't work for colleges. Those schools that require SATs feel that they are an important indicator of your ability to succeed in college. Specifically, they use your scores in one or both of two ways:

- To help them make admissions decisions
- To help them make placement decisions

Like the SAT I, the SAT II: Subject Tests provide schools with a standard measure of academic performance, which they use to compare you to applicants from different high schools and different educational backgrounds. This information helps them to decide whether you're ready to handle their curriculum.

SAT II scores may also be used to decide what course of study is appropriate for you once you've been admitted. A low score on the Writing Test, for example, may mean that you have to take a remedial English course. Conversely, a high score on the Math Level IIC Test may mean that you'll be exempted from an introductory math course.

What SAT IIs Should I Take?

The simple answer is: Take the ones that you'll do well on. High scores, after all, can only help your chances for admission. Unfortunately, many colleges demand that you take particular tests, usually the Writing Test and/or one of the Math Tests. Some schools will give you some choice in the matter, especially if they want you to take a total of three Subject Tests. So before you register to take any tests, check with colleges to find out exactly which tests they require. Don't rely on high school guidance counselors or admissions handbooks for this information. They might not give you accurate details.

When Can I Take the SAT IIs?

Most of the SAT II: Subject Tests are administered six times a year: in October, November, December, January, May, and June. A few of the Subject Tests are offered less frequently. Due to admissions deadlines, many colleges insist that you take SAT IIs no later than December or January of your senior year in high school. You may even have to take them sooner if you're interested in applying for "early admission" to a school. Those schools that use scores only for placement decisions may allow you to take the Subject

Tests as late as May or June of your senior year. You should check with colleges to find out which test dates are most appropriate for you.

You can take up to three Subject Tests on the same day. If you register for the Writing Test, it must be taken first on test day.

How Do I Register for the SAT IIs?

The College Board administers the SAT II: Subject Tests, so you must sign up with them. The easiest way to register is to obtain copies of the *SAT Registration Bulletin* and *Taking the SAT II: Subject Tests*. These publications contain all of the necessary information, including current test dates and fees. They can be obtained at any high school guidance office or directly from the College Board. You can re-register by telephone if you have previously registered for an SAT I or SAT II test.

How Are the SAT IIs Scored?

Like the SAT I, SAT II Subject Tests are scored on a 200–800 scale. In the case of the Writing Test, you'll receive separate subscores for both the essay and multiple-choice sections. You'll also receive an overall score on the 200–800 scale, which is calculated by combining the two separate subscores. Later chapters of this book will have more to say about scoring.

What's a "Good" Score?

That's tricky. The obvious answer is: the score that the college of your choice demands. Keep in mind, though, that SAT II scores are just one piece of information that colleges will use to evaluate you. The decision to accept or reject you will be based on many criteria, including your high school transcript, your SAT I score, your recommendations, your personal statement, your interview (where applicable), your extracurricular activities, and the like. So, failure to achieve the necessary score doesn't automatically mean that your chances of getting in have been damaged. For those who want a numerical benchmark, a score of 600 is considered very solid. (Note that as of 2002, the Score Choice option to withold a score you're unhappy with has been eliminated for the SAT II subject tests.)

If you take the Writing Test, you can order three graded copies of your essay through College Board's Writing Sample Copy Service. If you get a high score on the essay section, it's in your interest to use this service. Adding another piece of strong writing to your application, it goes without saying, will help your chances for admission.

What Should I Bring to the SAT IIs?

It's a good idea to get your test materials together the day before the tests. You'll need an admission ticket; a form of identification (check the *Registration Bulletin* to find out what is and what is not permissible); a few sharpened No. 2 pencils; a good eraser; and a calculator (for Math Levels IC

Do the Legwork

Want to register for the SAT II or get more info? Ask your school counselor's office for the *SAT Registration Bulletin*, which contains a Registration Form, test dates, fees, and instructions.

By mail: Mail in the Registration Form to the College Board.

Online: If you have a credit card, you can register online at http://www.collegeboard.com

By phone: You can register by phone *only if* you have registered for an SAT I or SAT II test in the past.

College Board SAT Program
P.O. Box 6200
Princeton, NJ 08541–6200
(609) 771–7600
www.collegeboard.com

Early Bird

If you intend to use Score Choice and/or the Writing Sample Copy Service, make sure that you take your SAT II: Subject Tests well in advance of college deadlines.

Not Like High School

The SAT II: Subject Tests are very different from the ones you've taken in high school. All questions are worth the same number of points, and you don't get any credit for showing your work.

Don't Get Lost

Learn SAT II directions as you prepare for the tests. You'll have more time to spend answering the questions on test day.

and IIC). If you'll be registering as a standby, collect the appropriate forms beforehand. Also, make sure that you have good directions to the test center. (We even recommend that you do a dry run getting to the site prior to test day—it can save you the grief of getting lost!)

SAT II Mastery

Now that you know a little about the SAT II: Subject Tests, it's time to let you in on a few basic test taking skills and strategies that can improve your scoring performance. You should practice these skills and strategies as you prepare for your SAT IIs.

Use the Test Structure to Your Advantage

The SAT II: Subject Tests are different from the tests that you're used to taking. On your high school exams, you probably go through the questions in order. You probably spend more time on hard questions than on easy ones, since hard questions are generally worth more points. And you often show your work since your teachers tell you that how you approach questions is as important as getting the right answers.

Well, forget all that! None of this applies to the SAT IIs. You can benefit from moving around within the tests, hard questions are worth the same points as easy ones, and it doesn't matter how you answer the questions or what work you did to get there—only what your answers are.

The SAT IIs are highly predictable. Because the format and directions of the SAT II: Subject Tests remain unchanged from test to test, you can learn how the tests are set up in advance. On test day, the various question types on the tests shouldn't be new to you.

One of the easiest things you can do to help your performance on the SAT IIs is to understand the directions before taking the test. Since the instructions are always the same, there's no reason to waste a lot of time on test day reading them. Learn them beforehand, as you work through this book and study the College Board publications.

Many SAT II questions are arranged by order of difficulty. Not all of the questions on the SAT IIs are equally difficult. The questions often get harder as you work through different parts of the test. This pattern can work to your benefit. As you work, you should always be aware of where you are in the test.

When working on more basic problems, you can generally trust your first impulse—the obvious answer is likely to be correct. As you get to the end of a test section, you need to be a bit more suspicious. Now the answers probably won't come as quickly and easily—if they do, look again because the obvious answers may be wrong. Watch out for answers that just "look right." They may be distracters—wrong answer choices deliberately meant to entice you.

You don't need to answer the questions in order. You're allowed to skip around on the SAT II: Subject Tests. High scorers know this fact. They move through the tests efficiently. They don't dwell on any one question, even a hard one, until they've tried every question at least once.

When you run into questions that look tough, circle them in your test booklet and skip them for the time being. Go back and try again after you've answered the more basic ones—if you've got time. On a second look, troublesome questions can turn out to be remarkably simple.

If you've started to answer a question but get confused, quit and go on to the next question. Persistence may pay off in high school, but it usually hurts your SAT II scores. Don't spend so much time answering one hard question that you use up three or four questions' worth of time. That'll cost you points, especially if you don't even get the hard question right.

The SAT IIs have a "guessing penalty" that can actually work in your favor. The College Board likes to talk about the guessing penalty on the SAT IIs. That's a misnomer. It's really a wrong answer penalty. If you guess wrong, you get penalized. If you guess right, you're in great shape.

The fact is, if you can eliminate one or more answer choices as definitely wrong, you'll turn the odds in your favor and actually come out ahead by guessing. The fractional points that you lose are meant to offset the points you might get "accidentally" by guessing the correct answer. With practice, however, you'll see that it's often easy to eliminate several answer choices on some of the questions.

The SAT II answer grid has no heart. It sounds simple, but it's extremely important: Don't make mistakes filling out your answer grid. When time is short, it's easy to get confused going back and forth between your test booklet and your grid. If you know the answers, but misgrid, you won't get the points. Here's how to avoid mistakes.

Always circle the questions you skip. Put a big circle in your test booklet around any question numbers that you skip. When you go back, these questions will be easy to relocate. Also, if you accidentally skip a box on the grid, you can check your grid against your booklet to see where you went wrong.

Always circle the answers you choose. Circling your answers in the test booklet makes it easier to check your grid against your booklet.

Grid five or more answers at once. Don't transfer your answers to the grid after every question. Transfer them after every five questions. That way, you won't keep breaking your concentration to mark the grid. You'll save time and gain accuracy.

Look for Clues

Where a question appears on an SAT II test can tell you something about how to approach it. Many questions on the Subject Tests are arranged in order of difficulty—easier questions first, harder questions last.

Skipping Allowed

You should do the questions in the order that's best for you. Don't pass up the chance to score easy points by wasting time on hard questions. Skip hard questions until you've gone through every question once. Come back to them later, time permitting.

Guessing Rule

Don't guess, unless you can eliminate at least one answer choice. Don't leave a question blank, unless you have absolutely no idea about it.

Hit the Spot

A common cause of major SAT II disasters is filling in all of the questions with the right answers—in the wrong spots. Every time you skip a question, circle it in your test booklet and be double sure that you skip it on the answer grid as well.

Think First

Always try to think of the answer to a question before you shop among the answer choices. If you've got some idea of what you're looking for, you're less likely to be fooled by "trap" choices.

Speed Limit

Work quickly on easier questions to leave more time for harder questions. But not so quickly that you lose points by making careless errors. And it's okay to leave some questions blank if you have to— even if you leave a few blank, you can still get a high score.

A Strategic Approach to SAT II Questions

Apart from knowing the setup of the SAT II: Subject Tests that you'll be taking, you've got to have a system for attacking the questions. You wouldn't travel around an unfamiliar city without a map, and you shouldn't approach the SAT IIs without a plan. What follows is the best method for approaching SAT II questions systematically.

Think about the questions before you look at the answers. The College Board loves to put distracters among the answer choices. Distractors are answers that look like they're correct, but aren't. If you jump right into the answer choices without thinking first about what you're looking for, you're much more likely to fall for one of these traps. And on the Writing Test essay, think about the topic before you begin to write.

Guess—when you can eliminate at least one answer choice. You already know that the "guessing penalty" can work in your favor. Don't simply skip questions that you can't answer. Spend some time with them in order to see whether you can eliminate any of the answer choices. If you can, it pays for you to guess.

Pace yourself. The SAT II: Subject Tests give you a lot of questions in a short period of time. To get through the tests, you can't spend too much time on any single question. Keep moving through the tests at a good speed. If you run into a hard question, circle it in your test booklet, skip it, and come back to it later if you have time.

You don't have to spend the same amount of time on every question. Ideally, you should be able to work through the more basic questions at a brisk, steady clip, and use a little more time on the harder questions. One caution: Don't rush through easier questions just to save time for the harder ones. The basic questions are points in your pocket, and you're better off not getting to some harder questions if it means losing easy points because of careless mistakes. Remember, you don't get extra credit for answering hard questions.

Locate quick points if you're running out of time. Some questions can be done more quickly than others because they require less work or because choices can be eliminated more easily. If you start to run out of time, locate and answer any of the quick points that remain.

CHAPTER 2

WRITING TEST OVERVIEW

Now that you know the basics about SAT II: Subject Tests, it's time to focus on the Writing Test. What's on it? How's it scored? After reading this chapter, you'll know just what to expect on test day.

Test Structure and Scoring

The hour-long SAT II: Writing Test is divided into two sections—an essay section and a multiple-choice section. The essay section, Part A, is 20 minutes long, while the multiple-choice section, Part B, is 40 minutes long. If you finish Part A in less than 20 minutes, you may move right into Part B.

In Part A, your task is to produce a well-organized and well-written essay on the assigned topic. You don't need any specific knowledge to complete the essay. In fact, the topic will be so broad in scope that you'll be able to write about what you know and are interested in. On recent Writing Tests, the topic has been presented in one of two basic forms. We'll show you both forms in this chapter.

In Part B, your task is to answer correctly as many of the multiple-choice questions as you can by applying your knowledge of standard written English to them. This section of the Writing Test consists of 60 questions. You'll get 30 "Usage" questions, 18 "Sentence Correction" questions, and 12 "Paragraph Correction" questions. They'll be arranged in the following order.

In a Nutshell

The Writing Test includes a 20-minute essay section and a 40-minute multiple-choice section. The essay section consists of a single assigned topic. The multiple-choice section consists of 60 questions, so you've got approximately 40 seconds to spend on each multiple-choice question.

How Part B Is Organized

- 20 Usage questions
- 18 Sentence Correction questions
- 12 Paragraph Correction questions
- 10 more Usage questions

Total: 60 Multiple-Choice Questions

The 48 Usage and Sentence Corrections are based on single, unrelated sentences on a variety of topics. The 12 Paragraph Correction questions are based on two brief essays, with six questions per essay.

Two-Timing

On test day, you'll be timed separately on Parts A and B. So you won't have to worry about accidently spending the whole 60 minutes on the essay.

Part A: The Essay

The directions for the essay come in two slightly different forms—you'll see one or the other. On test day, your test booklet may contain a set of essay directions that looks like the one below.

You have 20 minutes to write an essay on the following topic.

DO NOT WRITE AN ESSAY ON ANY OTHER TOPIC. AN ESSAY ON A DIFFERENT TOPIC IS UNACCEPTABLE.

This essay provides you with an opportunity to demonstrate how well you write. Therefore, you should express your ideas clearly and effectively. How much you write is much less important than how well you write; but to express your thoughts on the topic adequately you may want to write more than a single paragraph. Your essay should be specific.

Your essay must be written in the lines provided on your answer sheet. No other paper will be given to you. There is enough space to write your essay on the answer sheet if you write on every line, avoid wide margins, and keep your handwriting to a reasonable size.

Consider the following statement and assignment. Then write an essay as directed.

> **"Every cloud has a silver lining."**

<u>Assignment:</u>   Choose one example from personal experience, current events, or history, literature, or any other discipline and use this example to write an essay in which you agree or disagree with the statement above. Your essay should be specific.

WHEN THE PROCTOR ANNOUNCES THAT 20 MINUTES HAVE PASSED, YOU MUST STOP WRITING AND GO ON TO PART B OF THE TEST. IF YOU FINISH YOUR ESSAY BEFORE 20 MINUTES PASS, YOU MAY GO ON TO PART B.

YOU MAY MAKE NOTES ON THIS AND THE OPPOSITE PAGES. BUT YOU MUST WRITE YOUR ESSAY ON THE ANSWER SHEET.

Essentially, you've got to agree or disagree with the given statement by discussing an example of your choice.

On the other hand, your test booklet may contain a set of essay directions that looks like the one on the following page.

You have 20 minutes to write an essay on the following topic.

DO NOT WRITE AN ESSAY ON ANY OTHER TOPIC. AN ESSAY ON A DIFFERENT TOPIC IS UNACCEPTABLE.

This essay provides you with an opportunity to demonstrate how well you write. Therefore, you should express your ideas clearly and effectively. How much you write is much less important than how well you write; but to express your thoughts on the topic adequately you may want to write more than a single paragraph. Your essay should be specific.

Your essay must be written in the lines provided on your answer sheet. No other paper will be given to you. There is enough space to write your essay on the answer sheet if you write on every line, avoid wide margins, and keep your handwriting to a reasonable size.

Consider the following statement and assignment. Then write an essay as directed.

"I have learned many things that have helped me in life, but one thing that was especially valuable was _____."

Assignment: Write an essay that completes the statement above. Explain the reasons behind your choice.

WHEN THE PROCTOR ANNOUNCES THAT 20 MINUTES HAVE PASSED, YOU MUST STOP WRITING AND GO ON TO PART B OF THE TEST. IF YOU FINISH YOUR ESSAY BEFORE 20 MINUTES PASS, YOU MAY GO ON TO PART B.

YOU MAY MAKE NOTES ON THIS AND THE OPPOSITE PAGES. BUT YOU MUST WRITE YOUR ESSAY ON THE ANSWER SHEET.

Two Flavors

On test day, you've got to be prepared to handle either kind of essay topic. Keep in mind that the task in both is basically similar, despite their different appearances.

In this case, you've got to finish the statement first. Once you've got a complete statement, you must support it with evidence. At first, this kind of essay topic may look quite different to you than the other kind of essay topic. But your job is really the same in both—to develop an argument, to support it with evidence, and to write up the argument and evidence in a clear and effective way. Chapter 3 will show you how to do that.

Essay Scoring

Writing Test essays are scored "holistically." What does *holistically* mean? Simply put, your essay gets a single score—a number—that indicates its overall quality. This number takes into account such essay characteristics as organization, content, and grammar.

The number assigned to your essay will range from a high of 6 to a low of 1. The following chart illustrates the main criteria used to score your essay.

Essay Grading Criteria

⑥ **Outstanding Essay**—convincingly and insightfully fulfills the writing assignment; ideas are well developed, clearly presented, and logically organized; superior command of vocabulary, grammar, style, and accepted conventions of writing; a few minor flaws may occur.

⑤ **Solid Essay**—convincingly fulfills the writing assignment; ideas are adequately developed, clearly presented, and logically organized; strong command of vocabulary, grammar, style, and accepted conventions of writing; some minor flaws may occur.

④ **Adequate Essay**—fulfills the writing assignment; ideas are adequately developed, presented, and organized; satisfactory command of vocabulary, grammar, style, and accepted conventions of writing; some flaws may occur.

③ **Limited Essay**—doesn't adequately fulfill the writing assignment; ideas aren't adequately developed, clearly presented, or logically organized; unsatisfactory command of vocabulary, grammar, style, and accepted conventions of writing; contains many flaws.

② **Flawed Essay**—doesn't fulfill the writing assignment; ideas are vague; poorly presented, and not logically organized; poor command of vocabulary, grammar, style, and accepted conventions of writing; contains numerous serious flaws.

① **Deficient Essay**—doesn't fulfill the writing assignment; ideas are extremely vague, very poorly presented, and not logically organized; extremely poor command of vocabulary, grammar, style, and accepted conventions of writing; is so seriously flawed that basic meaning is obscured.

Your essay will be read and scored by two people. The scores that they assign to your essay will be added together to get a total score. This total score will range from a high of 12 to a low of 2. It will then be converted into a scaled score ranging from 20–80. This scaled score will account for one-third of your final Writing Test score.

Sample Essays

Below, you'll find six sample essays based on the two types of essay prompts. For each topic, we've shown a strong (5–6 range), a mediocre (3–4 range), and a weak (1–2 range) essay, along with "grader comments." Use these essays both to get a sense of the scoring process and as a standard by which to judge your writing. Revisit them as you work through chapter 3. In fact, you should write essays based on these topics after you've finished the material in chapter 3. Practice, after all, makes perfect!

Topic 1

<u>Directions:</u> You have 20 minutes to write an essay on the following topic.

DO NOT WRITE AN ESSAY ON ANY OTHER TOPIC. AN ESSAY ON A DIFFERENT TOPIC IS UNACCEPTABLE.

This essay provides you with an opportunity to demonstrate how well you write. Therefore, you should express your ideas clearly and effectively. How much you write is much less important than how well you write; but to express your thoughts on the topic adequately you may want to write more than a single paragraph. Your essay should be specific.

Your essay must be written in the lines provided on your answer sheet. No other paper will be given to you. There is enough space to write your essay on the answer sheet if you write on every line, avoid wide margins, and keep your handwriting to a reasonable size.

Consider the following statement and assignment. Then write an essay as directed.

> **"Every cloud has a silver lining."**

<u>Assignment:</u>   Choose one example from personal experience, current events, or history, literature, or any other discipline and use this example to write an essay in which you agree or disagree with the statement above. Your essay should be specific.

WHEN THE PROCTOR ANNOUNCES THAT 20 MINUTES HAVE PASSED, YOU MUST STOP WRITING AND GO ON TO PART B OF THE TEST. IF YOU FINISH YOUR ESSAY BEFORE 20 MINUTES PASS, YOU MAY GO ON TO PART B.

YOU MAY MAKE NOTES ON THIS AND THE OPPOSITE PAGES. BUT YOU MUST WRITE YOUR ESSAY ON THE ANSWER SHEET.

Sample Grade 6 Essay

When my mother and father divorced, I felt like it was the end of the world. It seemed as if a cloud had settled over me, and that there was no such thing as a reliable relationship anymore. But as I've grown older, I've actually come to appreciate the breakup. That's because the divorce has served to bring my family closer together than we might have been had my parents not separated.

❻ Is Outstanding

Six is the top of the scale. A grade 6 essay shows a superior command of vocabulary, grammar, and style. But an essay doesn't have to be perfect to merit a 6.

My parents divorced when I was around 11 years old. I never thought I'd see my father again. However, he didn't just vanish from sight. He lived in the same neighborhood, and he'd see my brother and me pretty much every weekend. We would go to a movie or out to dinner, and I discovered sides of him I never knew before. My father seemed happier, and in return he lavished affection on me and my brother, something he'd never really done before.

As I got older, I found my older brother was quickly becoming my best friend and advisor, something that wouldn't have happened to me had my father still been living at home. My brother helped me when I needed to know how to ask out girls or how to fight, and he even helped me with my calculus homework at night when my mother would be at school. If my dad had been there all the time, I wouldn't have had these experiences. Now that I'm almost a "man," I see how I have become what I am by learning from my father's mistakes and from the resourceful advice of my brother.

My relationship with my mother is also extremely close, closer than it would have been had my father lived at home and persevered in the negative behavior that ultimately led to their divorce. I'm not saying that the divorce was a wonderful event, but I believe that the bond between my mother, brother, and myself is much stronger since we had to depend on one another and not on some kind of Ward Cleaver father-husband figure. My mom is a strong woman, and she's always been honest and supportive. There have been hard times without my father around, but in the end, my developing relationships with my mother and brother proved to me that there was a silver lining in the cloud caused by my parents' divorce.

Grader's comments: This essay is outstanding. It addresses the topic statement in a thorough and imaginative way. Its ideas are extremely well organized, very clearly stated, and amply supported by evidence. Finally, the essay displays an excellent command of the conventions of standard written English.

Sample Grade 3 Essay

I remember the way my teacher's face looked when she entered the classroom and saw its condition. She sat down starting to cry. The sight of the vandalized room, with broken glass and books everywhere, was too much for her. Me and the other students decided we had to get together and help her fix up the place.

Who or why destroyed the room? This question didn't matter in the end. The class was motivated to figure out ways to fix and replace everything. Of course we cleaned up first. Glass and other dangerous things were disposed of. Then we replace all the posters and other educational material. We held town car-washes and bake sales to raise money for these things. I was really happy after a month of this kind of work we even had enough money to get new text-books. By working through this misfortune we figured out how to work together. Also, our teacher got to know us as people, not just students. We showed her how we could take charge of a situation and make it better. When we finally got to take classes again in our old classroom I felt that we proved that proverb listed above, "every cloud has a silver lining."

❸ Is Limited

A grade 3 essay doesn't totally accomplish what the assignment asks. It doesn't do an acceptable job of presenting ideas logically and arguing a convincing case. It contains many flaws.

Grader's comments: While this essay reflects a basic understanding of the topic statement, it doesn't address that statement in a convincing or direct way. Its ideas are neither well developed nor well organized. Its use of evidence to support those ideas is unsophisticated. Furthermore, this essay displays an unsatisfactory command of the conventions of standard written English.

❶ Is Deficient

A grade 1 essay fails to do what the assignment asks. It shows a lack of command of conventions of standard written English.

Sample Grade 1 Essay

I've had bad things happen to me and good things have come out of it. Sometimes when something terrible hapens you have to look for a sign that proves not everything is so bad.

In the book The Good Earth written by Pearl Buck their are many examples of this situation. The main character starts off really poor as a result of a terrible draught and no food. But then all sorts of terrible things hapen to him, however he meets a wonderful woman and becomes rich! So the main character proves that even when you think their is no hope their might be a lesson to be learned out of it all. If a person thinks that things couldn't get any worse, he/she should take a look around and you will see that life has some nice surprises in store for you.

Grader's comments: This essay is extremely poor. It's very vague, very repetitive, and almost completely devoid of evidence. It's also riddled with grammatical problems. In fact, this essay is basically an incoherent piece of writing.

Topic 2

<u>Directions:</u> You have 20 minutes to write an essay on the following topic.

DO NOT WRITE AN ESSAY ON ANY OTHER TOPIC. AN ESSAY ON A DIFFERENT TOPIC IS UNACCEPTABLE.

This essay provides you with an opportunity to demonstrate how well you write. Therefore, you should express your ideas clearly and effectively. How much you write is much less important than how well you write; but to express your thoughts on the topic adequately you may want to write more than a single paragraph. Your essay should be specific.

Your essay must be written in the lines provided on your answer sheet. No other paper will be given to you. There is enough space to write your essay on the answer sheet if you write on every line, avoid wide margins, and keep your handwriting to a reasonable size.

Consider the following statement and assignment. Then write an essay as directed.

"I have learned many things that have helped me in life, but one thing that was especially valuable was _____."

<u>Assignment:</u>   Write an essay that completes the statement above. Explain the reasons behind your choice.

WHEN THE PROCTOR ANNOUNCES THAT 20 MINUTES HAVE PASSED, YOU MUST STOP WRITING AND GO ON TO PART B OF THE TEST. IF YOU FINISH YOUR ESSAY BEFORE 20 MINUTES PASS, YOU MAY GO ON TO PART B.

YOU MAY MAKE NOTES ON THIS AND THE OPPOSITE PAGES. BUT YOU MUST WRITE YOUR ESSAY ON THE ANSWER SHEET.

Sample Grade 5 Essay

> I have learned many things that have helped me in life, but one which was especially valuable was learning how to play the violin. Learning how to create music provided me not only with a special skill, but ended up teaching me important lessons that I could never have gotten in regular school.
>
> Making music became a way to improve my self-confidence, which was personally important to me since I always tended to stutter and shake whenever I had to say something in front of a crowd. My violin teacher taught me tactics to stop my hands from shaking. He also advised me to think about performance as a way to actually stop thinking about myself so I could become "as one" with the beauty of the music. The more I followed his advice, the less qualms I had about performing and subsequently the less problems I had in presenting myself in other public situations.
>
> For example, I remember the first debate I had—this happening after having played violin successfully in public a couple of times. I was literally trembling with fear. The audience in front of me

Need Help With Your Writing?

Chapter 3 contains step-by-step strategies for writing a winning essay. And chapter 4 provides you with 22 principles of good writing.

⑤ Is Solid

A grade 5 essay fulfills the writing assignment convincingly. It presents its ideas clearly and logically. Any mistakes it contains are minor.

seemed like an enemy poised to attack. Suddenly, I had an epiphany. I could treat this like I treated the concerts I gave. I relaxed my body the way my music teacher had advised me to. I breathed deeply. Then, I realized I knew everything I needed too and concentrated entirely on letting my point come across. After I was done, the entire audience started clapping and cheering.

I've even used playing violin as a way to relieve the stress I get from life's daily situations. For example, I can get really angry. Instead of screaming and shouting, though, I run up to my room and play the violin. I can feel all that anger and stress flowing into theinstrument and out through the musical notes. What would I havedone had I not been introduced to music?

So, playing the violin has proved to be an outlet for irrational bursts of temper as well as teaching me lessons regular school never taught me. I really think it helps me do well in academic sub-jects too, since playing an instrument uses parts of the brain that are not otherwise exercised. Its obvious to me that learning the violin is the most valuable experience I've had yet.

Grader's comments: Overall, this essay is solid. It addresses the topic in a novel and thoughtful way. Its ideas are well developed, clearly presented, and well organized. It also contains plenty of evidence to support those ideas. On the other hand, it does contain a number of grammatical errors. While they aren't grave mistakes, they are sufficient in number to keep this essay from falling into the outstanding category.

Sample Grade 4 Essay

    I grew up in a neighborhood where everyone around me was from the same upbringing. I didn't really know anyone who was "different," be it skin color, religion, etc. I was what you could call sheltered. But then my family and I moved to Philadelphia, where I met this person who I am really good friends with now. He is a Muslim.

    I never thought about religion in the way I did before I became friends with him. He is devoted to the rituals of his religion, and he has taught me much about them. I have learned a lot about Muslim philosophy and holidays from him. In my old neighborhood, I only knew people who went to church, so I was familiar only with Christian ways. Because of my new friend, I learned that there are many ways to practice devotion to God and family.

    My friendship also introduced me to the fact that there are many different types of people living together in this country. In the past, I never really understood the idea of the "melting pot." My Muslim friend has shown me that people who behave differently— who eat different food, read different books, play different sports, wear different clothes, etc.—can live together in friendship. This lesson will be especially valuable to me as I meet people from different backgrounds in college and later life.

❹ Is Adequate

A grade 4 essay fulfills the writing assignment and shows an acceptable command of vocabulary, grammar, and style. The mistakes it contins are minor.

Grader's comments: This essay adequately addresses the topic statement. It contains sensible ideas, which are presented in an essentially clear and organized manner. But the evidence it provides in support of those ideas is a bit thin. Moreover, the essay contains some obvious grammatical problems. While they don't make the essay unintelligible, they do indicate an unfamiliarity with the conventions of standard written English.

❶ Is Deficient

Grade 1 is the bottom of the scale. A grade 1 essay fails to fulfill the assignment. It contains many mistakes and is poorly organized. A grade 1 essay doesn't make much sense.

Sample Grade 1 Essay

I think that many things I have learned have helped me alot. For example learning how to drive. This means that I can go anywhere without having to rely on parents or friends. With a driver's license you can travel to places and you wouldn't have to spend all that time wundering how your going to get somewhere. This is very valuable to anyone who likes their freedom. Wether you want to go out on a date, see a ball-game or a concert you definitely need to know how to drive. I would definitely say that I "have learned many things that have helped me in life, but one which was especially valuable was learning how to drive."

Grader's comments: Another extremely poor essay. The ideas are unsophisticated and not supported with significant evidence. Moreover, the author displays a lack of familiarity with the rules of standard written English.

Part B: Multiple-Choice Questions

There are three different types of multiple-choice questions. Take a moment to make sure you know the directions now. You don't want to waste precious time reading the directions on test day.

Usage Questions

The directions for Usage questions will look like this:

<u>Directions:</u> The following sentences contain problems in grammar, usage, diction (choice of words), and idiom.

Some of the sentences are correct.

None of the sentences contains more than one error.

The error, if there is one in the sentence, is underlined and lettered. Parts of the sentence that are not underlined are correct and cannot be changed. In selecting answers, follow the requirements of standard written English.

If there is an error, choose the <u>one underlined part</u> that must be changed to make the sentence correct and fill in the corresponding oval on your answer grid.

If there is no error, fill in oval E.

EXAMPLE:

<u>Even though</u> he <u>had to</u> supervise a
    A   B

large staff, his salary <u>was no greater</u>
                        C

than <u>a clerk</u>. <u>No error</u>
     D   E

SAMPLE ANSWER

Ⓐ Ⓑ Ⓒ ● Ⓔ

Half the Battle

Thirty Usage questions account for 50 percent of your score on the multiple-choice section of the test.

These sample Usage questions are just like what you'll see on Test Day. Give them a try. The answers and explanations appear at the end of the chapter.

1. <u>Nearly</u> all scientists believe that the
   A

  current threat <u>to</u> the environment
              B

  <u>could be abated</u> if the general public
     C

  consumed more <u>wiser</u>. <u>No error</u>
               D   E

Ⓐ Ⓑ Ⓒ Ⓓ Ⓔ

2. The Dean and the Curriculum

  Committee plan <u>increasing</u> the number
               A

  of credits <u>required</u> <u>for graduation</u>,
          B   C

  <u>beginning</u> with the incoming freshman
     D

  class. <u>No error</u>
      E

Ⓐ Ⓑ Ⓒ Ⓓ Ⓔ

Sentence Correction Questions

The directions for Sentence Correction questions will look like the directions that follow. Read them now so that you don't have to waste time trying to figure out what to do with Sentence Corrections on Test Day.

Directions: The following sentences test accuracy and effectivenss of expression. In selecting answers, follow the rules of standard written English; in other words, consider grammar, choice of words, sentence construction, and punctuation.

In each of the following sentences, a portion or all of the sentence is underlined. Under each sentence you will find five ways of phrasing the underlined portion. Choice A repeats the original underlined portion; the other four choices provide alternative phrasings.

Select the choice that best expresses the meaning of the original sentence. If the original sentence is better than any of the alternative phrasings, choose A; otherwise select one of the alternatives. Your selection should construct the most effective sentence—clear and precise with no awkwardness or ambiguity.

EXAMPLE: **SAMPLE ANSWER**

Ⓐ Ⓑ Ⓒ ⬤ Ⓔ

Wanting to reward her assistant for

loyalty, <u>Sheila gave a bonus to him</u>

<u>as large as his paycheck.</u>

   (A) Sheila gave a bonus to him as
          large as his paycheck

   (B) given to him by Sheila was a
          bonus as large as his paycheck

   (C) he was given a bonus as large as
          his paycheck by Sheila

   (D) Sheila gave him a bonus as
          large as his paycheck

   (E) Sheila gave him a paycheck to
          him as large as his bonus

The questions will look like the following sample items. Give them a try: the answers and explanations appear at the end of the chapter.

3. <u>The workers searched for trapped survivors, digging as fast as they could in the rubble of the collapsed building.</u>

   (A) The workers searched for trapped survivors, digging as fast as they could in the rubble of the collapsed building.

   (B) Digging, the workers searched for trapped survivors, as fast as they could in the rubble of the collapsed building.

   (C) Digging as fast as they could in the rubble of the collapsed building, trapped survivors were searched for by the workers.

   (D) The workers, searching for trapped survivors, while digging as fast as they could in the rubble of the collapsed building.

   (E) Digging as fast as they could in the rubble of the collapsed building, the workers searched for trapped survivors.

4. Doctors have been advising their patients to eat less fat, exercise more, <u>and reducing stress</u>.

   (A) and reducing stress

   (B) and stress is reduced

   (C) also reducing stress

   (D) and they should reduce stress

   (E) and reduce stress

It Adds Up

Eighteen Sentence Correction questions will account for 30 percent of your score on the multiple-choice section of the test.

Paragraph Correction Questions

The third and final multiple-choice question type on the SAT II: Writing Test is Paragraph Correction. The directions below are basically what you'll see on test day. Read through them and try the sample Paragraph Correction questions that follow. The answers appear at the end of the chapter.

Directions: The following passages are first drafts of student essays. Some portions of the essays have to be rewritten.

   Read the essays and answer the questions that follow them. Some of the questions concern particular sentences or fragments of sentences and require you to make choices about sentence structure, word choice, and usage. Other questions pertain to the entire essay or pieces of the essay and require you to think about organization, development, and appropriateness of language. Pick the answer that most effectively conveys the meaning and follows the rules of standard written English. Once you have chosen an answer, fill in the corresponding oval on your answer sheet.

Final Fifth

Twelve Paragraph Correction questions account for 20 percent of your score on the multiple-choice section of the test. Chapters 5, 6, and 7 will cover the multiple-choice questions in detail. They'll show you exactly what you need to know to handle successfully this part of the test.

<u>Questions 5–7</u> are based on the following essay.

(1) Our urban public schools need to be smaller. (2) In an environment where streets are crowded and sometimes unsafe, it's necessary that schools offer an intimate sense of community so that students can learn in a nurturing atmosphere.

(3) Some people argue that creating smaller schools will be expensive. (4) We don't have to spend lots of money to achieve this vision. (5) A school-building that already exists can be partitioned into two or three smaller schools. (6) And depleting funds by bying state-of-the-art equipment won't be necessary. (7) School boards can find other ways to get supplies. (8) A private business or bank can donate anything from money to computers. (9) And such donations would be beneficial for both parties involved. (10) The bank or business would gain valuable publicity by investing in the community, and the schools would get the products they need. (11) Parents can play a more active role in the school system, and then chaperone for school trips or volunteer to teach.

(12) We need to change the way our schools are built because students need a sense of community in our large cities. (13) Such a reformation might be difficult, but if we work together and we would have invested our time and energy, we can improve the schools for good.

5. Which of the following options is the best way to edit the underlined portions of sentences 3 and 4 (reproduced below) so that the two sentences are changed into one?

    Some people argue that creating smaller schools <u>will be expensive. We don't have to spend</u> lots of money to achieve this vision.

    (A) is expensive, and we don't have to spend

    (B) will be expensive, so we don't have to spend

    (C) will be expensive, but we don't have to spend

    (D) are expensive, but we don't have to spend

    (E) are expensive, yet we will not be spending

6. In terms of context, which version of the underlined section of sentence 11 is the clearest?

    Parents can play a more active role <u>in the school system, and then chaperone for school trips or volunteer to teach</u>.

    (A) by chaperoning in the school system for school trips and volunteering to teach

    (B) in the school system, as a chaperone for school trips or volunteer to teach

    (C) in the school system, then chaperoning for school trips and volunteering to teach

    (D) in the school system by chaperoning for school trips or volunteering to teach

    (E) as chaperones for school trips or volunteers to teach in the school system

    Ⓐ Ⓑ Ⓒ Ⓓ Ⓔ

7. Which of the versions of the underlined section of sentence 13 (reproduced below) is best?

    Such a reformation might be difficult, <u>but if we work together and we would have invested</u> our time and energy, we can improve the schools for good.

    (A) (As it is now)

    (B) and if we work together and we invest

    (C) but if we work together and invest

    (D) furthermore, if we work together, also investing

    (E) although if we are working together and will be investing

    Ⓐ Ⓑ Ⓒ Ⓓ Ⓔ

Educated Guessing

Remember, if you can eliminate one answer choice as definitely wrong, you should try to guess the answer to the question. Omit a question only if you have absolutely no clue about any of the choices.

Real World

The mean SAT II: Writing Test score for 2003 college-bound seniors was 596.

Source: College Board

Chapters 5, 6, and 7 will cover the multiple-choice questions in detail. They'll show you exactly what you need to know to handle this part of the test successfully.

How Multiple-Choice Questions Are Scored

If you get a multiple-choice question right, you will earn 1 point. If you omit a multiple-choice question, you will neither earn nor lose anything. And if you get a multiple-choice question wrong, you will lose one-quarter of a point. Once your raw score has been tallied, it will be converted into a scaled score ranging from 20–80. This scaled score will account for two-thirds of your final Writing Test score.

Your Overall Score

After your essay and multiple-choice raw scores have been converted into scaled scores, they will be combined into a single scaled score that reflects the different weight given to each section. This new scaled score will then be converted into a final score ranging from 200–800.

Answers to Sample Questions

1. (D)—*Wiser* should be *wisely* because *wiser* is intended to describe how the general public consumed an action. The verb *consumed* needs the adverb *wisely*.

2. (A)—The gerund form of the verb is not idiomatic with the verb *plan*. *Plan* requires the infinitive form of the verb: in this case, *to increase*.

3. (E)—*Digging as fast as they could in the rubble of the collapsed building* is a long modifying phrase. It modifies the noun *workers*. Only choice (E) places the modifying phrase right next to the noun that it modifies. Choice (D) might have been tempting, but it doesn't have any verb, so it's not a valid sentence.

4. (E)—This sentence requires parallel construction because it presents a list. Only choice (E) presents the last item in a manner parallel to the first two items.

5. (C)—This choice sets up the contrast between *some people* who argue that creating the schools will be expensive and the author's belief that creating smaller schools won't be expensive.

6. (D)—This choice is the only one that clearly shows how parents can work as volunteers or chaperones within the school system.

7. (C)—This choice is grammatically consistent with the rest of the paragraph. Notice that it's the shortest, simplest, and clearest choice.

SECTION TWO:
The Essay

WRITING A WINNING ESSAY

In this chapter, you'll learn how to approach the Essay section of the SAT II: Writing Test strategically. We'll show you how to plan your essay before writing. We'll give you lots of practice with sample topics. We've included sample essays to show how the grading system works. This will help you evaluate your own skill level. But before you learn the Kaplan approach to writing a winning essay, there's a bit of general advice that you need to be made aware of.

Essay Basics

The information that the College Board gives out doesn't tell you the whole story about how your essay will be evaluated. Here's what you need to know.

Essay Length

The College Board claims that what you write is much more important than how much you write. That's true—to a point. If you look over the sample essays that the College Board provides in its publications, you should notice a clear pattern. Those essays given high scores—that is, essays with total scores ranging from 10–12—are generally longer than those essays given lower scores. In fact, essays in the 10–12 range are three to five paragraphs long, and those paragraphs usually contain more than one or two sentences.

What does this mean to you? Quite simply, it means that you should try to write at least three substantial paragraphs on test day. One or two paragraphs, no matter how sophisticated, just won't cut it with the graders. In other words, fill up as many of the answer sheet's lines as possible, and create new paragraphs whenever possible. But say something in every sentence that you write! Don't fill up lines just to fill up lines. It's better to leave lines blank if you have nothing more to say than to fill them up with meaningless or repetitive sentences. On the other hand, you don't want your essay to be so ambitious in scope that you don't have the space or the time to finish it. A complete essay is certainly better than one that's incomplete.

No Fluff

Your essay should be three to five paragraphs long. But don't drag it out just to reach a particular number of paragraphs. A long essay that repeats itself or is filled with fluff isn't going to earn you extra points.

Get Over Yourself

If possible, your essay should discuss current events, history, literature, or some other discipline. Going beyond your personal experience in the essay will impress the graders.

Neatness Counts

An essay that's difficult to read may not get the score it deserves.

Essay Content

The College Board also claims that you don't need any specific knowledge to write the essay. They're correct. Writing Test essay topics are so broad that you can always write about a subject that you're familiar with, just as long as you address the topic at hand. But you must be specific. To that end, it's a good idea for you to include references to current events, history, or literature in your essay if at all possible. It will be graded by high school teachers or college professors—people who want to see what you know about the world. They'll be impressed by an essay that goes beyond your personal experience.

For example, let's assume that you're very knowledgeable about World War II. Well, then, you might want to make World War II the focus of your essay. On test day, you'll most likely get a topic that will allow you to discuss this subject. You've just got to come up with an angle to tie World War II to the topic. Similarly, let's assume that you're very familiar with the works of T. S. Eliot. Well, then, you might want to make T. S. Eliot the focus of your essay. The bottom line: Write about what you know and are interested in. The best writing is informed and engaged.

Essay Neatness

Your essay must be readable. If you edit what you've written, do it neatly. If you add a word, change a phrase, or cross out a sentence, do it carefully. It may sound silly, but neatness matters. In fact, it matters a lot.

Why? Simply put, the graders will have many essays to read and evaluate. That means they aren't going to spend much time judging any particular essay. They aren't going to read an essay three or four times in order to decipher hard-to-read words or sentences. Consequently, if the flow of an essay is difficult to follow because it's messy, graders may simply conclude that the essay's just not very good. The score that it receives will reflect this negative impression. An essay that's otherwise outstanding may not get the score it deserves because of the way it's presented. Thus, it's very much in your interest to make your essay readable.

To sum up: You're not expected to produce a brilliant piece of writing. After all, the College Board and the graders know that you have only 20 minutes to think about, write, and proofread your work. What they expect is an organized and readable piece of writing that makes a well-supported argument. The remainder of this chapter will show you how to accomplish that task.

The Kaplan Method for Writing a Winning Essay

The bad news is that the essay topic may appear in one of two basic forms (as we described in Chapter 2). The good news is that Kaplan's Three-Step Method—the THINK-ACT-REPAIR method—applies equally well to both forms. Here's how the method works.

Step 1: THINK

Don't start to write immediately. Take time to read the topic statement and assignment carefully. The topic statement's going to be very broad, so you've got to narrow it down. How? You need to come up with an argument that addresses the topic in some specific context. For instance, let's say that you get the following topic statement:

"The strong do what they wish."

Furthermore, let's say that the assignment asks you to take a specific example from your personal experience, from current events, or from history, literature, or any other discipline, and use this example to compose an essay that either agrees or disagrees with the above statement.

What do you do? Well, the first thing you should do is choose an example. You could discuss a historical case (e.g., a relationship between one of the superpowers and a less powerful country). Or you could discuss a scientific case (e.g., the behavior of a predatory species). Or you could discuss a personal experience (e.g., the relationship your employer has with you and other workers). Just pick something that you can write about intelligently and passionately.

Once you've got an example, you must develop an argument. In this instance, you must decide either to agree or disagree with the topic statement. You might agree with the statement by arguing that superpower X pushed around country Y in order to advance its own interests. Or you might agree with the statement by arguing that a predator can cause havoc among native species when it's introduced into a new ecosystem. Or you might disagree with the statement by explaining what a nice guy or gal your boss is.

You've also got to cite evidence to support your argument. You might want to discuss superpower X's invasion of country Y. Or you might want to discuss how several animal species native to Australia were adversely affected when British colonists introduced the domestic cat to the island. Or you might want to discuss how nicely your boss treats you and your fellow workers. Whatever your argument, be sure to include plenty of supporting evidence. An argument without evidence simply isn't convincing.

Kaplan's Three-Step Method for Essay Writing

1. THINK
2. ACT
3. REPAIR

Take Five

Take about five minutes to plan your essay. Know exactly what you want to say and exactly how you want to say it before you start to write. Make an outline of your thoughts and refer to it as you write.

Little Things

You shouldn't have to do anything more than make minor corrections to your first draft during this final step of the writing process.

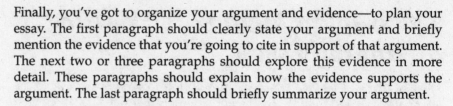

Finally, you've got to organize your argument and evidence—to plan your essay. The first paragraph should clearly state your argument and briefly mention the evidence that you're going to cite in support of that argument. The next two or three paragraphs should explore this evidence in more detail. These paragraphs should explain how the evidence supports the argument. The last paragraph should briefly summarize your argument.

You should, of course, outline your essay on the scratch paper that is provided for you; and you should refer to your outline as you write your essay.

The thinking step of the writing process should take about five minutes. That may seem like a lot of time to spend before your write a single sentence. But taking a few minutes to outline your essay is definitely worth the time. If you take a few minutes to think about and organize what you want to write, the words should flow smoothly from the end of your pencil once you actually begin to write.

Step 2: ACT

This step is the one in which you transform your outline into a fleshed-out essay. To write a strong essay, you need more than just a good outline, however. You also must understand the mechanics of good writing. A bit later on, this chapter will provide you with 22 principles of good writing. If you use them on test day, your essay is bound to be well written.

The writing step of your essay should take about 13 minutes. That's enough time to write three to five solid paragraphs if you work from a prepared outline.

Step 3: REPAIR

This step involves proofreading and fixing your essay. If you've done steps 1 and 2 correctly, this step should be a breeze. All you'll need to do is fix minor grammatical and/or spelling errors, change a few words here and there, and, maybe, add a sentence or two for clarity's sake.

This step of your essay should take no more than two minutes. If you spend the bulk of the 20 minutes thinking about and writing the essay, the repair step should entail nothing more than putting the finishing touches on an already strong essay.

It's very important to get a handle on outlining an essay as early in your test preparation as possible. Try the following drill before you dive into writing an essay.

Outline an Essay

Read the essay directions below and outline an essay on the topic statement. Your outline should include the argument that you wish to make, the evidence that you wish to cite in support of that argument, and an indication of where in the essay all of this information will appear.

Directions: You have 20 minutes to write an essay on the following topic. **DO NOT WRITE AN ESSAY ON ANY OTHER TOPIC. AN ESSAY ON A DIFFERENT TOPIC IS UNACCEPTABLE.**

This essay provides you with an opportunity to demonstrate how well you write. Therefore, you should express your ideas clearly and effectively. How much you write is much less important than how well you write; but to express your thoughts on the topic adequately you may want to write more than a single paragraph. Your essay should be specific.

Your essay must be written in the lines provided on your answer sheet. No other paper will be given to you. There is enough space to write your essay on the answer sheet if you write on every line, avoid big margins, and keep your handwriting to a reasonable size.

Consider the following statement and assignment. Then write an essay as directed.

"The strong do what they wish."

Assignment: Choose one example from personal experience, current events, or history, literature, or any other discipline and use this example to write an essay in which you agree or disagree with the statement above. Your essay should be specific.

WHEN THE PROCTOR ANNOUNCES THAT 20 MINUTES HAVE PASSED, YOU MUST STOP WRITING AND GO ON TO PART B OF THE TEST. IF YOU FINISH YOUR ESSAY BEFORE 20 MINUTES PASS, YOU MAY GO ON TO PART B.

YOU MAY MAKE NOTES ON THIS AND THE OPPOSITE PAGES. BUT YOU MUST WRITE YOUR ESSAY ON THE ANSWER SHEET.

Mechanics

Good writing involves more than just clear ideas and clear organization. You must also familiarize yourself with the mechanics of good writing. Check out the next chapter for 22 tips for writing better.

THE ESSAY

You may use this page to outline your essay. Remember, though, that your essay MUST be written on the lined pages of your answer sheet.

KAPLAN

Now that you've created an outline, compare it to the sample outline that appears below. Don't worry if your outline isn't as thorough as this one. It's your first try, after all. At the end of this chapter, you'll have several more opportunities to hone your outlining skills.

¶1 (Introduction)

a. General Argument: Rome, which was the greatest military power in the ancient world, routinely invaded and conquered its weaker neighbors in order to increase its own territory and wealth.

b. Examples: Punic Wars that led to destruction of Carthage; conquest of Gaul; conquest of Eastern Mediterranean lands

¶s 2, 3, and 4 (Body)

¶2:

a. Punic Wars were a series of wars that lasted over 100 years and ended with the complete destruction of Carthaginian Empire, which was located in North Africa

b. Wars finally ended in 146 B.C., when city of Carthage was sacked and burned and its surviving population was sold into slavery

c. Why did Rome fight these wars: to strip Carthage, its major political and economic rival in the Mediterranean, of its territory and wealth—over the course of a century, Rome took all of Carthage's territory in the Mediterranean and North Africa, and took control of seaborne commerce in the Mediterranean, which Carthage had formerly dominated

¶3:

a. The Romans initially moved into Gaul in order to retaliate against the Gauls, who were Celtic tribesman, for earlier sacking Rome and aiding the Carthaginians in the Punic Wars

b. But Romans also had territorial and commercial ambitions in their later drives to capture more of Gaul—they wanted to control the rich agricultural lands of southern Europe, as well as to dominate regional trade

¶4:

a. Rome took advantage of civil strife in Eastern Mediterranean lands in order to conquer them

b. Why was Rome interested in these lands—they contained more wealth than Western Mediterranean lands due to the antiquity of urban civilization in here, and they served a vital strategic purpose in securing Rome's undisputed control over the Mediterranean Sea

¶5 (Conclusion):

a. Restate general argument in different words

b. Quickly refer to any additional evidence

Write the Essay You've Outlined

Now that you're done with your outline, you're ready to start writing. Start your practice with the essay topic that you just outlined. Here's the topic again, with the directions like the ones you'll see on test day. Write your essay on the next page.

<u>Directions:</u> You have 20 minutes to write an essay on the following topic.

DO NOT WRITE AN ESSAY ON ANY OTHER TOPIC. AN ESSAY ON A DIFFERENT TOPIC IS UNACCEPTABLE.

This essay provides you with an opportunity to demonstrate how well you write. Therefore, you should express your ideas clearly and effectively. How much you write is much less important than how well you write; but to express your thoughts on the topic adequately you may want to write more than a single paragraph. Your essay should be specific.

Your essay must be written in the lines provided on your answer sheet. No other paper will be given to you. There is enough space to write your essay on the answer sheet if you write on every line, avoid wide margins, and keep your handwriting to a reasonable size.

Consider the following statement and assignment. Then write an essay as directed.

"The strong do what they wish."

<u>Assignment:</u>   Choose one example from personal experience, current events, or history, literature, or any other discipline and use this example to write an essay in which you agree or disagree with the statement above. Your essay should be specific.

WHEN THE PROCTOR ANNOUNCES THAT 20 MINUTES HAVE PASSED, YOU MUST STOP WRITING AND GO ON TO PART B OF THE TEST. IF YOU FINISH YOUR ESSAY BEFORE 20 MINUTES PASS, YOU MAY GO ON TO PART B.

YOU MAY MAKE NOTES ON THIS AND THE OPPOSITE PAGES. BUT YOU MUST WRITE YOUR ESSAY ON THE ANSWER SHEET.

THE ESSAY

Write your essay here. (The answer sheet for the SAT II: Writing Test provides two pages for the essay.)

KAPLAN

Sample Grade 6 Essay

To help you get a sense of how your essay might be graded, we have included a sample high-scoring essay. Compare your essay to the one below, which merits a grade of 6. By asking and answering these questions, you'll get a sense of how well you've done.

- Is your essay's argument as clear and straightforward?

- Does your essay use supporting evidence as effectively?

- Is your essay as well written?

- Is your essay nearly the same length?

Rome, which was the greatest military power in the ancient world, routinely invaded and conquered its weaker neighbors. It did so in order to increase its territory and wealth. That Rome was ruthless in pursuit of its own self-interest is illustrated by its treatment of the Carthaginians, the Gauls, and the peoples of the Near East.

The Punic Wars between Rome and Carthage lasted for over 100 years and ended with the complete destruction of the Carthaginian empire. In 146 B.C., Roman legions finally captured and burned Carthage itself, selling the city's survivors into slavery. As a result of its victory, Rome acquired territory in the Mediterranean and North Africa that it had long wanted to dominate. It also took control of seaborne trade in the region—trade that Carthage had previously dominated. In other words, Rome fought the Punic Wars in order to eliminate its major territorial and commercial rival in the Mediterranean and North African region.

The Romans initially invaded Gaul (located in southern France and northern Italy) in order to retaliate against "barbarian" tribes that had earlier sacked Rome and aided the Carthaginians in the Punic Wars. But later Roman attacks and conquests, which result-

ed in much suffering among the people of Gaul, were motivated by territorial and commercial ambitions. Gaul's land was very fertile, and control of it provided Rome with a secure source of food. Furthermore, Rome's treasury grew by heavily taxing those who used the area's well-developed trade routes.

Rome also exploited civil unrest in the Near East in order to expand its empire. Those who came under its control received harsh treatment, with many being killed or sold into slavery. Why was Rome interested in Near Eastern lands? It had two reasons. First, these lands contained great wealth, which Rome needed to run its empire. Second, control of the Near East served a vital strategic purpose; it prevented other powers from threatening Roman dominance of the Mediterranean Sea.

In sum, then, Rome did not hesistate to use force to accomplish its territorial and economic goals. In the short run, militaristic behavior enabled the empire to become stronger and more prosperous. In the long run, however, Rome's ruthless behavior was its undoing. The hatred that Roman conquests generated among non-Romans led to constant revolts, which eventually undermined the very foundations of the empire.

Practice Essay Topics

The following pages contain three practice essay topics for you to work on. Outline the topics, write the essays, and then proofread them. After each topic, you'll find three sample essays—a strong essay, a mediocre essay, and a weak essay. You'll also find sample grader comments explaining why these essays are strong, mediocre, or weak. Use these essays and comments to judge the quality of your own essays. Determine your strengths and weaknesses, and then reprep the weak spots.

Topic 1

<u>Directions:</u> You have 20 minutes to write an essay on the following topic.

DO NOT WRITE AN ESSAY ON ANY OTHER TOPIC. AN ESSAY ON A DIFFERENT TOPIC IS UNACCEPTABLE.

This essay provides you with an opportunity to demonstrate how well you write. Therefore, you should express your ideas clearly and effectively. How much you write is much less important than how well you write; but to express your thoughts on the topic adequately you may want to write more than a single paragraph. Your essay should be specific.

Your essay must be written in the lines provided on your answer sheet. No other paper will be given to you. There is enough space to write your essay on the answer sheet if you write on every line, avoid wide margins, and keep your handwriting to a reasonable size.

Need to Brush Up?

If you feel you need to brush up on the rules of standard written English, you may want to check out the material in Kaplan's Writing Clinic (chapter 4) before you try these practice essay topics.

Consider the following statement and assignment. Then write an essay as directed.

> **"I've done some brave things in my life, but I really learned the meaning of courage when _____."**

<u>Assignment:</u> Write an essay that completes the statement above. Explain the reasons behind your choice.

WHEN THE PROCTOR ANNOUNCES THAT 20 MINUTES HAVE PASSED, YOU MUST STOP WRITING AND GO ON TO PART B OF THE TEST. IF YOU FINISH YOUR ESSAY BEFORE 20 MINUTES PASS, YOU MAY GO ON TO PART B.

YOU MAY MAKE NOTES ON THIS AND THE OPPOSITE PAGES. BUT YOU MUST WRITE YOUR ESSAY ON THE ANSWER SHEET.

THE ESSAY

Write your essay here. (The answer sheet for the SAT II: Writing Test provides two pages for the essay.)

KAPLAN

Topic 1 Sample Essays

"I've done some brave things in my life, but I really learned the meaning of courage when _____."

Sample Grade 5 Essay

Some people learn about courage on the battlefield. Some learn courage in natural disasters like earthquakes and floods. I've done some brave things in my life, but I really learned the meaning of courage from my grandmother, her life and death.

My grandmother's name was Francine, but everyone called her Pip. She once told me that when she was growing up, if something was cool, people would say, "it's a pip." And she deserved the nickname. In the few faded snapshots of her childhood, you can see she was pretty, always smiling, and had a lively personality.

Unfortunately, the man Pip married was killed in a car accident. She was alone with her two small children, my mother and my Aunt Jenny. Pip's husband had left behind a sizeable debt and no insurance. But with the help of kind relatives, Pip managed to raise the two girls, working two, and sometimes three, jobs to pay off the debts. In those days, a single mother and working, that took real courage. When her children were grown up, Pip took classes at a local college and got her diploma. She always said graduating was the proudest day of her life.

When I was 13, Pip got sick with cancer. We'd go and visit her in the hospital, and she'd while away the time telling us stories about her life, from girlhood to being the oldest "kid" in her college class. It was like she was making us feel better, instead of the other way around. Cheerful in the face of death, she was the best example of courage I know.

Grader's comments: This is a solid essay. It's well organized and flows logically. Moreover, the evidence cited in the passage supports the author's ideas. There are some minor errors in spelling and diction, but the overall grammar is effective.

Sample Grade 3 Essay

I'm not sure I personally know what courage is yet. Not that I'm a coward. But my life has been, not easy, but not threatened by a war or poverty. Suffering is the thing that teaches courage.

There are many examples all around. Firemen risk their lives every day. Policemen get shot at, even paramedics and doctors who treat AIDS. Astronauts could blow up or be lost in space. The writer who wrote satanic verse had courage. They put a price on his head. Hiding everyday, not knowing if the next stranger on th e street is going to kill you because of that which you wrote. Getting out of bed in the morning takes courage in his shoes.

And school teaches you that scientists also are brave when people don't believe their ideas but they stick to their guns and history proves them right. Like Galileo, he thought the earth went around the sun. The authorites said you can't say that, but of course he was right. Other examples of courage are a fighter pilot behind enemy lines and the person who fights off a mugging. I hope when the time comes I will know what courage

Grader's comments: This essay is limited. It's filled with evidence, but the author neglects to develop his ideas. The author simply provides a string of unconnected facts. Moreover, this essay contains numerous and significant grammatical problems.

Sample Grade 1 Essay

I've done some brave things in my life but I really learned the meaning of courage when I faced my fear. That was the key to my first back dive.

From the time since childhood, I could do a front dive but not a back one. No way! It just was just to scary. But thanks to my brother one day he showed me. We were at this pool but before the diving board. He put his hands on my back and said lean back and I did. Now I felt how to do it right, and got up on the board. I was scared, but my brother said breath and I did and did the dive!

Other examples of courage are Gandhi and Martin Luther King.

Grader's comments: This essay doesn't really fulfill the writing assignment. The author's story of overcoming his fear of a back dive is potentially a good example, but is poorly developed, thinly supported, and contains many major errors in grammar, style and spelling. Furthermore, in an abrupt transition from personal experience to history, the final sentence simply names two men of courage without explaining why they were courageous.

Topic 2

<u>Directions:</u> You have 20 minutes to write an essay on the following topic.

DO NOT WRITE AN ESSAY ON ANY OTHER TOPIC. AN ESSAY ON A DIFFERENT TOPIC IS UNACCEPTABLE.

This essay provides you with an opportunity to demonstrate how well you write. Therefore, you should express your ideas clearly and effectively. How much you write is much less important than how well you write; but to express your thoughts on the topic adequately you may want to write more than a single paragraph. Your essay should be specific.

Your essay must be written in the lines provided on your answer sheet. No other paper will be given to you. There is enough space to write your essay on the answer sheet if you write on every line, avoid wide margins, and keep your handwriting to a reasonable size.

Consider the following statement and assignment. Then write an essay as directed.

"Every obstacle is an opportunity."

<u>Assignment:</u>   Choose one example from personal experience, current events, or history, literature, or any other discipline and use this example to write an essay in which you agree or disagree with the statement above. Your essay should be specific.

WHEN THE PROCTOR ANNOUNCES THAT 20 MINUTES HAVE PASSED, YOU MUST STOP WRITING AND GO ON TO PART B OF THE TEST. IF YOU FINISH YOUR ESSAY BEFORE 20 MINUTES PASS, YOU MAY GO ON TO PART B.

YOU MAY MAKE NOTES ON THIS AND THE OPPOSITE PAGES. BUT YOU MUST WRITE YOUR ESSAY ON THE ANSWER SHEET.

Write your essay here. (The answer sheet for the SAT II: Writing Test provides two pages for the essay.)

Topic 2 Sample Essays

"Every obstacle is an opportunity."

Sample Grade 5 Essay

Every obstacle is an opportunity, if one has the right attitude or perspective. People with this attitude are bouyant, not easily discouraged, and welcome challenges and adversity. I can think of no better example than in sixth grade, when I broke my hand. I fell off my bicycle one day and broke it, and the doctor put it in a cast.

Now the cast was a real obstacle. It was on my right hand, the one I write with. It looked like homework would be impossible, but I learned to type with one hand and did my English and Social Studies work on the typewriter, and my Mom wrote out my math homework based on answers I gave her. The experience sure helped my typing! It also made me learn the value of work, and gave me a chance to really learn to appreciate my mother.

In addition, having the cast was an excuse to improve my basketball game. I was a decent dribbler, but most comfortable with my right hand. But with the cast on I was forced to practice dribbling with my left hand, and now I can go either way.

Finally there was one other unexpected benefit. In Art Class, I was never very good. But one day, with my hand still in the cast, I tried drawing with my left hand. To my surprise, I was much better at it than ever before! The cast is long gone, but I still draw left-handed and am really quite good at it. Maybe I'd never have known about this ability if I hadn't made my obstacle into my opportunity

Grader's comments: This essay demonstrates a strong grasp of the writing assignment. The author states a thesis, provides a relevant example, and discusses that example in a clear and convincing way. There are a few minor grammatical errors; but these mistakes don't affect the generally high quality of the essay.

Sample Grade 3 Essay

To say that every obstacle is an opportunity is to be an optimist. Some people just always look on the bright side, and are able to overcome there obstacles.

Dorothy in The Wizard of Oz is stranded by the tornado and can't go home. So she takes the opportunity to make friends with Scarecrow etc, and to rid the world of wicked witches. Her optimism wins her the right to go back to Kansas. Ophelia in Hamlet however, is not an optimist. She and Hamlet fall in love but then he pushes her away. She doesn't understand why and kills herself.

In the real world, Marie Curie was told women couldn't be scientists but perservered and discovered radium. Now there are more woman scientists than ever.

I like to think I'm an optimist too. If somebody tells me I can't do something, I just try harder until I can. Take field hockey. I went out as a freshman and barely made the team, but worked and worked and this year was a starter on the varsity. We came in second in the league. Life is like that if you look on the bright side. Don't get discouraged. Every cloud has a silver lining. So if you are an optimist, every obstacle is an opportunity.

Grader's comments: Even though the author attempted with some success to fulfill the assignment, her essay contains many grammatical problems. Moreover, the examples from literature and history are underdeveloped, especially in paragraph 3, and confused. The author doesn't really explain how the obstacles she mentions became opportunities for the individuals in question. Finally, the author's personal experience of overcoming an obstacle doesn't tell us much about how she overcame it.

Sample Grade 1 Essay

I don't agree with this statement, that "every obstacle is an opportunity". Some obstacles are just that. Like if I wanted to be a NBA basketball player. In the NBA you have to be tall as a tree, and I'm the shortest person in the whole school. Back in elementery school too. So I'm never going to opportunity to play the NBA.

And if you die young like from lukemia, that obstacle doesn't give you the opportunity to do anything with your life. So it depends on the obstacle. It should have said MANY obstacles or SOME obstacles. It just depends.

Grader's comments: This essay is deficient in both development and presentation. It's perfectly acceptable for the author to disagree with the stimulus statement, but she provides hardly any argument in support of that position. The ideas that are presented are extremely thin, and there's no logical organization to them. Finally, this essay's prose seriously violates the rules of standard written English. For example, it's filled with sentence fragments.

Topic 3

<u>Directions:</u> You have 20 minutes to write an essay on the following topic.

DO NOT WRITE AN ESSAY ON ANY OTHER TOPIC. AN ESSAY ON A DIFFERENT TOPIC IS UNACCEPTABLE.

This essay provides you with an opportunity to demonstrate how well you write. Therefore, you should express your ideas clearly and effectively. How much you write is much less important than how well you write; but to express your thoughts on the topic adequately you may want to write more than a single paragraph. Your essay should be specific.

Your essay must be written in the lines provided on your answer sheet. No other paper will be given to you. There is enough space to write your essay on the answer sheet if you write on every line, avoid wide margins, and keep your handwriting to a reasonable size.

Consider the following statement and assignment. Then write an essay as directed.

"Some people believe that war is never justified. Other people believe that war is justified under certain circumstances."

<u>Assignment:</u> Choose one example from personal experience, current events, or history, literature, or any other discipline and use this example to write an essay in which you agree or disagree with the statement above. Your essay should be specific.

WHEN THE PROCTOR ANNOUNCES THAT 20 MINUTES HAVE PASSED, YOU MUST STOP WRITING AND GO ON TO PART B OF THE TEST. IF YOU FINISH YOUR ESSAY BEFORE 20 MINUTES PASS, YOU MAY GO ON TO PART B.

YOU MAY MAKE NOTES ON THIS AND THE OPPOSITE PAGES. BUT YOU MUST WRITE YOUR ESSAY ON THE ANSWER SHEET.

THE ESSAY

Write your essay here. (The answer sheet for the SAT II: Writing Test provides two pages for the essay.)

KAPLAN

Topic 3 Sample Essays

"Some people believe that war is never justified. Other people believe that war is justified under certain circumstances."

Sample Grade 4 Essay

We are a violent species. We have been fighting wars since before recorded history. The first wars were fought over territory, or perhaps for possession of precious natural resources, such as the use of a stream. In the past several thousand years, inumerable wars have been fought for the acquisition of political or religious supremacy.

I am totally against war, and would like to see it banished from human affairs. It is my belief, however, that fighting a war is justified in a few special circumstances, such as when freedom or survival is at stake. The American Revolution, for instance, was justifiable. The colonists rebelled in order to gain the right to worship as they pleased and to gain freedom from taxation without representation. World War II was a just war, with the Allies fighting to stop Hitler from achieving world domination. But wars fought in the name of religious freedom can become unjustified, and lead to persecution and massacres. Starting the war in what was formerly Yugoslavia wasn't justified. Ethnic prejudice is not the same as fighting for self-rule or survival. "Ethnic cleansing" led to the kind of massacres mentioned above.

There should be a world court to peacefully mediate disputes between countries or groups of people. The United Nations has tried to fill this role for 50 years, but doesn't have enough power to enforce its decisions. If we had a global organization powerful enough to do so, we might have a world with only justified wars or, better still, no wars at all.

Grader's comments: This is an adequate essay. The author has responded to the stimulus with an argument; but not one that precisely fulfills the writing assignment. The writing itself shows a reasonable familiarity with the conventions of standard written English.

Sample Grade 3 Essay

War is justified in certain circumstances, such as self-defense. If one country attacks another country, the second country has the right to defend itself in order to survive. When the Japanese attacked Pearl Harbor, this gave us the right to fight World War II.

Aggression not in self-defense is not justified. All Quiet on the Western Front by Remarque is a prime example of the horrors of unjustified war. The German soldiers in World War 1 are portrayed in the novel like lambs to the slaughter, pawns in their leader's unjust war for domination of Europe.

What holds true for countries also holds true for people. A person only has the right to defend him or her self with deadly force if their life is threatened. It's called justifiable homicide. Personal freedom is also worth fighting for. That's why Black South Africans were justified to fight against apartheid.

Life in the United States, however does not require most of us to fight for survival. This is probably why people like violent movies. They watch stars (Stallone, Shwarzenegger, Van Damme) act out their own private fantasies of destruction, and no one gets hurt. Buildings get blown up with no loss of innocent life, it's just a set. The bullets aren't real. Maybe we could put end to wars if leaders of countries would watch more violent movies!

Grader's comments: Here's another example of an essay in which the author doesn't precisely fulfill the writing assignment. Moreover, this essay wanders from idea to idea without much linkage. Also, it's filled with grammatical flaws—to the point of damaging its presentation of ideas.

Sample Grade 2 Essay

It is hard to choose between these statements! I am against loss of life in any form. So war is never justified. But what about in the case of attack. Somebody attacks you, its right to fight back even if they die in the process. So the second statement is true too.

The Viet Nam war was not justified. We sent young Americans over there and alot of them didn't come back. There was alot of unrest at home with the antiwar Movement. Veterans had night mares for years and trouble getting jobs. And the VietNamese had to rebuild there country because it was all bombed out. So the circumstances were not right for us in this case. But if during the cold war the Russians had bombed us, we would be justified in bombing back. It's a matter of self-defense.

So if I have to choose, I'd take the second statement. That way you keep your options open.

Grader's comments: This essay doesn't really address the writing assignment. Moreover, it's seriously flawed by its vague ideas, unsatisfactory organization, and poor grammar. The author would have been better served by choosing one side or the other, instead of waffling on the issue. Nevertheless, the essay contains the kernel of a coherent argument and does provide a bit of evidence in support of that argument; hence, it merits a 2 instead of a 1.

CHAPTER 4

KAPLAN'S WRITING CLINIC

In the last chapter, you learned how to analyze an essay topic, organize your thoughts, and outline an essay. Once you have an overall idea of what you want to say in your essay, you can start thinking about how to say it. This chapter emphasizes the skills you need for the second stage of the writing process: producing a well-written essay.

Perhaps the single most important thing to bear in mind when writing an essay is: keep it simple. This applies to word choice, sentence structure, and argument. Obsessing over how to spell a word correctly can throw off your flow of thought. The more complicated and wordy your sentences, the more likely they will be plagued by errors. The more convoluted your argument, the more likely you will get bogged down in convoluted sentence structure. Yet simple does not mean simplistic. A clear, straightforward approach can be sophisticated.

Many students mistakenly believe that their essays will be "downgraded" by such mechanical errors as misplaced commas, poor choice of words, misspellings, faulty grammar, and so on. Occasional problems of this type won't affect your essay score. To reiterate, the graders understand that you're writing under extreme time pressure. They will not be looking to take points off for such errors, provided that you don't display a demonstrable pattern of such errors.

Your objective in taking the SAT II is admission to the college(s) of your choice. To achieve that goal, give schools what they want. They don't expect eloquence in a 20-minute assignment, but they do want to see effective writing. As you attempt to write an effective essay, it helps to follow these four golden rules of good writing.

- Be Concise (or Cut the Fat)
- Be Forceful (or Be Strong or Be Firm or Take a Stand)
- Be Correct (or Follow the Rules)
- Be Polished (or Attend to Details)

An effective essay is concise: It wastes no words. An effective essay is forceful: It makes its point. And an effective essay is correct: It conforms to the generally accepted rules of grammar and form.

Keep Your Essay Simple

Use simple words, use simple sentences, and use a simple argument. You can express sophisticated thoughts with simple prose.

Dos and Don'ts

Don't worry excessively about writing mechanics.

Do try to train yourself out of poor habits.

Do proofread your essays for obvious errors.

Four Major Goals

An effective essay is concise, forceful, correct, and polished.

The following pages contain 22 specific principles that will help you achieve the four broad goals of concision, forcefulness, and correctness. Don't panic! Many of the principles will already be familiar to you. And, besides, you will have many chances to learn and practice them. Indeed, some of what you'll be exposed to here will be reinforced in the sections of this book that deal with Usage and Sentence Correction questions. After all, the grammar that you need to apply to your own writing is the same grammar that you need to know to spot problems in others' writing.

We've grouped the 22 principles according to which of the four goals they relate to.

- Principles 1 through 4 relate to concise writing.
- Principles 5 through 10 relate to forceful writing.
- Principles 11 through 15 relate to grammatically correct writing.
- Principles 16 through 22 relate to polished, perfected writing.

The three goals are interrelated, though. For instance, a forceful sentence is usually not wordy, and correct sentences tend to be more forceful than incorrect ones.

The principles of concise and forceful writing are generally not as rigid as the principles of grammatically correct writing. Concision and forcefulness are matters of art and personal style as well as common sense and tradition. But if you are going to disregard a principle, do so sparingly and out of educated choice. On the Writing Test, sticking closely to the principles of standard written English will help you produce a concise, forceful, and correct essay.

Be Concise (or Cut the Fat)

The first four principles of good writing relate to the goal of expressing your points clearly in as few words as possible. Each principle represents a specific way to tighten up your writing.

1. Avoid Wordiness

Do not use several words when one will do. Wordy phrases are like junk food: they add only fat, no muscle. Many people make the mistake of writing *at the present time* or *at this point* in time instead of the simpler *now*, or *take into consideration* instead of simply *consider*, in an attempt to make their prose seem more scholarly or more formal. It doesn't work. Instead, their prose ends up seeming inflated and pretentious. Don't waste your words or your time.

The Big Four

An effective essay is concise, forceful, correct, and polished.

Wordy:

I am of the opinion that the aforementioned managers should be advised that they will be evaluated with regard to the utilization of responsive organizational software for the purpose of devising a responsive network of customers.

Concise:

We should tell the managers that we will evaluate their use of flexible computerized databases to develop a customer's network.

Waste Not

Don't use more words than are necessary.

Writing Drill 1

Improve the following sentences by omitting or replacing wordy phrases. Write your repaired sentence on the line underneath the original sentence. (Suggested repairs appear at the end of this chapter.)

1. The agency is not prepared to undertake expansion at this point in time.

Rewrite: _____

_____

2. In view of the fact that John has prepared with much care for this presentation, it would be a good idea to award him with the project.

Rewrite: _____

_____

3. The airline has a problem with always having arrivals that come at least an hour late, despite the fact that the leaders of the airline promise that promptness is a goal which has a high priority for all the employees involved.

Rewrite: _____

_____

4. In spite of the fact that she only has a little bit of experience in photography right now, she will probably do well in the future because she has a great deal of motivation to succeed in her chosen profession.

Rewrite: _____

_____

5. The United States is not in a position to spend more money to alleviate the suffering of the people of other countries considering the problems of its own citizens.

Rewrite: _____

_____

6. Although not untactful, George is a man who says exactly what he believes.

Rewrite: _____

_____

7. Accuracy is a subject that has great importance to English teachers and company presidents alike.

Rewrite: _____

_____

8. The reason why humans kill each other is that they experience fear of those whom they do not understand.

Rewrite: _____

_____

9. Ms. Miller speaks with a high degree of intelligence with regard to many aspects of modern philosophy.

Rewrite: _____

_____

10. The best of all possible leaders is one who listens and inspires simultaneously.

Rewrite: _____

_____

2. Don't Be Redundant

Redundancy means that the writer needlessly repeats an idea. It's redundant to speak of "a beginner lacking experience." The word *beginner* by itself implies lack of experience. You can eliminate redundant words or phrases without changing the meaning of the sentence. Watch out for words that add nothing to the sense of the sentence. The chart below lists some common redundant phrases and how to fix them.

Easy to Fix

Redundancy is a common (and widespread) problem in student essays. But don't worry: You can easily eliminate redundant elements when proofreading.

Redundant	Concise
refer back	refer
few in number	few
small-sized	small
grouped together	grouped
in my own personal opinion	in my opinion
end result	result
serious crisis	crisis
new initiatives	initiatives

Writing Drill 2

Repair the following sentences by crossing out redundant elements. (Suggested repairs appear at the end of the chapter.)

1. All these problems have combined together to create a serious crisis.

2. A staff that large in size needs an effective supervisor who can get the job done.

3. He knows how to follow directions and he knows how to do what he is told.

4. The writer's technical skill and ability do not mask his poor plot line.

5. That monument continues to remain a significant tourist attraction.

6. The recently observed trend of spending on credit has created a middle class that is poorer and more impoverished than ever before.

7. Those who can follow directions are few in number.

8. She has deliberately chosen to change careers.

9. Dialogue opens up many doors to compromise.

10. The ultimate conclusion is that environmental and economic concerns are intertwined.

3. Avoid Needless Qualification

Since the object of your essay is to convince your reader, you will want to adopt a reasonable tone. There won't be any single, clear-cut "answer" to the essay topic, so don't overstate your case. Occasional use of such qualifiers as *fairly*, *rather*, *somewhat*, *relatively* and of such expressions as *seems to be*, *a little*, and *a certain amount of* will let the reader know that you are reasonable, but using such modifiers too often weakens your argument. Excessive qualification makes you sound hesitant. Like wordy phrases, qualifiers can add bulk without adding substance.

Wordy:
This rather serious breach of etiquette may possibly shake the very foundations of the diplomatic community.

Concise:
This serious breach of etiquette may shake the foundations of the diplomatic community.

Just as bad is the overuse of the word *very*. Some writers use this intensifying adverb before almost every adjective in an attempt to be more forceful. If you need to add emphasis, look for a stronger adjective (or verb).

Weak:
Novak is a very good pianist.

Piling It On

Don't try to qualify words that are already absolute.

Strong:

Novak is a virtuoso pianist. OR Novak plays beautifully.

Wrong	Correct
more unique	unique
the very worst	the worst
completely full	full

Writing Drill 3

Although reasonable qualification benefits an essay, excessive qualification debilitates your argument. The excessive qualification used below might occasionally be appropriate, but it won't usually be. Practice tightening up your prose by eliminating needless qualification in the sentences below. Write your repaired sentence below the original sentence. (Suggested rewrites appear at the end of the chapter.)

1. She is a fairly excellent teacher.

Rewrite: _____

_____

2. Ferrara seems to be sort of a slow worker.

Rewrite: _____

_____

3. There are very many reasons technology has not permeated all countries equally.

Rewrite: _____

_____

4. It is rather important to pay attention to all the details of a murder trial as well as to the "larger picture."

Rewrite: _____

_____

5. You yourself are the very best person to decide what you should do for a living.

Rewrite: _____

_____

6. It is possible that the author overstates his case somewhat.

Rewrite: _____

_____

7. The president perhaps should use a certain amount of diplomacy before he resorts to force.

Rewrite: _____

_____

Don't Be Timid

Overusing qualifiers like *fairly*, *rather*, *seems to be*, or *somewhat* makes you sound hesitant.

8. In Italy I found about the best food I have ever eaten.

Rewrite: _____

_____

9. Needless to say, children should be taught to cooperate at home and in school.

Rewrite: _____

_____

10. The travel agent does not recommend the trip to Tripoli, since it is possible that one may be hurt.

Rewrite: _____

_____

4. Don't Write Sentences Just to Fill Up Space

This principle suggests several "Don'ts."

- Don't write a sentence that gets you nowhere.
- Don't ask a question only to answer it.
- Don't merely copy the essay's directions.
- Don't write a whole sentence only to announce that you're changing the subject.

If you have something to say, say it without preamble. If you need to smooth over a change of subject, do so with a transitional word or phrase, rather than with a meaningless sentence.

Cut the Fat

If your proofreading reveals wasted sentences, neatly cross them out.

Wordy:
    Which idea of the author's is more in line with what I believe? This is a very interesting . . . .

Concise:
    The author's beliefs are similar to mine.

The author of the previous wordy example is just wasting words and time. Get to the point quickly and stay there. Simplicity and clarity win points.

Writing Drill 4

Can you rewrite each of these two-sentence statements as one concise sentence? Use the lines below the original sentences. (Suggested rewrites appear at the end of the chapter.)

1. In the late twentieth century, the earth can be characterized as a small planet. Advanced technology has made it easy for people who live vast distances from each other to communicate.

Rewrite: _____

_____

2. What's the purpose of getting rid of the chemical pollutants in water? People cannot safely consume water that contains chemical pollutants.

Rewrite: _____

_____

3. Napoleon suffered defeat in Russia because most of his troops perished in the cold. Most of his men died because they had no winter clothing to protect them from the cold.

Rewrite: _____

_____

4. Third, I do not believe those who argue that some of Shakespeare's plays were written by others. There is no evidence that other people had a hand in writing Shakespeare's plays.

Rewrite: _____

_____

5. Which point of view is closest to my own? This is a good question. I agree with those who say that the United States should send soldiers to areas of conflict.

Rewrite: _____

_____

6. Frank Lloyd Wright was a famous architect. He was renowned for his ability to design buildings that blend into their surroundings.

Rewrite: _____

_____

7. Who was Julius Caesar? He was a leader of the Roman Empire.

Rewrite: _____

_____

8. He was not in class today. The teacher refused to let him into class because he showed up ten minutes late.

Rewrite: _____

_____

9. The fire burned thousands of acres of forest land. Many trees were destroyed by the fire.

Rewrite: _____

_____

10. A lot of people find math a difficult subject to master. They have trouble with math because it requires very precise thinking skills.

Rewrite: _____

_____

Be Forceful/Take a Stand

The next group of principles aim at the goal of producing forceful writing. If you follow these principles, your writing will be much more convincing to the reader.

5. Avoid Needless Self-Reference

Avoid such unnecessary phrases as *I believe, I feel,* and *in my opinion.*

Weak:

    I am of the opinion that air pollution is a more serious problem than the government has led us to believe.

Forceful:

    Air pollution is a more serious problem than the government has led us to believe.

Self-reference is another form of qualifying what you say—a very obvious form. A few self-references in an essay might be appropriate, just as the use of qualifiers like *probably* and *perhaps* can be effective if you practice using them *sparingly.* Practice is the only sure way to improve your writing.

Take a Stand

An effective essay is forceful, not wishy-washy.

Keep a Low Profile

There is no need to remind your reader that what you are writing is your opinion.

Writing Drill 5

Rephrase these sentences to eliminate needless self-references. Rewrite the sentence on the line underneath it. (Suggested rewrites appear at the end of the chapter.)

1. I feel we ought to pay teachers more than we pay senators.

Rewrite: _____

_____

2. The author, in my personal opinion, is stuck in the past.

Rewrite: _____

_____

3. I do not think this argument can be generalized to most business owners.

Rewrite: _____

_____

4. My own experience shows me that food is the best social lubricant.

Rewrite: _____

_____

5. I doubt more people would vote even if they had more information about candidates.

Rewrite: _____

_____

6. Although I am no expert, I do not think privacy should be valued more than social concerns.

Rewrite: _____

_____

7. My guess is that most people want to do good work, but many are bored or frustrated with their jobs.

Rewrite: _____

_____

8. I must emphasize that I am not saying the author does not have a point.

Rewrite: _____

_____

9. If I were a college president, I would implement several specific reforms to combat apathy.

Rewrite: _____

_____

10. It is my belief that either alternative would prove disastrous.

Rewrite: _____

_____

Be Active

Use active verbs, not passive ones, whenever possible.

6. Use the Active Voice

Using the passive voice is a way to avoid accountability. Put verbs in the active voice whenever possible. In the active voice, the subject performs the action: *We should decide now.* In the passive voice, the subject is the receiver of the action and is often only implied: *It should be decided now.*

You should avoid the passive voice EXCEPT in the following cases.

- When you do not know who performed the action: *The letter was opened before I received it.*

- When you prefer not to refer directly to the person who performs the action: *An error has been made in computing this data.*

Passive:
> The estimate of this year's tax revenues was prepared by the General Accounting Office.

Active:
> The General Accounting Office prepared the estimate of this year's tax revenues.

Passive sentences are weak. They are usually the product of writing before you think. Avoid this by prewriting. Take a few minutes to find out what you want to say before you say it. Your prewriting, especially the game plan in which you begin to outline ideas for sentences, should give you an idea of your essay's purpose. To change from the passive to the active voice, ask yourself who or what is performing the action. In the sentence above, the *General Accounting Office* is performing the action. Therefore, the *GAO* should be the subject of the sentence.

Writing Drill 6

Replace the passive voice with active wherever possible. Use the line below the original sentence for your rewrite. (Suggested rewrites appear at the end of the chapter.)

1. The Spanish-American War was fought by brave but misguided men.

   Rewrite: _____

   _____

2. The bill was passed in time, but it was not signed by the president until the time for action had passed.

   Rewrite: _____

   _____

3. Advice is usually requested by those who need it least; it is not sought out by the truly lost and ignorant.

   Rewrite: _____

   _____

4. That building should be relocated where it can be appreciated by the citizens.

   Rewrite: _____

   _____

5. Garbage collectors should be generously rewarded for their dirty, smelly labors.

   Rewrite: _____

   _____

6. The conditions of the contract agreement were ironed out minutes before the strike deadline.

   Rewrite: _____

   _____

7. The minutes of the City Council meeting should be taken by the city clerk.

   Rewrite: _____

   _____

8. With sugar, water, or salt, many ailments contracted in less-developed countries could be treated.

   Rewrite: _____

   _____

★

Don't Rush

If you take the time to plan before you write, you can avoid weak sentences.

9. Test results were distributed with no concern for confidentiality.

Rewrite: _____

_____

10. The report was compiled by a number of field anthropologists and
    marriage experts.

Rewrite: _____

_____

**Think Before You
Write**

Think about what you want to
accomplish in a sentence
before you actually write it.

7. Avoid Weak Openings

Try not to begin a sentence with *there is*, *there are*, or *it is*. These roundabout
expressions usually indicate that you are trying to distance yourself from
the position you are taking. Again, weak openings usually result from writing before you think, hedging until you find out what you want to say.
(Suggested rewrites appear at the end of the chapter.)

Writing Drill 7

Rewrite these sentences to eliminate weak openings. Use the lines below
the original sentence for your rewrite.

1. It would be unwise for businesses to ignore the illiteracy problem.

Rewrite: _____

_____

2. It can be seen that in many fields experience is more important than
    training.

Rewrite: _____

_____

3. There are several reasons why this plane is obsolete.

Rewrite: _____

_____

4. It would be of no use to fight a drug war without waging a battle
    against demand for illicit substances.

Rewrite: _____

_____

5. There are many strong points in the candidate's favor; intelligence,
    unfortunately, is not among them.

Rewrite: _____

_____

Be Concrete

Specific language is always better than vague language.

6. It is difficult to justify building a more handsome prison.

Rewrite: _____

_____

7. It has been decided that we, as a society, can tolerate homelessness.

Rewrite: _____

_____

8. There seems to be little doubt that Americans like watching television better than conversing.

Rewrite: _____

_____

9. It is clear that cats make better pets than mice.

Rewrite: _____

_____

10. It is obvious that intelligence is a product of environment and heredity.

Rewrite: _____

_____

8. Avoid Needlessly Vague Language

Don't let words flow uncontrolled from the end of your pencil. Choose specific, descriptive words. Vague language weakens your writing because it forces the reader to guess what you mean instead of allowing the reader to concentrate fully on your ideas and style. The essay topics you're given aren't going to be obscure. You will be able to come up with specific examples and concrete information about the topics. Your argument will be more forceful if you stick to this information.

Weak:
Brown is highly educated.

Forceful:
Brown has a master's degree in business administration.

Weak:
She is a great communicator.

Forceful:
She speaks persuasively.

Notice that sometimes, to be more specific and concrete, you will have to use more words than you might with vague language. This principle is not in conflict with the general goal of concision. Being concise may mean eliminating *unnecessary* words. Avoiding vagueness may mean adding *necessary* words.

Writing Drill 8

Rewrite these sentences to replace vague language with specific, concrete language. Use the lines below the sentence for your rewrite. (Suggested rewrites appear at the end of the chapter.)

1. Water is transformed into steam when the former is heated up to 100 degrees C.

    Rewrite: _____

    _____

2. The diplomat was required to execute an agreement that stipulated that he would live in whatever country the federal government thought necessary.

    Rewrite: _____

    _____

3. Arthur is a careless person.

    Rewrite: _____

    _____

4. Many economists think that banks are contributing to the current economic downturn by constantly raising their interest rates.

    Rewrite: _____

    _____

5. She told us that she was going to go to the store as soon as her mother came home.

    Rewrite: _____

    _____

6. A radar unit is a highly specialized piece of equipment.

    Rewrite: _____

    _____

7. The principal told John that he shouldn't even think about coming back to school until he changed his ways.

    Rewrite: _____

    _____

Tired

Don't use worn-out phrases in your essay. (Clichés are a dime a dozen.)

8. The police detective had to seek the permission of the lawyer to question the suspect.

Rewrite: _____

_____

9. Thousands of species of animals were destroyed when the last ice age occurred.

Rewrite: _____

_____

10. The secretary was unable to complete the task that had been assigned.

Rewrite: _____

_____

9. Avoid Clichés

Clichés are overused expressions, expressions that may once have seemed colorful and powerful but are now dull and worn-out. Time pressure and anxiety may make you lose focus; that's when clichés may slip into your writing. A reliance on vague or meaningless clichés will suggest you are a lazy thinker. Keep them out of your essay.

Weak:
Performance in a crisis is the acid test for a leader.

Forceful:
Performance in a crisis is the best indicator of a leader's abilities.

Putting a cliché in quotation marks in order to indicate your distance from the cliché does not strengthen the sentence. If anything, it just makes weak writing more noticeable. Notice whether or not you use clichés. If you do, ask yourself if you could substitute more specific language for the cliché.

Writing Drill 9

Make the following sentences more forceful by replacing clichés. Use the lines below the original sentence for your rewrites. (Suggested rewrites appear at the end of the chapter.)

1. Beyond the shadow of a doubt Jefferson was a great leader.

Rewrite: _____

_____

2. I have a sneaking suspicion that families spend less time together than they did fifteen years ago.

Rewrite: _____

_____

3. The pizza delivery man arrived in the sequestered jury's hour of need.

Rewrite: _____

_____

4. Trying to find the employee responsible for this embarrassing information leak is like trying to find a needle in a haystack.

Rewrite: _____

_____

5. Both strategies would be expensive and completely ineffective, so it's six of one and half a dozen of the other.

Rewrite: _____

_____

6. The military is putting all its eggs in one basket by relying so heavily on nuclear missiles for the nation's defense.

Rewrite: _____

_____

7. Older doctors should be required to update their techniques, but you can't teach an old dog new tricks.

Rewrite: _____

_____

8. You have to take this new fad with a grain of salt.

Rewrite: _____

_____

9. The politician reminds me of Abraham Lincoln: He's like a diamond in the rough.

Rewrite: _____

_____

10. A ballpark estimate of the number of fans in the stadium would be 120,000.

Rewrite: _____

_____

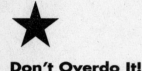

Don't Overdo It!

Don't use overtechnical language that a reader with no special training can't understand.

10. Avoid Jargon

Jargon includes two categories of words that you should avoid. First is the specialized vocabulary of a group, such as that used by doctors, lawyers, or baseball coaches. Second is the overly inflated and complex language that burdens many students' essays. You will not impress anyone with big words that do not fit the tone or context of your essay, especially if you misuse them.

If you are not certain of a word's meaning or appropriateness, leave it out. An appropriate word, even a simple one, will add impact to your argument. As you come across words you are unsure of, ask yourself, "Would a reader in a different field be able to understand exactly what I mean from the words I've chosen?" "Is there any way I can say the same thing more simply?"

Weak:
> The international banks are cognizant of the new law's significance.

Forceful:
> The international banks are aware of the new law's significance.

Wrong:
> The new law would negatively impact each of the nations involved.

Correct:

> The new law would hurt each of the nations involved.
> (*Impact* is also used to mean *affect* or *benefit*.)

Jargon Hit List

prioritize	parameter (boundary, limit)
optimize	user-friendly
time frame	utilize (use)
input/output	finalize (end, complete)
mutually beneficial	bottom line
conceptualize (imagine, think)	assistance
maximize	target (v.)
designate	blindside
originate (start, begin)	downside
facilitate (help, speed up)	ongoing (continuing)

Writing Drill 10

Replace the jargon in the following sentences with more appropriate language. Use the lines below each sentence for your rewrite. (Suggested rewrites appear at the end of the chapter.)

1. We anticipate utilizing hundreds of paper clips in the foreseeable future.

   Rewrite: _____

   _____

2. The research-oriented person should not be hired for a people-oriented position.

   Rewrite: _____

   _____

3. Educationwise, our schoolchildren have been neglected.

   Rewrite: _____

   _____

4. Foreign diplomats should always interface with local leaders.

   Rewrite: _____

   _____

5. Pursuant to your being claimed as a dependent on the returns of another taxpayer or resident wage earner, you may not consider yourself exempt if your current income exceeds five hundred dollars.

   Rewrite: _____

   _____

6. There is considerable evidentiary support for the assertion that Vienna sausages are good for you.

   Rewrite: _____

   _____

7. With reference to the poem, I submit that the second and third stanzas connote a certain despair.

   Rewrite: _____

   _____

8. Allow me to elucidate my position: This horse is the epitome, the very quintessence of equine excellence.

   Rewrite: _____

   _____

9. In the case of the recent railway disaster, it is clear that governmental regulatory agencies obfuscated in the preparation of materials for release to the public through both the electronic and print media.

Rewrite: _____

_____

10. Having been blindsided by innumerable unforeseen crises, this office has not been able to prepare for the aforementioned exigencies.

Rewrite: _____

_____

Be Correct (or Follow the Rules)

Correctness is perhaps the most difficult goal for writers to achieve. The complex rules of standard written English can leave you feeling unsure of your writing and more than a bit confused. But remember, the most important lesson you can take from this chapter is how to organize your thoughts into a *strong*, well-supported argument. Style and grammar are important but *secondary* concerns on the essay portion of the Writing Test. Your readers will *not* mark you down for occasional errors common to first-draft writing. So just think of this section as helping you to improve the details of good writing. If it begins to overwhelm you, stop and take a break. You need time to absorb this information.

Do the exercises and then compare your answers to ours. Make sure you understand what the error was in each sentence.

As you work through this section, you will come across a few technical words that describe particular functions that words have in a sentence. You will not be expected to know these terms on the Writing Test, only to understand the essence of a word's function in the sentence so that you can recognize an error when you see one.

11. Pay Attention to Subject-Verb Agreement

Many of the rules of English usage are designed to force the writer to stick with one structure or usage throughout a sentence or even an entire essay in order to give the reader as many clues as possible about meaning. Perhaps the most basic example of this is subject-verb agreement. Singular subjects and plural subjects take different forms of the verb in the present tense. Usually the difference lies in the presence or absence of a final -*s* (for example, *he becomes* and *they become*), but sometimes the difference is more radical (for example, *he is, they are*). You can usually trust your ear to give you the correct verb form, but certain situations cause difficulty:

Don't You Agree?

Singular subjects go with singular verbs, and plural subjects with plural verbs.

- When the subject and verb are separated by a number of words
- When the subject is an indefinite pronoun
- When the subject consists of more than one noun

Don't let the words that come between the subject and the verb confuse you as to the number (singular or plural) of the subject. Usually one word can be pinpointed as the grammatical subject of the sentence. The verb, no matter how far removed, must agree with that subject in number.

Incorrect:

> The *joys* of climbing mountains, especially if one is a novice climber without the proper equipment, escapes me.

Correct:

> The *joys* of climbing mountains, especially if one is a novice climber without the proper equipment, escape me.

Incorrect:

> A *group* of jockeys who have already finished the first race and who wish to have their pictures taken are blocking my view of the horses.

Correct:

> A *group* of jockeys who have already finished the first race and who wish to have their pictures taken is blocking my view of the horses. (The long prepositional phrase beginning with the preposition of qualifies the noun *group*. The subject of the sentence is the noun "group," which takes the singular verb *is*).

Look out for prepositional phrases intervening between subject and verb. In both examples, the phrases and clauses between subject and verb do not affect the grammatical relationship between subject and verb. An intervening phrase does not change a singular subject into a plural one.

Don't Lose Track of the Subject

A verb must agree with its subject in number regardless of intervening phrases.

Some Common Prepositions

after	by	from	onto	under
against	concerning	in	out	until
before	despite	off	over	up
between	down	on	through	with

Also, watch out for collective nouns like *group, audience, committee,* or *majority*. These take a singular noun unless the individuals forming the group are to be emphasized. The word *number* takes a singular verb when preceded by *the* and a plural verb when preceded by *a*.

Correct:

> A majority of the committee *have* signed their names to the report.

Correct:

A majority of the jury *thinks* that the defendant is guilty.

Correct:

A *number* of fans *hope* for a mere glimpse of his handsome face; unfortunately, they are rarely satisfied with a mere glimpse.

Correct:

The *number* of fans who hope to catch a glimpse of his handsome face *seems* to grow exponentially each time the tabloids write a story of his seclusion.

Keep this rule in mind: A subject that consists of two or more nouns connected by *and* takes the plural form of the verb.

Correct:

Karl, who is expert in cooking Hunan spicy duck, *and George,* who is expert in eating Hunan spicy duck, *have* combined their expertise to start a new restaurant.

When the subject consists of two or more nouns connected by *or* or *nor*, the verb agrees with the closest noun.

Correct:

Either the senators or the president *is* misinformed.

Correct:

Either the president or the senators *are* misinformed.

There are some connecting phrases that look as though they should make a group of words into a plural but actually do not. The only connecting word that can make a series of singular nouns into a plural subject is *and*. In particular, the following connecting words and phrases do not result in a plural subject:

Connecting Words That Don't Create a Plural Subject

along with	in addition to
as well as	together with
besides	

Incorrect:

The chairman, along with the treasurer and the secretary, are misinformed.

Correct:

The chairman, along with the treasurer and the secretary, is misinformed.

If a sentence that is grammatically correct still sounds awkward, you should probably rephrase your thought.

Less Awkward:
Along with the treasurer and the secretary, the chairman is misinformed.

A note on the subjunctive: After verbs such as *recommend, require, suggest, ask, demand,* and *insist* and after expressions of requirement, suggestion, and demand (for example, I demand that), use the subjunctive form of the verb—that is, the form of the verb used after such expressions as "I want *to* _____."

Correct:
I recommend that the chocolate cake *be* reinstated on your menu.

Correct:
It is essential that the reader *understand* what you are trying to say.

Writing Drill 11

Fix or replace incorrect verbs. Use the lines below each sentence for your rewrite. (Suggested repairs appear at the end of the chapter.)

1. The logical structure of his complicated and rather tortuous arguments are always the same.

Rewrite: _____

_____

2. The majority of the organization's members is over 60 years old.

Rewrite: _____

_____

3. Both the young child and her grandfather was depressed for months after discovering that the oldest ice cream parlor in the city had closed its doors forever.

Rewrite: _____

_____

4. Hartz brought the blueprints and model that was still on the table instead of the ones that Mackenzie had returned to the cabinet.

Rewrite: _____

_____

5. A case of bananas have been sent to the local distributor in compensation for the fruit that was damaged in transit.

Rewrite: _____

_____

6. A total of 50 editors read each article, a process that takes at least a week, sometimes six months.

Rewrite: _____

_____

7. Neither the shipping clerk who packed the equipment nor the truckers who transported it admits responsibility for the dented circuit box.

Rewrite: _____

_____

8. Either Georgette or Robespierre are going to be asked to dinner by the madcap Calvin. I dread the result in either case.

Rewrite: _____

_____

9. I can never decide whether to eat an orange or a Belgian chocolate; each of them have their wondrous qualities.

Rewrite: _____

_____

10. Everyone in the United States, as well as the Canadians, expect the timber agreement to fall through.

Rewrite: _____

_____

12. Use Modifiers Correctly

In English, the position of the word within a sentence often establishes the word's relationship to other words in the sentence. This is especially true with modifying phrases. Modifiers, like pronouns, are generally connected to the nearest word that agrees with the modifier in person and number. If a modifier is placed too far from the word it modifies, the meaning may be lost or obscured. Notice in the following sentences that ambiguity results when the modifying phrases are misplaced in the sentence.

Ambiguous:
Gary and Martha sat talking about the movie in the office.

Ambiguous:
They wondered how much the house was really worth when they bought it.

Avoid ambiguity by placing modifiers as close as possible to the words they are intended to modify.

Clear:

Gary and Martha sat in the office talking about the movie.

Clear:

When they bought the house, they wondered how much it was really worth.

Modifiers can refer to words that either precede or follow them. Ambiguity can also result when a modifier is squeezed between two possible referents and the reader has no way to know which is the intended referent.

Ambiguous:

The dentist instructed him regularly to brush his teeth.

Ambiguous:

Tom said in the car he had a map of New Jersey.

Be sure that the modifier is closest to the intended referent and that there is no other possible referent on the other side of the modifier.

Clear:

The dentist instructed him to brush his teeth regularly.

Clear:

Tom said he had a map of New Jersey in the car.

All the ambiguous sentences above are examples of misplaced modifiers: Modifiers whose placement makes the intended reference unclear. In addition to misplaced modifiers, watch for dangling modifiers: Modifiers whose intended referents are not even present.

Incorrect:

Coming out of context, Peter was startled by Julia's perceptiveness.

The modifying phrase *coming out of context* is probably not intended to refer to *Peter*, but if not, then to whom or what? *Julia? Perceptiveness?* None of these makes sense as the referent of *coming out of context*. What came out of context was more likely a *statement* or *remark*. The sentence is incorrect because there is no word or phrase that can be pinpointed as the referent of the opening modifying phrase. Rearrangement and rewording solve the problem.

Correct:

Julia's remark, coming out of context, startled Peter with its perceptiveness.

Remember

Modifiers should be placed as close as possible to what they modify.

Writing Drill 12

Rewrite these sentences to put modifiers closer to the words they modify. Rewrite each sentence on the line below it. (Suggested rewrites appear at the end of the chapter.)

1. Bentley advised him quickly to make up his mind.

Rewrite: _____

_____

2. I agree with the author's statements in principle.

Rewrite: _____

_____

3. Coming out of the woodwork, he was surprised to see termites.

Rewrite: _____

_____

4. The governor's conference met to discuss racial unrest in the audi-torium.

Rewrite: _____

_____

5. Hernandez said in her office she had all the necessary documents.

Rewrite: _____

_____

6. All of his friends were not able to come, but he decided that he pre-ferred small parties anyway.

Rewrite: _____

_____

7. Margolis remembered she had to place a telephone call when she got home.

Rewrite: _____

_____

8. George told Suzette he did not like to discuss politics as they walked through the museum.

Rewrite: _____

_____

9. Having worked in publishing for ten years, Stokely's résumé shows that he is well qualified.

Rewrite: _____

_____

10. A politician would fail to serve her constituents without experience in community service.

Rewrite: _____

_____

13. Use Pronouns Correctly

A pronoun is a word that replaces a noun in a sentence. Every time you write a pronoun—*he, him, his, she, her, it, its, they, their, that,* or *which*—be sure there can be absolutely no doubt what its antecedent is. (An antecedent is the particular noun a pronoun refers to or stands for). Careless use of pronouns can obscure your intended meaning.

Ambiguous:
The teacher told the student he was lazy.
(Does *he* refer to *teacher* or *student*?)

Ambiguous:
Sara knows more about history than Irina because she learned it from her father.
(Does *she* refer to *Sara* or *Irina*?)

You can usually rearrange a sentence to avoid ambiguous pronoun reference.

Clear:
The student was lazy, and the teacher told him so.

Clear:
The teacher considered himself lazy and told the student so.

Clear:
Since Sara learned history from her father, she knows more than Irina does.

Clear:
Because Irina learned history from her father, she knows less about it than Sara does.

If you are worried that a pronoun reference will be ambiguous, rewrite the sentence so that there is no doubt. Do not be afraid to repeat the antecedent (the noun that the pronoun refers to) if necessary.

Grammar Reference

Pronoun: a word that replaces a noun in a sentence.

Antecedent: the noun a pronoun stands for.

Be Agreeable

A pronoun must agree with its antecedent. Make sure each pronoun refers clearly to one and only one antecedent.

Ambiguous:

> I would rather settle in Phoenix than in Albuquerque, although it lacks wonderful restaurants.

Clear:

> I would rather settle in Phoenix than in Albuquerque, although Phoenix lacks wonderful restaurants.

A reader must be able to pinpoint the pronoun's antecedent. Even if you think the reader will know what you mean, do not use a pronoun without a clear and appropriate antecedent.

Incorrect:

> When you are painting, be sure not to get it on the floor. (*It* could refer to only the noun *paint*. But pronouns cannot refer to implied nouns.)

Correct:

> When you are painting, be sure not to get any paint on the floor.

Avoid using *this*, *that*, *it*, or *which*, to refer to a whole phrase, sentence, or idea. Even when these pronouns are placed very close to their intended antecedents, the references may still be unclear.

Unclear:

> Consumers use larger amounts of nonrecyclable plastic every year. This will someday turn the earth into a giant trash can.

Clear:

> Consumers use larger amounts of nonrecyclable plastic every year. This ever-growing mass of waste products will someday turn the earth into a giant trash can.

A good rule of thumb is to try not to begin a sentence with *that* or *this* unless the word accompanies a noun. For example, it's fine to say *this problem*, or *that situation*.

Unclear:

> The salesman spoke loudly, swayed back and forth, and tapped the table nervously, which made his customers extremely nervous.

Clear:

> The salesman spoke loudly, swayed back and forth, and tapped the table nervously, mannerisms which made his customers extremely nervous.

Also, unless you are talking about the weather, avoid beginning a sentence with *it*.

Weak:

It is difficult to distinguish between the rights of criminals and those of victims.

Better:

To distinguish between the rights of criminals and those of victims is difficult.

A few of the indefinite pronouns that can be either singular or plural are *some, all, most, any,* and *none.* When using one of these words as the subject, you must check to see whether the antecedent is singular or plural.

Correct:

He was unable to finish his *work* last night. *Some remains* to be done today. *None* of it *is easy.* (Read: *Some* of his work *remains; none* of his work *is* easy.)

Incorrect:

His superiors have been following his progress. *Some are* more impressed than others. *None are* overwhelmed. (Read: *Some* of his superiors *are; none* of his superiors *are.*)

Other indefinite pronouns are invariable in number. Look at these examples.

Remember One Thing

Pronouns ending with *-body, -one,* and *-thing* are singular.

Singular Indefinite Pronouns

anybody	everybody	somebody	either	one
anyone	everyone	someone	neither	each
anything	everything	something	no one	

(Note: Just remember that *-body, -one,* and *-thing* pronouns are singular.)

Plural Indefinite Pronouns

both	few	many	several

A related problem arises when writers try to avoid using the traditionally generic pronoun *he.* Writers may mistakenly substitute *they* for *he.* But there are other ways to avoid using *he* as a generic pronoun.

Incorrect:

Each person must protect their individuality if one wants to remain truly free.

Correct:

People must protect their individuality if they want to remain truly free.

Relative Pronouns

who	whom	that	which

It may be difficult to decide which relative pronoun—*who, whom, that,* or *which*—to use.

Correct:
Those people, whom I have been calling all day, never returned my call.

Incorrect:
Those salespeople, whom have been calling all day, are harassing me.

One way to decide is to turn the clause into a question. Ask yourself, "I have been calling *who* or *whom*?" Answer your question, substituting a pronoun: "I have been calling *them*." In the second sentence, you would ask, "*Who* or *whom* has been calling all day?" Answer your question, substituting a pronoun: "*They* have been calling all day." If you use *her, him, them,* or *us* to answer the question, the appropriate relative pronoun is *whom*. If you use *she, he, they,* or *we* to answer the question, the appropriate relative pronoun is *who*.

That and *which* are often used interchangeably, but they shouldn't be. As a rule, use *which* if the relative clause is set off by commas (in other words, when the clause isn't crucial to the meaning of the sentence). Use *that* if the clause isn't set off by commas (when the clause is crucial to the meaning of the sentence).

Example:
The movie, *which* was released two years behind schedule, was one of the few *that* were real box office hits this spring.

Watch Out

Some nouns and pronouns are singular in one context and plural in another, depending on the number of the antecedent.

Writing Drill 13

Correct the following sentences, using the lines below each sentence for your rewrite. (Suggested rewrites appear at the end of the chapter.)

1. Clausen's dog won first place at the show because he was well bred.

Rewrite: _____

_____

2. The critic's review made the novel a commercial success. He is now a rich man.

Rewrite: _____

_____

3. The military advisor was more conventional than his commander, but he was a superior strategist.

Rewrite: _____

_____

4. Bertha telephoned her friends in California before going home for the night, which she had not done for weeks.

Rewrite: _____

_____

5. Although John hoped and prayed for the job, it did no good. When he called him the next morning, they had hired someone else.

Rewrite: _____

_____

6. You must pay attention when fishing—otherwise, you might lose it.

Rewrite: _____

_____

7. Zolsta Karmagi is the better musician, but he had more formal training.

Rewrite: _____

_____

14. Pay Attention to Parallelism

Matching constructions must be expressed in parallel form. It is often rhetorically effective to use a particular construction several times in succession, in order to provide emphasis. The technique is called *parallel construction*, and it is effective only when used sparingly. If your sentences are varied, a parallel construction will stand out. If your sentences are already repetitive, a parallel structure will further obscure your meaning. Here's how parallel construction should be used.

> *As a* leader, Lincoln inspired a nation to throw off the chains of slavery; *as a* philosopher, he proclaimed the greatness of the little man; *as a* human being, he served as a timeless example of humility.

The repetition of the italicized construction provides a strong sense of rhythm and organization to the sentence and alerts the reader to yet another aspect of Lincoln's character.

The most common mistake that students make in their essays with regard to parallelism is to fail to use parallel structure where it's needed. But sometimes students make the mistake of using parallel structure where it's not needed. Here's an example of how someone might make the mistake of using a parallel structure for dissimilar items.

Incorrect:
They are sturdy, attractive, and cost only a dollar each.

(The phrase *they are* makes sense preceding the adjectives *sturdy* and *attractive*, but cannot be understood before *cost only a dollar each*.)

Correct:
> They are sturdy and attractive, and they cost only a dollar each.

Parallel constructions must be expressed in parallel grammatical form: All nouns, all infinitives, all gerunds, all prepositional phrases, or all clauses.

Incorrect:
> All students should learn word processing, accounting, and how to program computers.

Correct:
> All students should learn word processing, accounting, and computer programming.

This principle applies to any words that might begin each item in a series: Prepositions (*in, on, by, with*, et cetera), articles (*the, a, an*), helping verbs (*had, has, would*, etc.) and possessives (*his, her, our*, et cetera). Either repeat the word before every element in a series or include it only before the first item. Anything else violates the rules of parallelism.

In effect, your treatment of the second element of the series determines the form of all subsequent elements. Look at these examples.

Incorrect:
> He invested his money in stocks, in real estate, and a home for retired performers.

Correct:
> He invested his money in stocks, in real estate, and in a home for retired performers.

Correct:
> He invested his money in stocks, real estate, and a home for retired performers.

When proofreading, check that each item in the series agrees with the word or phrase that begins the series. In the above example, *invested his money* is the common phrase that each item shares. You would read "He *invested his money in real estate, (invested his money) in stocks*, and *(invested his money) in a home for retired performers.*"

A number of constructions call for you to always express ideas in parallel form. These constructions include the following.

> *X* is as _____ as *Y*.
>
> *X* is more _____ than *Y*.
>
> *X* is less _____ than *Y*.
>
> Both *X* and *Y* . . .
>
> Either *X* or *Y* . . .
>
> Neither *X* nor *Y* . . .
>
> Not only *X* but also *Y* . . .

X and Y can stand for as little as one word or as much as a whole clause, but in any case the grammatical structure of X and Y must be identical.

Incorrect:
The view from this apartment is not nearly as spectacular as from that mountain lodge.

Correct:
The view from this apartment is not nearly as spectacular as *the one from that mountain lodge.*

Writing Drill 14

Correct the faulty parallelism in the following sentences. Use the line below each sentence for your rewrite. (Suggested rewrites appear at the end of the chapter.)

1. This organization will not tolerate the consumption, trafficking, or promoting the use of drugs.

Rewrite: _____

_____

2. The dancer taught her understudy how to move, how to dress, and how to work with choreographers and deal with professional competition.

Rewrite: _____

_____

3. Merrill based his confidence on the futures market, the bond market, and on the strength of the president's popularity.

Rewrite: _____

_____

4. The grocery baggers were ready, able, and were quite determined to do a great job.

Rewrite: _____

_____

5. The requirements for a business degree are not as stringent as a law degree.

Rewrite: _____

_____

Items in a List

Similar elements in a list should be in similar form.

Big Ego

Don't refer to yourself excessively in the essay, unless the topic calls for it.

15. Don't Shift Narrative Voice

Principle 5 advised you to avoid needless self-reference. Since you are asked to write an explanatory essay, however, an occasional self-reference may be appropriate. You may even call yourself *I* if you want, as long as you keep the number of first-person pronouns to a minimum. Less egocentric ways of referring to the narrator include *we* and *one*. If these more formal ways of writing seem stilted, stay with *I*.

1. In my lifetime, *I* have seen many challenges to the principle of free speech.

2. *We* can see many challenges to the principle of free speech.

3. *One* must admit that there have been many challenges to the principle of free speech.

The method of self-reference you select is called the narrative voice of your essay. Any of the above narrative voices are acceptable. Nevertheless, whichever you choose, you must be careful not to shift narrative voice in your essay. If you use *I* in the first sentence, for example, do not use *we* in a later sentence.

Incorrect:

In my lifetime, *I* have seen many challenges to the principle of free speech. *We* can see how a free society can get too complacent when free speech is taken for granted.

It is likewise wrong to shift from *you* to *one:*

Incorrect:

Just by following the news, *you* can readily see how politicians have a vested interest in pleasing powerful interest groups. But one should not generalize about this tendency.

To correct each of the above sentences, you need to change one pronoun to agree with the other, as follows.

Correct:

"*We* can readily see" (to agree with "though *we* should not generalize")

Correct:

"*I* can readily see" (to agree with "though *I* would not generalize")

Correct:

"*One* can readily see" (to agree with "though *one* should not generalize")

Writing Drill 15

Rewrite these sentences to give them consistent points of view. Use the lines below each sentence for your rewrite. (Suggested rewrites appear at the end of the chapter.)

1. I am disgusted with the waste we tolerate in this country. One cannot simply stand by without adding to such waste: Living here makes you wasteful.

Rewrite: _____

_____

2. You must take care not to take these grammar rules too seriously, since one can often become bogged down in details and forget why he is writing at all.

Rewrite: _____

_____

3. We all must take a stand against waste in this country; else how will one be able to look oneself in the mirror?

Rewrite: _____

_____

Be Polished (or Attend to Details)

Bright

Your essay will shine even more if you follow the last seven Principles of Good Writing.

Here are a few odds and ends that you need to pay attention to when you write your essay.

16. Avoid Slang and Colloquialisms

Conversational speech is filled with slang and colloquial expressions. However, you should avoid slang on the Writing Test. Slang terms and colloquialisms can be confusing to the reader, since these expressions are not universally understood. Even worse, such informal writing may give readers the impression that you are poorly educated or arrogant.

Inappropriate:
  He is really into gardening.

Correct:
  He enjoys gardening.

Inappropriate:
  She plays a wicked game of tennis.

Correct:
  She excels in tennis.

86 the Slang

Don't pepper your essay with words or phrases that aren't universally understood or accepted.

Inappropriate:
Myra has got to go to Memphis for a week.

Correct:
Myra must go to Memphis for a week.

Inappropriate:
Joan has been doing science for eight years now.

Correct:
Joan has been a scientist for eight years now.

Inappropriate:
The blackened salmon's been one of the restaurant's most popular entrées.

Correct:
The blackened salmon has been one of the restaurant's most popular entrées.

With a little thought you will find the right word. Using informal language is risky. Play it safe by sticking to standard usage.

Writing Drill 16

Replace the informal elements of the following sentences with more appropriate terms. Use the line below the sentence for your rewrite. (Suggested rewrites appear at the end of the chapter.)

1. Cynthia Larson sure knows her stuff.

Rewrite: _____

_____

2. The crowd was really into watching the fire-eating juggler, but then the dancing horse grabbed their attention.

Rewrite: _____

_____

3. As soon as the personnel department checks out his résumé, I am sure we will hear gales of laughter issuing from the office.

Rewrite: _____

_____

4. Having something funny to say seems awfully important in our culture.

Rewrite: _____

_____

5. The chef has a nice way with salmon: His sauce was simple but the effect was sublime.

Rewrite: _____

_____

6. Normal human beings can't cope with repeated humiliation.

Rewrite: _____

_____

7. The world hasn't got much time to stop polluting; soon, we all will have to wear face masks.

Rewrite: _____

_____

8. If you want a good cheesecake, you must make a top-notch crust.

Rewrite: _____

_____

9. International organizations should try and cooperate on global issues like hunger.

Rewrite: _____

_____

10. The environmentalists aren't in it for the prestige; they really care about protecting the spotted owl.

Rewrite: _____

_____

17. Watch Out For Sentence Fragments and Run-On Sentences

A sentence fragment has no independent clause; a run-on sentence has two or more independent clauses that are improperly connected. Under time pressure, you could lose track as you are writing a sentence and end up with a sentence fragment or a run-on sentence. Here's how to avoid this common problem.

Sentence fragments: Every sentence in formal expository writing must have an independent clause. An independent clause contains a subject and a predicate and does not begin with a subordinate conjunction such as one of the following words:

Run-Ons and Fragments

Avoid this:

Students often write run-on sentences, two independent clauses are joined without proper punctuation.

Avoid this, too:

A sentence fragment, lacking a main verb.

Subordinate Conjunctions

after	if	than	whenever
although	in order that	though	where
as	provided that	unless	whether
because	since	until	while
before	so that		

Incorrect:

Global warming. That is what the scientists and journalists are worried about this year.

Correct:

Global warming is the cause of concern for scientists and journalists this year.

Incorrect:

Seattle is a wonderful place to live. Having mountains, ocean, and forests all within easy driving distance. If you can ignore the rain.

Correct:

Seattle is a wonderful place to live, with mountains, ocean, and forests all within easy driving distance. However, it certainly does rain often.

Incorrect:

Why do I think the author's position is preposterous? Because he makes generalizations that I know are untrue.

Correct:

I think the author's position is preposterous because he makes generalizations that I know are untrue.

Note: Beginning single-clause sentences with coordinate conjunctions—*and, but, or, nor,* and *for*—is acceptable in moderation, although some readers may object to beginning a sentence with *and.*

Correct:

Most people would agree that indigent patients should receive wonderful health care. But every treatment has its price.

Run-On Sentences: Time pressure may also cause you to write two or more sentences as one. Watch out for independent clauses that are not joined with any punctuation at all or are only joined with a comma.

Run-On Sentence:

Current insurance practices are unfair they discriminate against the people who need insurance most.

You can repair run-on sentences in any one of three ways. First, you could use a period to make separate sentences of the independent clauses.

Correct:
Current insurance practices are unfair. They discriminate against the people who need insurance most.

Second, you could use a semicolon. A semicolon is a weak period. It separates independent clauses but signals to the reader that the ideas in the clauses are related.

Correct:
Current insurance practices are unfair; they discriminate against the people who need insurance most.

The third method of repairing a run-on sentence is usually the most effective. Use a conjunction to turn an independent clause into a dependent one and to make explicit how the clauses are related.

Correct:
Current insurance practices are unfair, in that they discriminate against the people who need insurance most.

One cause of run-on sentences is the misuse of adverbs like *however, nevertheless, furthermore, likewise,* and *therefore.*

Run-On Sentence:
Current insurance practices are discriminatory, furthermore they make insurance too expensive for the poor.

Correct:
Current insurance practices are discriminatory. Furthermore, they make insurance too expensive for the poor.

Writing Drill 17

Repair the following by eliminating sentence fragments and run-on sentences. Use the lines below the examples for your rewrites. (Suggested rewrites appear at the end of the chapter.)

1. The private academy has all the programs Angie will need. Except the sports program, which has been phased out.

Rewrite: _____

_____

2. Leadership ability. That is the elusive quality which our current government employees have yet to capture.

Rewrite: _____

_____

3. Antonio just joined the athletic club staff this year but Barry has been with us since 1993, therefore we would expect Barry to be more skilled with the weight-lifting equipment. What a surprise to find Barry pinned beneath a barbell on the weight-lifting bench with Antonio struggling to lift the 300-pound weight from poor Barry's chest.

Rewrite: _____

_____

4. There is time to invest in property. After one has established one-self in the business world, however.

Rewrite: _____

_____

5. Sentence fragments are often used in casual conversation, however they should not be used in written English under normal circumstances.

Rewrite: _____

_____

18. Use Commas Correctly

When using the comma, follow these rules.

1. Use commas to separate items in a series. If more than two items are listed in a series, they should be separated by commas; the final comma—the one that precedes the word *and*—is not strictly required.

Correct:
My recipe for buttermilk biscuits contains flour, baking soda, salt, shortening, and buttermilk.

Correct:
My recipe for chocolate cake contains flour, baking soda, sugar, eggs, milk and chocolate.

2. Do not place commas before the first element of a series or after the last element.

Incorrect:
My investment advisor recommended that I construct a portfolio of, stocks, bonds, commodities futures, and precious metals.

Incorrect:
The elephants, tigers, and dancing bears, were the highlights of the circus.

Comma Rules

There are six basic rules about comma use—learn them.

3. Use commas to separate two or more adjectives before a noun; do not use a comma after the last adjective in the series.

Correct:

I can't believe you sat through that long, dull, uninspired movie three times.

Incorrect:

The manatee is a round, blubbery, bewhiskered, creature whose continued presence in American waters is endangered by careless boaters.

4. Use commas to set off parenthetical clauses and phrases. (A parenthetical expression is one that is not necessary to the main idea of the sentence.)

Correct:

Gordon, who is a writer by profession, bakes an excellent cheese-cake.

The main idea is that Gordon bakes an excellent cheesecake. The intervening clause merely serves to identify Gordon; thus it should be set off with commas.

Correct:

The newspaper that has the most insipid editorials is the *Daily Times*.

Correct:

The newspaper, which has the most insipid editorials of any I have read, won numerous awards last week.

In the first of these examples the clause beginning with *that* defines which paper the author is discussing. In the second example, the main point is that the newspaper won numerous awards, and the intervening clause beginning with *which* identifies the paper.

5. Use commas after introductory participial or prepositional phrases.

Correct:

Having watered his petunias every day during the drought, Harold was very disappointed when his garden was destroyed by insects.

Correct:

After the banquet, Harold and Martha went dancing.

6. Use commas to separate independent clauses (clauses that could stand alone as complete sentences) connected by coordinate conjunctions such as *and, but, not, yet,* etcetera.

Correct:

Susan's old car has been belching blue smoke from the tailpipe for two weeks, but it has not broken down yet.

Correct:

Zachariah's pet frog eats 50 flies a day, yet it has never gotten indigestion.

Here's a final word on commas. Make sure the comma separates two *independent* clauses, joined by a conjunction. It is incorrect to use a comma to separate the two parts of a compound verb.

Incorrect:

Barbara went to the grocery store, and bought two quarts of milk.

Incorrect:

Zachariah's pet frog eats 50 flies a day, and never gets indigestion.

Writing Drill 18

Correct the punctuation errors in the following sentences by inserting the proper punctuation marks or crossing out unnecessary ones. (Suggested repairs are at the end of the chapter.)

1. Peter wants me to bring records games candy and soda to his party.

2. I need, lumber, nails, a hammer and a saw to build the shelf.

3. It takes a friendly energetic person to be a successful salesman.

4. I was shocked to discover that a large, modern, glass-sheathed, office building had replaced my old school.

5. The country club, a cluster of ivy-covered whitewashed buildings was the site of the president's first speech.

6. Pushing through the panicked crowd the security guards frantically searched for the suspect.

7. Despite careful analysis of the advantages and disadvantages of each proposal Harry found it hard to reach a decision.

19. Use Semicolons Correctly

1. Use a semicolon instead of a coordinate conjunction such as *and*, *or*, or *but* to link two closely related independent clauses.

Correct:

Whooping cranes are an endangered species; there are only 50 whooping cranes in New Jersey today.

Semicolon Rules

There are two basic rules about semicolon use—learn them.

Correct:

> Whooping cranes are an endangered species, and they are unlikely to survive if we continue to pollute.

Incorrect:

> Whooping cranes are an endangered species; and they are unlikely to survive if we continue to pollute.

2. Use a semicolon between independent clauses connected by words like *therefore, nevertheless,* and *moreover.*

Correct:

> The staff meeting has been postponed until next Thursday; therefore, I will be unable to get approval for my project until then.

Correct:

> Farm prices have been falling rapidly for two years; nevertheless, the traditional American farm is not in danger of disappearing.

Writing Drill 19

Fix the following, if necessary. Use the lines below each sentence for your rewrite. (Suggested rewrites are at the end of the chapter.)

1. Morgan has five years' experience in karate; but Thompson has even more.

Rewrite: _____

_____

2. Very few students wanted to take the class in physics, only the professor's kindness kept it from being canceled.

Rewrite: _____

_____

3. You should always be prepared when you go on a camping trip, however you must avoid carrying unnecessary weight.

Rewrite: _____

_____

20. Use Colons Correctly

1. In formal writing the colon is used only as a means of signaling that what follows is a list, definition, explanation, or concise summary of what has gone before. The colon usually follows an independent clause, and it will frequently be accompanied by a reinforcing expression like *the following, as follows,* or *namely,* or by an explicit demonstrative like *this.*

Colon Rules

There are three basic rules about colon use—learn them.

Correct:

Your instructions are as follows: Read the passage carefully, answer the questions on the last page, and turn over your answer sheet.

Correct:

This is what I found in the refrigerator: A moldy lime, half a bottle of stale soda, and a jar of peanut butter.

Correct:

The biggest problem with the country today is apathy: The corrosive element that will destroy our democracy.

2. Be careful not to put a colon between a verb and its direct object.

Incorrect:

I want: a slice of pizza and a small green salad.

Correct:

This is what I want: A slice of pizza and a small green salad. (The colon serves to announce that a list is forthcoming.)

Correct:

I don't want much for lunch: Just a slice of pizza and a small green salad. (Here what follows the colon defines what "don't want much" means.)

3. Context will occasionally make clear that a second independent clause is closely linked to its predecessor, even without an explicit expression like those used above. Here, too, a colon is appropriate, although a period will always be correct too.

Correct:

We were aghast: The "charming country inn" that had been advertised in such glowing terms proved to be a leaking cabin full of mosquitoes.

Correct:

We were aghast. The "charming country inn" that had been advertised in such glowing terms proved to be a leaking cabin full of mosquitoes.

Writing Drill 20

Rewrite these sentences so they use colons correctly, using the lines below the sentences. (Suggested repairs are at the end of the chapter.)

1. I am sick and tired of: your whining, your complaining, your nagging, your teasing, and, most of all, your barbed comments.

Rewrite: _____

_____

2. The chef has created a masterpiece, the pasta is delicate yet firm, the mustard greens are fresh, and the medallions of veal are melting in my mouth.

Rewrite: _____

_____

3. In order to write a good essay, you must: practice, get plenty of sleep, and eat a good breakfast.

Rewrite: _____

_____

21. Use Hyphens And Dashes Correctly

1. Use the hyphen to separate a word at the end of a line.

Correct:
> In this incredible canvas, the artist used only monochromatic elements.

2. Use the hyphen with the compound numbers twenty-one through ninety-nine, and with fractions used as adjectives.

Correct:
> Sixty-five students constituted a majority.

Correct:
> A two-thirds vote was necessary to carry the measure.

3. Use the hyphen with the prefixes *ex*, *all*, *self*, and *semi* and with the suffix *elect*.

Correct:
> Semi-retired executives are often called upon to assist others in starting new businesses.

Correct:
> The constitution protects against self-incrimination.

Correct:
> The president-elect was invited to chair the meeting.

4. Use the hyphen with a compound adjective when it comes *before* the word it modifies, but not when it comes *after* the word it modifies.

Correct:
> The no-holds-barred argument continued into the night.

Correct:
> The argument continued with no holds barred.

Hyphens and Dashes

There are seven basic rules about hyphen and dash use—learn them.

5. Use the hyphen with any prefix used before a proper noun or adjective.

Correct:
His pro-African sentiments were heartily applauded.

Correct:
They believed that his activities were un-American.

6. Use a hyphen to separate component parts of a word in order to avoid confusion with other words or to avoid the use of a double vowel.

Correct:
Most of the buildings in the ghost town are re-creations of the original structures.

Correct:
She took an anti-inflammatory drug for her sports injury.

7. Use the dash to indicate an abrupt change of thought. In general, however, in formal writing, it's better to plan what you want to say in advance and avoid abrupt changes of thought.

Correct:
The inheritance must cover the entire cost of the proposal—Gail has no other money to invest.

Correct:
To get a high score—and who doesn't want to get a high score—you need to devote yourself to prolonged and concentrated study.

Writing Drill 21

Insert hyphens and dashes in the correct places in these sentences.

1. The child was able to count from one to ninety nine.

2. The adults only movie was banned from commercial TV.

3. It was the first time she had seen a movie that was for adults-only.

4. John and his ex wife remained on friendly terms.

5. A two thirds majority would be needed to pass the budget reforms.

6. The house, and it was the most dilapidated house that I had ever seen was a bargain because the land was so valuable.

22. Use Apostrophes Correctly

1. Use the apostrophe with contracted forms of verbs to indicate that one or more letters have been eliminated in writing. But try to avoid contractions on the Writing Test.

One of the most common errors involving use of the apostrophe is using it in the contraction *you're* or *it's* to indicate the possessive form of *you* or *it*. When you write *you're*, ask yourself whether you mean *you are*. If not, the correct word is *your*. Similarly, are you sure you mean *it is*? If not, use the possessive form *its*. You spell *his* or *hers* without an apostrophe, so you should spell *its* without an apostrophe.

Incorrect:
> You're chest of drawers is ugly.

Incorrect:
> The dog hurt it's paw.

Correct:
> Your chest of drawers is ugly.

Correct:
> The dog hurt its paw.

Apostrophe Rules

There are three basic rules about apostrophe use—learn them.

2.   Use the apostrophe to indicate the possessive form of a noun.

Not Possessive: the boy, Harry, the children, the boys

Possessive: the boy's, Harry's, the children's, the boys'

Note: The word *boy's* could have one of three meanings:

1.   The boy's an expert at chess. (The boy is . . .)

2.   The boy's left for the day. (The boy has . . .)

3.   The boy's face was covered with pie. (possessive: the face of the boy)

The word *boys'* can have only one meaning—a plural possessive (the . . . of the boys).

Correct:
> I caught a glimpse of the fox's red tail as the hunters sped by.
> (The *'s* ending indicates that one fox is the owner of the tail.)

Correct:
> Ms. Fox's office is on the first floor.
> (One person possesses the office.)

Correct:
> The Foxes' apartment has a wonderful view.

(There are several people named Fox living in the same apartment. First you must form the plural, then add the apostrophe to indicate possession.)

3.   The apostrophe is used to indicate possession only with nouns; in the case of pronouns there are separate possessives for each person and number.

Pronoun	Possessive
her	hers
his	his
its	its
my	mine
our	ours
their	theirs
your	yours

The exception is the neutral *one*, which forms its possessive by adding an apostrophe and an *s*.

Writing Drill 22

In the following sentences, add apostrophes where needed and cross out unnecessary ones. (Suggested repairs are at the end of the chapter.)

1. The Presidents limousine had a flat tire.

2. You're tickets for the show will be at the box office.

3. The opportunity to change ones lifestyle does not come often.

4. The desks' surface was immaculate, but it's drawers were messy.

5. The cat on the bed is hers'.

Answers to Writing Drills

Many of the items in the writing drills could have more than one possible correct answer. In those cases, we've suggested sample correct answers. Keep that in mind as you compare your answers to ours.

Drill 1 Answers

1. The agency is not prepared to expand now.

2. Since John has prepared for this presentation so carefully, we should award him the project.

3. Flights are always at least an hour late on this airline, though its leaders promise that promptness is a high priority for all its employees.

4. Although she is inexperienced in photography, she will probably succeed because she is motivated.

5. The United States cannot spend more money to alleviate other countries' suffering when its own citizens suffer.

6. Although tactful, George says exactly what he believes.

7. Accuracy is important to English teachers and company presidents alike.

8. Humans kill each other because they fear those whom they do not understand.

9. Ms. Miller speaks intelligently about many aspects of modern philosophy.

10. The best leader is one who listens and inspires simultaneously.

Drill 2 Answers

1. All these problems have combined to create a crisis.

2. A staff that large needs an effective supervisor.

3. He knows how to follow directions.

4. The writer's technical skill does not mask his poor plot line.

5. That monument remains a significant tourist attraction.

6. The recent trend of spending on credit has created a more impoverished middle class.

7. Few people can follow directions.

8. She has chosen to change careers.

9. Dialogue opens many doors to compromise.

10. The conclusion is that environmental and economic concerns are intertwined.

Drill 3 Answers

1. She is a good teacher.

2. Ferrara is a slow worker.

3. For many reasons, technology has not permeated all countries equally.

4. In a murder trial, it is important to pay attention to the details as well as to the "larger picture."

5. You are the best person to decide what you should do for a living.

6. The author overstates his case somewhat.

7. The president should use diplomacy before he resorts to force.

8. In Italy I found the best food I have ever eaten.

9. Children should be taught to cooperate at home and in school. (If there's no need to say it, don't!)

10. The travel agent said not to go to Tripoli, since one may be hurt. (Saying it is possible that one may be hurt is an example of redundant qualification, since both possible and may indicate uncertainty.)

Drill 4 Answers

1. Advanced technology has made it easy for people who live vast distances from each other to communicate.

2. People cannot safely consume water that contains chemical pollutants.

3. Napoleon suffered defeat in Russia because most of his troops perished in the cold.

4. No present evidence suggests that Shakespeare's plays were written by others.

5. I agree with those who say that the United States should send soldiers to areas of conflict.

6. The architect Frank Lloyd Wright was famous for his ability to design buildings that blend into their surroundings.

7. Julius Caesar was a leader of the Roman Empire.

8. The teacher refused to let him into class because he showed up ten minutes late.

9. Many trees were destroyed by the fire that burned thousands of acres of forest land.

10. A lot of people find math a difficult subject because it requires very precise thinking skills.

Drill 5 Answers

1. We ought to pay teachers more than we pay senators.

2. The author is stuck in the past.

3. This argument cannot be generalized to most business owners.

4. Food is perhaps the best social lubricant.

5. More people would not vote even if they had more information about candidates.

6. Privacy should not be valued more than social concerns.

7. Most people want to do good work, but many are bored or frustrated with their jobs.

8. The author has a point.

9. College presidents should implement several specific reforms to combat apathy.

10. Either alternative would prove disastrous.

Drill 6 Answers

1. Brave but misguided men fought the Spanish-American War.

2. Congress passed the bill in time, but the President did not sign it until the time for action had passed.

3. Those who need advice least usually request it; the truly lost and ignorant do not seek it.

4. We should relocate that building where citizens can appreciate it.

5. City government should generously reward garbage collectors for their dirty, smelly labors.

6. Negotiators ironed out the conditions of the contract agreement minutes before the strike deadline.

7. The city clerk should take the minutes of the City Council meeting.

8. With sugar, water, or salt, doctors can treat many of the ailments that citizens of less-developed countries contract.

9. The teacher distributed test results with no concern for confidentiality.

10. A number of field anthropologists and marriage experts compiled the report.

Drill 7 Answers

1. Businesses ignore the illiteracy problem at their own peril.

2. Experience is more important than training in many fields.

3. This plane is obsolete for several reasons.

4. The government cannot fight a drug war effectively without waging a battle against demand for illicit substances.

5. The candidate has many strong points; intelligence, unfortunately, is not among them.

6. The city cannot justify building a more handsome prison.

7. We, as a society, have decided to tolerate homelessness.

8. Americans must like watching television better than conversing.

9. Cats make better pets than mice.

10. Intelligence is a product of environment and heredity.

Drill 8 Answers

1. When water is heated to 100° C, it turns into steam.

2. The diplomat had to agree to live wherever the government sent him.

3. Arthur often forgets to do his chores.

4. Many economists think that rising bank interest rates have contributed to the current economic downturn.

5. She told us that she would go to the store when her mother came home.

6. A radar unit registers the distance and characteristics of aircraft.

7. The principal told John that he could not return to school until his behavior improved.

8. The police detective had to ask the lawyer for permission to question the suspect.

9. Thousands of animal species were destroyed in the last ice age.

10. The secretary was unable to type the document.

Drill 9 Answers

1. Jefferson was certainly a great leader.

2. Families probably spend less time together than they did 15 years ago.

3. The pizza delivery man arrived just when the sequestered jury most needed him.

4. Trying to find the employee responsible for this embarrassing information leak may be impossible.

5. Both strategies would be expensive and completely ineffective: they have an equal chance of failing.

6. The military should diversify its defense rather than rely so heavily on nuclear missiles.

7. Older doctors should be required to update their techniques, but many seem resistant to changes in technology.

8. You need not take this new fad very seriously; it will surely pass.

9. The politician reminds me of Abraham Lincoln with his rough appearance and warm heart.

10. I estimate that 120,000 fans were in the stadium. (Even when a cliché is used in its original context, it sounds old.)

Drill 10 Answers

1. We expect to use hundreds of paper clips in the next two months.

2. A person who likes research should not be hired for a position that requires someone to interact with customers all day.

3. Our schoolchildren's education has been neglected.

4. Foreign diplomats should always talk to local leaders.

5. If someone claims you as a dependent on a tax return, you may still have to pay taxes on your income in excess of five hundred dollars.

6. Recent studies suggest that Vienna sausages are good for you.

7. When the poet wrote the second and third stanzas, he must have felt despair.

8. This is a fine horse.

9. Government regulatory agencies were not honest in their press releases about the recent railway accident.

10. Having spent our time responding to many unexpected problems this month, we have not been able to prepare for these longer-term needs.

Drill 11 Answers

1. The logical *structure* of his complicated and rather tortuous arguments *is* always the same.

2. The *majority* of the organization's members *are* over 60 years old.

3. *Both* the young child and her grandfather *were* depressed for months after discovering that the oldest ice cream parlor in the city had closed its doors forever.

4. Hartz brought the *blueprints and model* that *were* still on the table instead of the ones that Mackenzie had returned to the cabinet. (The restrictive phrase beginning with *that* defines the noun phrase *blueprints and model*.)

5. A *case* of bananas *has* been sent to the local distributor in compensation for the fruit that was damaged in transit.

6. A *total* of 50 editors *reads* each article, a process that takes at least a week, sometimes six months.

7. Neither the shipping clerk who packed the equipment nor the *truckers* who transported it *admit* responsibility for the dented circuit box.

8. *Either* Georgette or Robespierre *is* going to be asked to dinner by the madcap Calvin. I dread the result in either case.

9. I can never decide whether to eat an orange or a Belgian chocolate; *each* of them *has* its wondrous qualities. (Note that you must also change the possessive pronoun to the singular form.)

10. *Everyone* in the United States, as well the Canadians, *expects* the timber agreement to fall through.

Drill 12 Answers

1. *Quickly* is sandwiched between two verbs, and it could refer to either one.

Sample Rewrite:
Bentley advised him to make up his mind quickly.

2. *In principle* probably modifies *agreed*, but its placement makes it appear to modify *statement*.

Sample Rewrite:
I agree in principle with the author's statements.

3. Termites are probably coming out of the woodwork, not the man, but an introductory modifying phrase always refers to the grammatical subject of the sentence.

Sample Rewrite:
He was surprised to see termites coming out of the woodwork.

4. Was the racial unrest in the auditorium, or was the conference merely held there?

Sample Rewrite:
The Governor's conference met in the auditorium to discuss racial unrest.

5. Did she say it in her office? Were the documents in her office? Or both?

Sample Rewrite:
Hernandez said that she had all the necessary documents in her office.

6. If none of his friends came, it must have been a small party indeed.

Sample Rewrite:
Not all of his friends were able to come, but he decided that he preferred small parties anyway.

7. Did she remember when she got home? Or did she have to call when she got home?

Sample Rewrite:
When she got home, Margolis remembered she had to place a telephone call.

8. Either he didn't like discussing politics in the museum, or he didn't like discussing it at all.

Sample Rewrite:
As they walked through the museum, George told Suzette he did not like to discuss politics.

9. Was it Stokely's résumé that worked in publishing for ten years?

Sample Rewrite:
Stokely, who has worked in publishing for ten years, appears from his résumé to be well qualified.

10. It is the person holding the job, not her constituents, that requires experience in community service.

Sample Rewrite:
A politician without experience in community service would fail to serve her constituents.

Drill 13 Answers

1. The structure of the sentence might leave us wondering whether Clausen or his dog was well bred. Instead, use the impersonal *it*.

Sample Rewrite:
Clausen's dog won first place at the show because it was well bred.

2. It's not clear who "he" is. No antecedent exists in the sentence for it. *Critic's* can't be the antecedent of *he* because it's the possessive form.

Sample Rewrite:
The critic's review made the novel a commercial success, and the novelist is now a rich man.

3. We cannot tell from the context whether the military advisor or his superior was the superior strategist.

Sample Rewrite:
The military advisor was more conventional than his commander, but the advisor was a superior strategist.

4. *Which* is the problem here: We do not know whether Bertha had not spent the night at home in weeks or whether she had not telephoned her friends in weeks.

Sample Rewrite:
Because she had not telephoned her California friends in weeks, Bertha called them before she went home for the night.

5. Referring to some ambiguous *they* without identifying who *they* are beforehand is incorrect.

Sample Rewrite:
John wanted the job badly, but when he called the employer the next morning he found that the company had hired someone else.

6. We don't know exactly what it is, but we can assume that *it* is a fish.

Sample Rewrite:
You must pay attention when fishing—otherwise, you might lose your catch.

7. We do not know whether *he* refers to Zolsta or to the unnamed lesser musician.

Sample Rewrite:
Zolsta Karmagi is the better musician, but Sven Wonderup had more formal training.

Drill 14 Answers

1. This organization will not tolerate the consumption, trafficking, or promotion of drugs.

2. The dancer taught her understudy how to move, dress, work with choreographers, and deal with professional competition.

3. Merrill based his confidence on the futures market, the bond market, and the strength of the president's popularity.

4. The grocery baggers were ready, able, and quite determined to do a great job.

5. *The requirements for a business degree* are not as stringent as *those for a law degree.*

Drill 15 Answers

1. I am disgusted with the waste we tolerate in this country. We cannot simply stand by without adding to such waste: Living here makes all of us wasteful.

2. You must take care not to take these grammar rules too seriously, since you can often become bogged down in details and forget why you are writing at all.
   (Or use *one* consistently.)

3. We must all take a stand against waste in this country; else how will we be able to look ourselves in the mirror?
   (When using *we*, you must make sure to use the plural form of verbs and pronouns.)

Drill 16 Answers

1. Cynthia Larson is an expert.

2. The crowd was absorbed in watching the fire-eating juggler, but then the dancing horse caught their attention.

3. As soon as the personnel department tries to verify his résumé, I am sure we will hear gales of laughter issuing from the office.

4. Having something funny to say seems to be very important in our culture.

5. The chef prepares salmon skillfully: his sauce was simple but the effect was sublime.

6. Normal human beings cannot tolerate repeated humiliation.

7. The world does not have much time to stop polluting; soon, we all will have to wear face masks.
   (*Hasn't got* is both a contraction and an example of the colloquial substitution of *have got* for *have*.)

8. If you want a good cheesecake, you must make a superb crust.

9. International organizations should try to cooperate on global issues like hunger.

10. The environmentalists are not involved in the project for prestige; they truly care about protecting the spotted owl.

Drill 17 Answers

1. In this context, *except* is a conjunction, and as such makes the clause to which it is attached a dependent one.

Sample Rewrite:
The private academy has all the programs Angie will need, except that the sports program has been phased out.

2. *Leadership ability* is a sentence fragment, since it has no predicate.

Sample Rewrite:
Leadership ability: that is the elusive quality that our current government employees have yet to capture.

3. Here we have both a run-on sentence (two independent clauses linked by *therefore* and a comma) and a sentence fragment ("What a surprise to find . . ." that contains no subject or predicate).

Sample Rewrite:
Antonio just joined the athletic club staff this year, but Barry has been with us since 1993; therefore, we would expect Barry to be more skilled with the weight-lifting equipment. It was quite a surprise to find Barry pinned beneath a barbell on the weight-lifting bench with Antonio struggling to lift the 300-pound weight from poor Barry's chest.

4. The conjunction *after* makes the second group of words a sentence fragment.

Sample Rewrite:
There is time to invest in property, but only after one has established oneself in the business world.

5. Since transitional words like *however* do not subordinate a clause, this is a run-on sentence. You could either change the first comma to a semicolon or separate the clauses with a period.

Sample Rewrite:
Sentence fragments are often used in casual conversation. They should not, however, be used in written English under normal circumstances.

Drill 18 Answers

1. Peter wants me to bring records, games, candy, and soda to his party.

2. I need lumber, nails, a hammer and a saw to build the shelf. (OR . . . a hammer, and a saw . . .).

3. It takes a friendly, energetic person to be a successful salesman.

4. I was shocked to discover that a large, modern, glass-sheathed office building had replaced my old school.

5. The country club, a cluster of ivy-covered whitewashed buildings, was the site of the president's first speech.

6. Pushing through the panicked crowd, the security guards frantically searched for the suspect.

7. Despite careful analysis of the advantages and disadvantages of each proposal, Harry found it hard to reach a decision.

Drill 19 Answers

1. Morgan has five years' experience in karate, but Thompson has even more.

2. Very few students wanted to take the class in physics; only the professor's kindness kept it from being canceled.

3. You should always be prepared when you go on a camping trip; however, you must avoid carrying unnecessary weight.

Drill 20 Answers

1. I am sick and tired of your whining, your complaining, your nagging, your teasing, and, most of all, your barbed comments.

2. The chef has created a masterpiece: the pasta is delicate yet firm, the mustard greens are fresh, and the medallions of veal are melting in my mouth.

3. In order to write a good essay, you must do the following: practice, get plenty of sleep, and eat a good breakfast.

Drill 21 Answers

1. The child was able to count from one to ninety-nine.

2. The adults-only movie was banned from commercial TV.

3. It was the first time she had seen a movie that was for adults only.

4. John and his ex-wife remained on friendly terms.

5. A two-thirds majority would be needed to pass the budget reforms.

6. The house—and it was the most dilapidated house that I had ever seen—was a bargain because the land was so valuable.

Drill 22 Answers

1. The president's limousine had a flat tire.

2. Your tickets for the show will be at the box office.

3. The opportunity to change one's lifestyle does not come often.

4. The desk's surface was immaculate, but its drawers were messy.

5. The cat on the bed is hers.

SECTION THREE:
Multiple-Choice Section

CHAPTER 5

USAGE QUESTIONS

Some students panic at the prospect of Usage questions because today's high schools don't teach much grammar. But Kaplan's careful analysis of recent Writing Tests reveals that a large majority of Usage questions relate to a surprisingly limited number of grammatical issues. You don't need to panic if you familiarize yourself with the typical test questions. The following pages will give you a good idea of what to expect and will more than adequately prepare you for Usage questions on the Writing Test.

What Usage Questions Test

Standard written English is somewhat more formal than the average person's spoken English: Things that you're used to saying in everyday conversation may well be considered wrong on the Writing Test. Standard written English is the kind of English that you find in textbooks and the kind of English your professors will expect you to use in your college papers.

You don't have to use or define grammatical terms, so don't worry if your grasp of grammatical terminology is a little shaky. The Writing Test measures only your ability to recognize acceptable and unacceptable uses of language. It doesn't even test you on every aspect of language use. It tests you in three main areas: Basic grammar, sentence structure, and choice of words. The Writing Test doesn't test spelling or capitalization. Punctuation is tested only as a secondary matter in connection with questions of sentence structure.

How to "Spot the Mistake"

Kaplan calls Usage questions "spot-the-mistake" questions because that's basically all that they require you to do. In these questions, you're given a sentence with four words or phrases underlined. The underlined parts are labeled (A) through (D). One of the underlined pieces may contain a grammar mistake. You're supposed to spot it and fill in the corresponding oval on your grid. If the sentence is mistake-free, the correct answer is (E), No error. Here's an example.

Relax!

To score well on the Usage sections of the Writing Test, you need to master only a relatively small number of grammar issues.

Spot the Mistakes

Usage questions ask you only to identify grammar mistakes. You don't have to explain the mistakes in formal, grammatical terms.

One in Five

About 20 percent of your answers to Usage questions on test day should be choice (E), *No error*.

Although the number of firms declaring
 A
bankruptcy keep growing, the mayor claims that the
             B   C
city is thriving. No error
    D   E

Ⓐ Ⓑ Ⓒ Ⓓ Ⓔ

You're asked to decide which (if any) underlined word or phrase needs to be changed to make the sentence grammatically correct. Assume that the parts of the sentence that are not underlined are correct, since they can't be changed. Here's a simple three-step method for answering these questions.

> **The Kaplan Method for Usage Questions**
>
> 1. Read the sentence, "listening" for a mistake.
>
> 2. Read each underlined part again.
>
> 3. Use the process of elimination to find the mistake. Don't be afraid to pick (E).

Let's try this out on our example. Start by reading it to yourself. Did you hear the mistake? If so, your work is done for this question; fill in the appropriate oval and move on. If you didn't hear the mistake on the first reading, simply go back and read each underlined part again. The word *although* seems fine in this context. The word *keep* is a plural verb, but its subject is *number*, which is singular. That seems to be a mistake. On the other hand, the phrase *claims that* sounds all right, and it has a singular verb for a singular subject, *mayor*. Similarly, is *thriving* sounds all right, and it too provides a singular verb for the singular subject *city*. Choice (B) contains the mistake, so (B) is the correct answer.

This is a classic example because errors of subject-verb agreement are common on the Writing Test. You'll learn more about the most common errors in the following pages. This information is valuable, since it's easier to spot errors when you know what to look for.

And keep in mind that not all the Usage questions on the Writing Test contain errors. When you're reading each sentence critically in an effort to spot the mistakes, you may fall into the trap of spotting mistakes where there are none. Choice (E), *No error*, is the correct answer to Usage questions about one-fifth of the time. If you find that for the 30 Usage questions you have chosen (E) only a couple of times, chances are that you're spotting mistakes that aren't there. Expect about six of the answers to be (E).

The Classic Mistakes

Answering Usage questions correctly begins with simply reading the sentence carefully. The error, if there is one, will often be obvious to you at the first reading.

If it isn't, remember that only a rather limited range of grammar rules is tested. For this reason, we won't burden you with an exhaustive review of English grammar. What follows instead is a comprehensive survey of the grammatical problems that actually occur with some frequency on Writing Test Usage questions. Rather than emphasize abstract rules of grammar, which you don't have to regurgitate on the Writing Test, we'll show you the types of grammatical errors that appear in every edition of the Writing Test. Once your inner ear has become attuned to the Writing Test's classic grammar mistakes, you'll have an easier time spotting them on test day.

On the following pages you'll find descriptions and examples of 16 classic Usage mistakes. You'll also find drills to give you experience spotting these typical goofs. At the end of the chapter is a drill with 30 Usage questions, the same number you'll see on test day.

Subject-Verb Agreement Problem when Subject Follows Verb

Singular subjects call for singular verbs, and plural subjects call for plural verbs. Subject-verb agreement under normal circumstances is not difficult for native speakers of English. You know better than to say *Americans is . . .* or *The building are . . .* In certain situations, however, subject-verb agreement can be tricky even for native speakers because it is not so obvious what the real subject of the sentence is. One of these situations arises when the subject comes *after* the verb, as it does in a clause beginning with the word *there*. Take a look at this example.

> Despite an intensive campaign to encourage conservation, there *is* many Americans who have not accepted recycling as a way of life.

This sentence presents the most common of all subject-verb agreement errors found on the Writing Test in recent years, generally occurring once and often twice on each test. The subject of the sentence is not *there*, but *Americans*, which is plural. Therefore, the singular verb *is* is incorrect; *is* should be replaced by the plural verb *are*. Watch out whenever you see *there* on the Writing Test.

Here's another example in which the subject follows the verb.

> High above the Hudson River *rises* the gleaming skyscrapers of Manhattan.

This sentence is tricky because there is a singular noun before the verb: *the Hudson River*. But the later noun *gleaming skyscrapers* is actually the subject.

Spot the Classics

Master the 16 classic mistakes: you'll score well on Usage questions if you do.

Check the Number

Subjects and verbs must agree in number. Subjects and verbs that do not agree in number appear very frequently on the Writing Test.

Think about it. What's doing the rising? The subject is plural, and so the verb should be *rise*.

Usage Drill 1

Underline the italicized verbs in the sentences that contain errors in subject-verb agreement. (Answers are at the end of the chapter.)

1. According to a noted meteorologist, there *is* various explanations for the accelerating rate of global warming.

2. In this critically acclaimed film, there *is* a well-developed plot and an excellent cast of characters.

3. Through the locks of the Panama Canal *passes* more than fifty ships each day.

4. There *are* a number of state legislatures currently debating strict environmental laws.

5. If there *is* competing proposals, your idea may not be acted upon until next week.

6. There *is* at least five types of climbing rose and a unique variety of small fir in the Botanical Gardens.

7. Despite numerous professed sightings, there *is* still no conclusive evidence of extraterrestrial beings.

Verbs First

When you're checking subject-verb agreement, remember that the subject doesn't always come before the verb.

Subject-Verb Agreement Problem when Subject and Verb Are Separated

The test makers have another way to complicate a simple thing like subject-verb agreement. They'll insert some additional information about the subject before the verb appears. Expect to see at least one question of this type on the Writing Test.

> The local congressman, a reliable representative of both community and statewide interests, *are* among the most respected persons in the public sector.

Once again, the way to determine whether the verb agrees with the subject is to identify the subject of the sentence. You see the plural *community and statewide interests* right in front of the verb, but that's not the subject. It's part of the modifying phrase that's inserted between the subject *congressman*, which is singular, and the verb, which should also be singular—*is*. Don't let intervening phrases fool you. In this example, the commas are a tip-off that the verb is separated from the subject. Another tip-off is a preposition like *of*:

The collection of paintings entitled "Matisse in Morocco" *are* one of the most widely traveled exhibits in recent years.

Again, you should first find the subject of the sentence. It's *collection*. The phrases that follow the subject, *of paintings* and *entitled "Matisse in Morocco"* merely modify the subject. The true subject is singular and so the verb should be *is*. The writers of the Writing Test like this type of question because the intervening modifying phrases or clauses may cause you to lose sight of the subject and its number. These phrases simply modify the subject they follow, without changing its number. Don't be fooled by the placement of these phrases.

Usage Drill 2

Underline the verb that agrees with the subject. (Answers are at the end of the chapter.)

1. Multipurpose vehicles, which can be very useful on rough terrain, (is/are) now banned in many states.

2. The level of chemicals and other air pollutants (is/are) now monitored in many offices.

3. The fundamental hitting skills of Rick Reuschel (goes/go) largely unnoticed by the average fan.

4. A community as diverse as Los Angeles (attracts/attract) immigrants from many countries.

5. One-way tickets for domestic travel (is/are) often more expensive than round-trip fares.

6. So-called bullet trains from Tokyo to Osaka (completes/complete) the 300-mile trip in about two hours.

7. Donations to the church-sponsored orphanage (is/are) up by 50 percent over last year.

8. Einstein's theory of relativity (ranks/rank) with the most developed hypotheses involving space and time.

Subject-Verb Agreement Problem when the Subject Seems Plural

Sometimes the sentence in a Usage question includes what appears to be, but in fact is not, a plural subject. This is another situation in which subject-verb agreement can be tricky. Here's an example.

Neither country music nor heavy metal *were* a part of mainstream listening habits in the United States ten years ago.

Comma Trick

Commas often signal that the verb is separated from the subject. And you can learn to recognize groups of words that can come between the subject and verb.

Separation Anxiety

It's harder to recognize intervening phrases and clauses when they're not set off by commas, but if you remember to check each sentence carefully for such things, you'll be

Be Suspicious

When the subject seems plural, check for an agreement problem.

This sentence is tricky because it has two subjects, but these two singular subjects do not add up to a plural subject. When the subject of a sentence is in the form *neither* _____ *nor* ____ or in the form *either* _____ *or* ____ and the nouns in the blanks are singular, the verb should be singular. In the sentence above, it's as if *country music* and *heavy metal* act as subjects one at a time, and so the verb should be the singular *was*. If the nouns in a *neither-nor* or *either-or* construction are plural, then a plural verb is correct.

Here are some other constructions that seem to make plural subjects, but actually don't.

- _____   *along with*   _____
- _____   *as well as*   _____
- _____   *in addition to* _____

In these constructions, the noun in the first blank is the true subject and what follows is, grammatically speaking, just an intervening modifying phrase. If the first noun is singular, the verb should be singular. Look at this sentence.

> Poor pitching, along with injuries and defensive lapses, *are* among the problems that plague last year's championship team.

The phrase *along with injuries and defensive lapses* is a modifying phrase that separates the subject *poor pitching* from the verb. This sentence is tricky because there seem to be three problems that plague the baseball team. But in fact, phrases like *along with*, or *in addition to*, do not work in the same way as the conjunction *and* does. If the above sentence had begun *Poor pitching, injuries, and defensive lapses* the plural verb *are* would have been correct. As written, however, the sentence has only one subject, *poor pitching*, and its verb should be *is*. Beware those pseudocompound subjects!

Usage Drill 3

Underline the verb that agrees with the true subject. (Answers are at the end of the chapter.)

1. The fishing industry, along with railroad safety issues, (is/are) of great concern to the state assembly.

2. Either the manager or one of his coaches usually (removes/remove) a pitcher from the mound.

3. Both the word *scuba* and the word *radar* (is/are) acronyms.

4. Auto exhaust, in addition to industrial pollution, (is/are) a cause of smog in southern California.

5. It is said that neither poor weather nor poor health (keeps/keep) a postman from making his rounds.

Confusion of Simple Past and Past Participle

A typical error tested on the Writing Test is confusion between the simple past and the past participle forms of a verb. A past participle form may erroneously substitute for the simple past form, as in this sentence.

Several passersby *seen* the bank robber leaving the scene of his crime.

The verb form *seen* is the past participle and should be used only with a helping verb *have* or *be*. This sentence requires the simple past form *saw*.

Just about every edition of the Writing Test includes a Usage question in which the simple past is used erroneously with a helping verb, or in which the past participle is used erroneously without a helping verb. For regular verbs the simple past and past participle are identical, ending in *-ed*. But irregular verbs like see usually have two different forms for simple past and past participle. The following is a partial list of irregular verbs. These are the simple past and past participle forms that are most often confused. Instead of listing them alphabetically, we have grouped them by pattern.

IRREGULAR VERBS

Infinitive	Simple Past	Past Participle
break	broke	broken
speak	spoke	spoken
freeze	froze	frozen
forget	forgot	forgotten
get	got	gotten
ride	rode	ridden
rise	rose	risen
arise	arose	arisen
drive	drove	driven
write	wrote	written
eat	ate	eaten
fall	fell	fallen
give	gave	given
take	took	taken
shake	shook	shaken
see	saw	seen
ring	rang	rung
sing	sang	sung
sink	sank	sunk
shrink	shrank	shrunk
drink	drank	drunk
begin	began	begun
swim	swam	swum
run	ran	run
come	came	come

Irregular Customers

Familiarize yourself with the different irregular verbs in this chart. It's quite possible that you might see one of them on test day.

Trust Your Ear

Don't be afraid to trust your ear. Sometimes that's all there is to finding a mistake.

become	became	become
do	did	done
go	went	gone
blow	blew	blown
grow	grew	grown
know	knew	known
throw	threw	thrown
fly	flew	flown
draw	drew	drawn

Note the patterns. Verb forms that end in *-oke, -oze, -ot, -ode, -ose, -ove, -ote, -ang, -ank, -an, -an, -am, -ame, -ew,* or *-ook,* are simple past. Verb forms that end in *-en, -wn, -ung, -unk, -un, -um, -ome,* and *-one,* are past participles. But finally, the best method is simply to train your ear for irregular verb forms that aren't already second nature to you.

Confusion of Infinitive and Gerund

Some Writing Test questions test your sense of idiomatic use of English. That is, they test whether you know what combinations of words *sound* right, or which words sound right in particular contexts. For example, there is generally at least one Usage question in which the infinitive is used where a gerund would be appropriate, or vice versa.

> Team officials heralded Cap Day as an attempt *at attracting* a larger turnout of fans.

This sentence is unidiomatic. There's no grammar rule that explains why it's wrong to say an *attempt at attracting*. If you have a good sense of idiom, you ear tells you it should be *an attempt to attract*. This sentence confuses the *-ing* gerund form with the *to + verb* infinitive form. Here's another sentence that should sound wrong:

> Surveillance cameras are frequently placed in convenience stores to prevent customers to *shoplift*.

After *prevent* you don't use the infinitive but rather the word *from* plus the gerund. The sentence should end *to prevent customers from shoplifting*. Why? There's no real grammatical reason. That's just the way we say it in English. You have to train and to trust your ear on these. There's no way to list definitively all the infinitive/(preposition +) gerund combinations that could possibly appear on the Writing Test. But don't worry. You don't need to see every possible combination in advance. Just remember to prick up your ears whenever an infinitive or gerund is underlined on the test.

Usage Drill 4

Identify and correct the sentences that confuse gerund and infinitive. Write the correct form of the italicized verb on the line under the sentence. (Answers are at the end of the chapter.)

1. The International Olympic Committee does not allow professional tennis players over 21 years of age *to competing* in the Games.

   _____

2. Our directors plan *increasing* the number of workers in the plant by 500.

   _____

3. Any parent would see the value *to set* a curfew for his or her child.

   _____

4. Questioning a store owner's right *of carrying* a gun is not the purpose of this City Council meeting.

   _____

5. The trade agreement is designed to prevent Japan *from limiting* the amount of its imports.

   _____

6. Through this new ad campaign, we hope *for tripling* our gross income by the end of the year.

   _____

7. Widespread resistance to the councilman's proposed reforms did not succeed *to discourage* his innovative thinking.

   _____

8. The teachers' union is eager to resolve the contractual disagreement with the school board.

   _____

Non-Idiomatic Preposition After Verb

Here's another type of mistake that will give your ears a workout. The Writing Test also tests your recognition of the particular prepositions that combine idiomatically with certain verbs. Here's a sentence that uses the wrong preposition.

City Council members frequently meet until the early morning hours in order to *work in* their stalemates.

Winning Combinations

Certain prepositions follow certain verbs. Get to know the verbs and prepositions in the list on this page.

It's not always wrong to write *work in*. You might use *work in* to speak about the field one works in, or the place one works in. But this combination does not correspond to the meaning of this sentence. The writer means to say *work through* or *work out*, that is, overcome the stalemates.

Here's another sentence with the wrong preposition:

> The local band's new album was *frowned at* by many parents because of its suggestive lyrics.

That's just not the way we say it in English. The preferred verb-preposition combination is *frowned upon*. That's the idiomatic expression. Once again, this is an area where you'll have to trust your ear. Just remember to pay attention and think for a moment when you see an underlined preposition after a verb.

Here are some more verb-preposition idioms.

Commonly Tested Verbs and Prepositions

abide by	consist of	object to
abide in	contribute to	participate in
accuse of	count (up)on	pray for
agree to	cover with	prevent from
agree with	decide (up)on	prohibit from
agree on	depend (up)on	protect from
apologize for	differ from	provide with
apply to	differ with	recover from
apply for	differ over	rely (up)on
approve of	differ about	rescue from
argue with	discriminate against	respond to
argue about	distinguish from	stare at
arrive at	dream of	stop from
believe in	dream about	subscribe to
blame for	escape from	substitute for
care about	excel in	succeed in
care for	excuse for	thank for
charge for	forget about	vote for
charge with	forgive for	wait for
compare to	hide from	wait on
compare with	hope for	work with
complain about	insist (up)on	worry about

Wrong Word

The English language contains many pairs of words that sound alike but are spelled differently and have different meanings. Expect to encounter one or two Usage questions that test your ability to distinguish between these problematic word pairs. Here are some examples.

ACCEPT/EXCEPT To *accept* is to take or receive something that is offered: "Dad said he would *accept* my apology for putting a dent in his new car, but then he grounded me for two weeks."

To *except* is to leave out or exclude: "The soldier was *excepted* from combat duty because he had poor field vision." *Except* is usually used as a preposition meaning, "with the exception of, excluding." "When the receptionist found out that everyone *except* him had received a raise, he demanded a salary increase as well."

ADAPT/ADOPT To *adapt* is to change oneself or change something to become suitable for a particular condition or use: "Fred tried to *adapt* his Volkswagen for use as a submarine by gluing the windows shut and attaching a periscope to the roof."

To *adopt* is to make something one's own: "My neighbors decided to *adopt* a child."

AFFECT/EFFECT To *affect* is to have an influence on something: "Al refused to let the rain *affect* his plans for a picnic, so he sat under an umbrella and ate potato salad."

To *effect* is to bring something about or cause something to happen: "The young activist received an award for *effecting* a change in her community." An *effect* is an influence or a result: "The newspaper article about homeless animals had such an *effect* on Richard that he brought home three kittens from the shelter."

AFFLICT/INFLICT To *afflict* is to torment or distress someone or something. It usually appears as a passive verb: "Jeff is *afflicted* with severe migraine headaches."

To *inflict* is to impose punishment or suffering on someone or something: "No one dared displease the king, for he was known to *inflict* severe punishments on those who upset him."

ALLUSION/ILLUSION An *allusion* is an indirect reference to something, a hint: "I remarked that Sally's boyfriend was unusual looking; this *allusion* to his prominent tattoos did not please Sally."

An *illusion* is a false, misleading, or deceptive appearance: "A magician creates the *illusion* that something has disappeared by hiding it faster than the eye can follow it."

EMIGRATE/IMMIGRATE To *emigrate* is to leave one country for another country, and is usually used with the preposition *from*: "Many people *emigrated* from Europe in search of better living conditions."

To *immigrate* is to enter a country to take up permanent residence there, and is usually used with the preposition *to*: "They *immigrated* to North America because land was plentiful."

EMINENT/IMMINENT Someone who is *eminent* is prominent or outstanding: "The *eminent* archeologist Dr. Wong has identified the artifact as prehistoric in origin."

Something that is *imminent* is likely to happen soon, or is impending: "After being warned that the hurricane's arrival was *imminent*, beachfront residents left their homes immediately."

LAY/LIE To *lay* is to place or put something, and this verb usually does have a "something," a direct object, following it. One form, *laid*, serves as the simple past and the past participle of *lay*. "Before she begins her pictures, Emily *lays* all of her pencils, brushes, and paints on her worktable to avoid interruptions while she draws and paints."

To *lie* is to recline, to be in a lying position or at rest. This verb never takes a direct object: you do not *lie* anything down. The simple past form of *lie* is *lay*; the past participle is *lain*. Notice that the past form of *lie* is identical with the present form of *lay*. This coincidence complicates the task of distinguishing the related meaning of *lay* and *lie*. "Having *laid* the picnic cloth under the sycamore, they *lay* in the shady grass all last Sunday afternoon."

LEAVE/LET To *leave* is to depart, or to allow something to remain behind after departing, or to allow something to remain as it is. One irregular verb form serves as the simple past and the past participle: *left*. "I boarded my plane and it *left*, *leaving* my baggage behind in Chicago." When *leave* is used in the third sense—to allow something to remain as it is—and followed by alone, this verb does overlap with *let*: "If parents *leave* (or *let*) a baby with a new toy alone, she will understand it as quickly as if they demonstrated how the toy works."

To *let* is to allow, or to rent out. These are the verb's core meanings, but it also combines with several different prepositions to produce various specific senses. *Let* is irregular. One form serves as present, past, and past participle. "The French border police would not *let* the Dutch tourist pass without a passport."

RAISE/RISE To *raise* is to lift up, or to cause to rise or grow, and it usually has a direct object: You *raise* dumbbells, roof beams, tomato plants, children. *Raise* is a completely regular verb. "The trade tariff on imported leather goods *raised* the prices of Italian shoes."

To *rise* is to get up, to go up, to be built up. This verb never takes a direct object: You do not *rise* something. The past and past participle forms are irregular; *rose* is the simple past, *risen* the past participle. "Long-distance commuters must *rise* early and return home late."

SET/SIT The difference between *set* and *sit* is very similar to the difference between *lay* and *lie*, and the difference between *raise* and *rise*. To *set* is to put or place something, to settle or arrange it. But *set* takes on other specific meanings when it combines with several different prepositions. *Set* is an irregular verb in that one form serves as present, past, and past participle.

Set usually takes a direct object: You *set* a ladder against the fence, a value on family heirlooms, a date for the family reunion. "The professor *set* the students' chairs in a semicircle in order to promote open discussion."

To *sit* is to take a seat or to be in a seated position, to rest somewhere, or to occupy a place. This verb does not usually take a direct object, although you can say, "The usher *sat* us in the center seats of the third row from the stage." The irregular form *sat* serves as past and past participle. Usually, no direct object follows this verb: "The beach house *sits* on a hill at some distance from the shoreline."

Wrong Tense

An error typically tested on the Writing Test is the use of a verb in the wrong tense. Here's a sentence in which the verb is in the wrong tense.

> Over the last half-century, the building of passenger airliners *had grown* into a multibillion-dollar industry.

In a one-verb sentence like this one, time-descriptive phrases help you determine what the time frame of a sentence is. The action being described is a process which began during *the last half-century*, and which is continuing to the present day. Any action starting in the past and continuing today is expressed by a verb in the present perfect tense. The present perfect form of this verb is *has grown*. Using the verb *had* makes it seem that passenger airliners aren't being made anymore. That can't be what the sentence is trying to say. With practice, you'll be able to spot mistakes like this with confidence.

Another type of sentence testing verb tense might have two verbs in it. Here's an example.

> Many superb tennis players turn professional at an alarmingly early age, but because of their lack of physical stamina, *suffered* early in their careers.

When there are two verbs in a sentence, first study the time relation between the verbs, and determine whether it is logical as presented. In this sentence, the verb in the first clause of this sentence is *turn*, a present tense verb. The action is not occurring at any specified occasion, but in the general present. The verb *suffered* is in the simple past, but it should remain in the general present, even though the phrase *early in their careers* may suggest a past time. Be sure that there is a logical relation between the verbs when two are presented in the same sentence.

Perilous Pairs

Learn to distinguish these commonly confused words. You're likely to see at least one of them on your test, and knowing the correct word could raise/rise your score.

Don't Get Tense

Verb tense errors are common on the Writing Test. Be on the lookout for them.

Usage Drill 5

Are the underlined words in the following sentences grammatically correct? Mark the incorrect phrase and replace it with the correct phrase in the blank. (Answers are at the end of the chapter.)

1. Scientists have noted how coastlines change subtly and land masses *will shrink* _____ infinitesimally as the polar ice caps begin to melt.

2. Accounts of their voyages reveal that some of the first Europeans to travel to the North American continent *think* _____ they had landed in Asia.

3. At art auctions during the last few years, paintings by some acknowledged masters *will have brought* _____ prices in the millions.

4. The country's land reform law *is* _____ first proposed by a coalition government in 1945, and included farmers who lost their farms during collectivization.

5. As a result of the recent economic recession, many graduating law students *have had* _____ difficulty finding jobs even in large, well-established firms.

6. The Port Huron Statement, an outline of the values and goals of the Students for a Democratic Society, *was having* _____ a major impact on social protest in the decade following its 1962 publication.

7. To get to the theater, which is on the East Side, wait at the corner until the express bus *came* _____.

8. As the ninth inning began, his manager reminded "Doc" Gooden that he *has hit* _____ the lead-off batter in the first inning.

Number Agreement Problems

The Writing Test also tests a particular error of modification involving number; for instance, a noun may be plural while a phrase describing the noun belongs with a singular noun. That sounds complicated, but fortunately, you don't need to be able to explain the grammar involved: You just need to be able to spot this type of mistake. Here's an example of what you need to look out for.

The advertisement in the newspaper requested that only persons *with a high school diploma* apply for the position.

Nouns in a sentence must have logical number relations. The noun in question, the subject of the second clause of this sentence, is *persons*, a plural noun. However, the noun *diploma* is singular. Because the phrase is singular, it seems to say that this group of people shares one diploma, when in fact each person should have his or her own diploma. The underlined phrase should read *with high school diplomas*.

Here's an example of number disagreement in which a singular noun is coupled with a plural subject:

> The economies of Romania and Albania are considered by many to be *a symbol* of the failure of the command market structure.

Again, identify the subject of the sentence, *economies*. The noun which corresponds to the subject is *symbol*, a singular noun. There is no agreement in number between *economies* and *symbol*. Each individual economy is a symbol; both economies wouldn't be a single symbol. The plural form, *symbols*, makes this sentence grammatically correct. Make sure that the nouns in a sentence that logically should agree in number do agree.

Usage Drill 6

Put a check mark next to any the following sentences that contains an error in number agreement. (Answers are at the end of the chapter.)

☐ 1. Rising stock value and capital liquidity are considered by financiers to be *a requirement* for healthy investment.

☐ 2. The two-piece bathing suit is considered by many to be *a throwback* to the 1960s.

☐ 3. The rubble of Berlin and the division of Germany were *a reminder* of the defeat of the Axis powers in World War II.

☐ 4. Many question the validity of laws that do not allow people *with a child* to rent certain apartments.

☐ 5. Students *in a college T-shirt* will be admitted to the concert for free.

☐ 6. Few could foresee the Model T and Model A, produced by Ford in the early twentieth century, *as the prototype* of today's automobile.

☐ 7. Armed *with their bank account*, corporate raiders schemed to overtake many of America's leading industries.

☐ 8. One of the eels of the Muraenidae family, the moray is feared *as a lethal aquatic vertebrate*.

Pronoun in the Wrong Number

You'll be tested on your ability to tell whether a noun and the pronoun that refers to that noun agree in number. A singular pronoun should be used to refer to a singular noun; a plural pronoun should be used with a plural noun. In these examples, the pronoun does not match its antecedent in number.

> The typical college student has difficulty adjusting to academic standards much higher than those of *their* school.

The subject of the sentence is *student*, a singular noun. The pronoun *their* should refer to a plural noun, but in this sentence it refers back to *student*. Therefore, the pronoun should be the singular form *his*, and not the plural form *their*. Look for the same kind of mistake in the next sentence.

> Most infants, even unusually quiet ones, will cry with greater intensity when it begins teething.

The error in this sentence is just the opposite from that in the first example. The subject is *infants*, a plural noun. But the pronoun that refers back to this plural noun is *it*, a singular form. The correct form of the pronoun is *they*, referring back to the plural subject. Be sure that a pronoun agrees with its antecedent in number.

Usage Drill 7

Are the following sentences grammatically correct? Mark the incorrect sentences and replace the underlined words with the correct forms using the blank lines. (Answers are at the end of the chapter.)

1. The appreciation shown to the dance troupe was a symbol of the school's gratitude for *their* _____ hard work.

2. The mayor welcomed the foreign delegation by presenting *them* _____ with a key to the city.

3. Crowds of tennis fans love his style of play, because the tennis star frequently appeals to *them* _____ for support.

4. The Internal Revenue Service is annually derided by critics who claim that *their* _____ instruction manuals for filing taxes are too cryptic.

5. A typical bank will reject an application for a loan if *their* _____ credit department discovers that the applicant is unemployed.

6. Investors who lost money in the stock market crash generally recouped *his* _____ losses over the next 18 months.

Beware of Pronouns

If you see a pronoun underlined in a Usage question, be very suspicious. Here are some of the pronoun errors that you'll be tested on:

- Errors in number
- Errors in case
- Shifts in person or number
- Ambiguous references

7. The committee asserts that the venture capitalist has not proven quite as philanthropic as *their* _____ public relations campaign suggests.

8. The waitresses in this elegant restaurant can receive up to eighty percent of *her* _____ salary in tips.

Case Study

To decide whether the subjective case form or the objective case form of a pronoun is correct, check how the pronoun is used in the sentence.

Pronoun in the Wrong Case in Compound Noun Phrases

Errors of pronoun choice in sentences with compound noun phrases are also favorites of the people who make the Writing Test. These are errors of the "between you and I" variety. Can you identify the compound in the sentence below, and the error in the choice of pronoun?

> Him and the rest of the team stopped by the malt shop for milk-shakes after the game.

In this sentence, the compound subject is *Him and the rest of the team*. To identify the error, you should isolate the pronoun from the compound. Take away the second part of the compound, and you are left with *him*. The pronoun *him* is the object form of the pronoun in the third person singular. This form is incorrect, because, as you can see from the sentence's word order, the pronoun is the subject of the sentence. The correct form for this sentence is *he*, the subject form.

Can you identify and isolate the incorrect pronoun in the following sentence?

> Uncle John and Aunt Rosie join my parents and I for dinner every Thursday.

In this sentence, the compound noun phrase in question is *my parents and I*, the object of the verb. Ignoring the phrase *my parents*, you can now read the sentence: *Uncle John and Aunt Rosie join I for dinner every Thursday*. The pronoun *I* is the incorrect form of the personal pronoun; the correct form is *me*, the object form. For the following exercise questions, single out the pronoun from the rest of the compound. Then determine what role the pronoun plays in the sentence, and put the pronoun into the correct form.

Usage Drill 8

Underline the pronoun that makes the sentence grammatically correct. (Answers are at the end of the chapter.)

1. The other drivers and (I/me) pulled over until the heavy rains passed.

Pick One

Pronouns must agree with their antecedents in person. Watch for shifts from *one* to *you*, and so on.

2. I did not receive the final draft of the report until it was approved by my supervisor and (he/him).

3. (We/Us) and the high school band accompanied the team to the stadium on the chartered bus.

4. Our professor forgot to distribute the new Bunsen burner kit to my lab partner and (I/me).

5. (She/Her) and her parents set off yesterday on a three-week cruise of the North Atlantic.

6. It was surprising to hear the minister address my new wife and (I/me) as "Mr. and Mrs. Murphy."

7. The legal authorities questioned (she/her) and the other students involved in the incident for two hours before dropping the charges.

8. (We/Us) and the other team combined for 16 runs and 23 hits in the seven-inning game.

Pronoun Shift

Here's another way in which your knowledge of the correct way to use pronouns will be tested. "Pronoun shift" is a switch in pronoun person or number within a given sentence. Here's an example.

> One cannot sleep soundly if *you* exercise vigorously before retiring to bed.

The sentence above is typical of errors in this category. The subject in the first clause is *one*, and the subject in the second clause is *you*. These two pronouns refer to the same performer of two actions, so they should be consistent in person and number. If you see the pronoun *one* in one part of a sentence, then elsewhere in the sentence, look for either *one*, or *he* or *she*, or *a person*—all in the third person singular form. The sentence should not shift to the second person, *you* form.

Look for another kind of pronoun shift in the next sentence.

> If someone loses his way in the airport, *they* can ask any employee for directions.

This pronoun shift is as glaring as the last. The subject is *someone* in the first clause, but *they* in the second clause. Clearly, both pronouns refer to the same agent; the performer(s) of both actions, *losing* and *asking*, is the same. This switch in number from singular to plural is not grammatical. In creating such a sentence, the Writing Test writers play on a common logical confusion. In English, singular words like *one*, *someone*, and *a person* can represent people in general. So can plural words like *people* or *they*. Be on the lookout when general statements use pronouns, and consider whether these pronouns are consistent.

Usage Drill 9

Identify the sentences that include a pronoun shift and replace the incorrect italicized words with the correct forms, using the blanks. (Answers are at the end of the chapter.)

1. When we gather during the Thanksgiving holidays, *you* _____ cannot help appreciating family and friends.

2. One cannot gauge the immensity of the Empire State Building until *you* _____ stand atop the building.

3. As you arrive in New York City's Grand Central Terminal, *one* _____ can easily imagine that station as the most elaborate in all of the United States.

4. You may not be fond of Shakespeare, but the theater company guarantees *you* _____ will be impressed with the quality of acting in this production.

5. You should not even attempt to pass your driving test unless *one* _____ has learned to parallel park.

6. When they grew up in my grandfather's neighborhood during the Great Depression, *you* _____ could feel the despair that gripped the nation.

7. Whenever we read about a plane crash, even as an infrequent flyer, *one* _____ becomes concerned about air safety.

8. When one considers the vastness of the universe, one cannot help being struck by *your* _____ own insignificance.

Pronoun with Ambiguous Reference

There are two ways the Writing Test might test your ability to recognize ambiguous pronoun reference. First, a sentence may be given in which it is impossible to determine to what noun the pronoun refers. Take a look at this example.

> The United States entered into warmer relations with China after *its* compliance with recent weapons agreements.

To which country does the pronoun *its* refer? Grammatically and logically, either country could be the antecedent of the pronoun. With the limited information provided by this sentence alone, the reader simply can't determine which country the pronoun stands in for; its reference is ambiguous.

Pronoun reference can also be ambiguous if the pronoun's antecedent is not explicitly stated in the sentence.

Pronoun

A *pronoun* is a word that is used in place of a noun.

After the derailment last month, *they* are inspecting trains for safety more often than ever before.

The question to ask about this sentence is, Who is *they*? There is no group of people identified in this sentence to whom the pronoun could refer. You can logically infer that *they* refers to agents of a railroad safety commission, but because these inspectors are not explicitly mentioned in the sentence, the personal pronoun cannot be clear. Be sure to locate the antecedent of any pronoun in Writing Test Usage sentences.

Usage Drill 10

Read the following sentences and circle the pronouns with ambiguous reference. (Answers are at the end of the chapter.)

1. The company chairman contacted the marketing director after he failed to attend the sales meeting.

2. Temporary loss of hearing is a common occurrence at rock concerts where they sit too close to the mammoth speakers.

3. The small claims court lawyer won the case for the defendant once she proved her innocence with legal documents.

4. Jurors are told to disregard the race of the participants in a trial when they come into the courtroom.

5. When an old friend came to town last week, he asked what plays they were presenting on Broadway.

6. The manager benched the star player after he criticized the pitcher's lack of intensity.

7. Dozens of students rallied against administration officials to protest the music they were playing on the college radio station.

8. When the painters work on your neighbors' laundry room, make sure that they do not get paint on their clothes.

Faulty Comparison

Most faulty comparisons occur when two things that logically cannot be compared, are compared. A comparison can be faulty either logically or grammatically. Look for the faulty comparison in the sentence below.

A Nobel Peace Prize winner and the author of several respected novels, Elie Wiesel's name is still less well known than last year's Heisman Trophy winner.

Antecedent

The noun that the pronoun stands for is called the *antecedent* of the pronoun.

Relationship Problems

Many of the pronoun problems on the Writing Test result from a faulty relationship between the pronoun and the antecedent. So checking the relationship between those two words will help you to catch many of the pronoun errors that you'll see on the test.

In every sentence, you should first identify what things or actions are being compared. In this sentence, *Elie Wiesel's name* is compared to *last year's Heisman Trophy winner*. This comparison is faulty because a person's name is compared to another person. If the first item were *Elie Wiesel*, then the comparison would be valid.

Try to identify the faulty comparison in the next sentence.

> To lash back at one's adversaries is a less courageous course than attempting to bring about a reconciliation with them.

The comparison in this sentence is logically correct in that two actions are compared. But the problem lies in the grammatical form of the words compared. An infinitive verb, *to lash*, expresses the first action, but a gerund, *attempting*, expresses the second action. These verb forms should match in order to make the comparison parallel. If *lashing* replaced *to lash*, the comparison would be grammatically parallel and logically valid. Check comparisons in Writing Test Usage questions for logic and grammatical consistency.

Usage Drill 11

Which of the following sentences contain faulty comparisons? Correct the phrases that contain errors of comparison, using the lines below the sentences. (Answers are at the end of the chapter.)

1. Like many politicians, the senator's promises sounded good but ultimately led to nothing.

Rewrite: _____

_____

2. As a manager and a problem solver, the Governor was considered as creative as, or more creative than, writing and painting.

Rewrite: _____

_____

3. Marine zoologists who have trained porpoises maintain that porpoises have powers of attention more sustained than chimpanzees.

Rewrite: _____

_____

4. The United States scientist's assumption, unlike Germany's Professor Heisenberg, was that the release of atomic energy would be sudden and violent.

Rewrite: _____

_____

Comparison Checklist

When you encounter a comparison on the Writing Test, ask yourself: Is the comparison logical? Are the things being compared expressed in similar grammatical forms?

5. Although some traditionalists still prefer typewriters to computers, most people agree that word processors are a great boon.

Rewrite: _____

_____

6. The nonviolent resistance philosophy of Thoreau, Ghandi, and King holds that it is better to go to jail than submitting to an unjust law.

Rewrite: _____

_____

7. The cost of a year at college these days is greater than a house was when my father was a boy.

Rewrite: _____

_____

8. According to some medievalists, women were treated with far greater respect during the Middle Ages than many countries in the twentieth century.

Rewrite: _____

_____

Grammar Reference

An adjective modifies, or describes, a noun or pronoun. An adverb modifies a verb, an adjective, or another adverb. Most, but not all adverbs end in -ly.

Misuse of Adjective or Adverb

Questions in this category are designed to test your ability to recognize misuses of one-word modifiers. Keeping in mind that adjectives modify nouns, and adverbs modify verbs, adjectives, and other adverbs, ask yourself what the *underlined* word is intended to modify as you look at the sentence below.

The applicants for low-interest loans hoped to buy *decent* built houses for their families.

The word *decent* is an adjective. However, a word in this position should describe how the houses were built. A word that modifies an adjective like *built* is an adverb. So the word needed in this sentence is an adverb, decently. Notice also that this adverb ends in -ly, the most common adverbial ending.

Now take a look at the second sentence:

The critics who reviewed both of Amy Tan's novels like the second one *best*.

The word *best* is a superlative modifier. (It's an adverb in this sentence, but *best* can also be an adjective.) Superlative adverbs and adjectives (adverbs and adjectives ending in -est, such as *biggest, loudest, fastest*) should express comparisons between three or more things or actions. This sentence compares critics' responses to two novels by Amy Tan. Comparative adverbs and adjectives (ending in -*er*, such as *bigger*, *louder*, *faster*) should express comparisons between two things or actions. Instead of *best*, this sentence needed the comparative modifier *better*. Remember that some adjectives and adverbs, usually those of two or more syllables, form the comparative with more instead of the -*er* ending. And *most* instead of the -*est* ending converts some modifiers to superlatives.

Trust your ear to distinguish adjectives from adverbs in Writing Test Usage questions, but do "listen" carefully. Pay close attention when you decide whether a sentence needs a comparative or superlative modifier.

Usage Drill 12

Underline the option that makes the sentence grammatically correct. (Answers are at the end of the chapter.)

1. Global warming would increase more (gradual/gradually) if solar energy sources were more fully exploited.

2. Eliminating (commercial/commercially) prepared sauces and seasonings is a good way to reduce the amount of sodium in your diet.

3. Although many people feel that parapsychology, the study of psychic phenomena, is completely frivolous, others take it very (serious/seriously).

4. Among the many problems facing the nation's schools today, the high dropout rate may be the (more/most) distressing.

5. The reading list for the course included short stories by five American authors, but most students found those by Poe (more/most) effective.

6. Archaeologists excavating the ancient Inca site removed soil very (slow/slowly) to protect any buried artifacts.

7. Although Delacroix is best known for the drama of his large canvases, many of his smaller works capture heroic themes just as (forceful/forcefully).

8. When movies were cheaper to produce than they are now, young directors were able to make films (easier/more easily).

Double Negative

A quick tip: Don't use no double negatives on the Writing Test! In standard written English, it is incorrect to use two negatives together unless one is intended to cancel out the other. That is, one negative word is enough to express a negative sense. Notice the two negative words in this sentence.

James easily passed the biology exam *without hardly* studying his lab notes.

No-Nos

Watch out for double negatives on Usage questions. Be sure to count less obviously negative words like *hardly*, *barely*, and *scarcely*.

Without is a negative, as is any word which indicates absence or lack. *Hardly* is a less familiar negative; it also denotes a scarcity of something, but perhaps not a total absence.

Now look at the next sentence.

In the history of the major leagues, *barely no one* has maintained higher than a .400 batting average for an entire season.

Clearly, *no one* is a negative, but so is *barely*. Just as *hardly* does, this word indicates a scarcity of something, almost a total absence. In Usage questions, be on the lookout for negatives which are not obviously negative, such as *hardly*, *barely*, and *scarcely*.

Usage Drill 13

Which of the following sentences contain inappropriate double negatives? Underline the double negatives.

1. Until Copernicus proposed his theory, scarcely no one believed that the sun was the center of the universe.

2. The decline of outmoded industries has resulted in an unstable economy, since no easy way of retraining workers has never been found.

3. Many submarine volcanoes lie at such great depth that eruptions occur without hardly any release of gas or steam.

4. Charles Dickens had not written fiction for scarcely three years when he became a bestselling novelist.

5. Practically no big-time college football team has enjoyed success on the gridiron without increasing overall athletic department revenues.

6. Because consumer electronics are so affordable today, hardly no college student needs to go without a personal stereo.

7. Last summer's extended drought means there may not be scarcely enough wheat to satisfy the growing demand.

8. The author's latest work is so powerfully written and emotionally charged that hardly any commentators have criticized it.

Usage Practice Quiz

30 Questions (12 minutes)

Directions: The sentences in this section test your knowledge of grammar, usage, diction (choice of words), and idiom.

Some of the sentences are correct.
None of the sentences contains more than one error.

The error, if there is one in the sentence, is underlined and lettered. Parts of the sentence that are not underlined are correct and cannot be changed. Follow the rules of standard written English when selecting your answers.

If the sentence contains an error, choose the <u>one underlined part</u> that must be changed to make the sentence correct. Then, fill in the corresponding oval on the answer grid.

If the sentence is correct and no changes are needed, fill in oval E.

SAMPLE QUESTION

<u>Even though</u> he <u>had to</u> supervise a
   A   B
large staff, his salary <u>was no greater</u>
                      C
than <u>a clerk</u>. <u>No error</u>
     D   E

SAMPLE ANSWER

Ⓐ Ⓑ Ⓒ ● Ⓔ

---

1. <u>Even when</u> shrouded by the morning fog,
    A
Mt. Hood <u>looked</u> more <u>dramatically</u> beautiful
           B   C
to us than <u>any mountain</u>. <u>No error</u>
            D   E

Ⓐ Ⓑ Ⓒ Ⓓ Ⓔ

2. <u>Today's</u> athlete may feel such <u>great</u> pressure
   A   B
<u>to succeed</u> at every level of competition that
  C
<u>they begin</u> taking drugs at an early age.
    D
<u>No error</u>
   E

Ⓐ Ⓑ Ⓒ Ⓓ Ⓔ

3. <u>Bicycling</u>, as well as walking and jogging,
    A
<u>reduce</u> <u>one's</u> <u>dependence on</u> motorized
  B   C   D
transportation. <u>No error</u>
           E

Ⓐ Ⓑ Ⓒ Ⓓ Ⓔ

4. Children from two-parent homes, <u>according</u> to
                               A
a <u>recent</u> clinical study, <u>are</u> as susceptible to
   B   C
peer pressure <u>as</u> children with only one parent.
          D
<u>No error</u>
   E

Ⓐ Ⓑ Ⓒ Ⓓ Ⓔ

5. The volunteer librarian <u>is</u> <u>extremely</u> concerned
                                A   B
    <u>in</u> the appallingly low rate of adult literacy in
    C
    <u>his</u> community. <u>No error</u>
    D   E
    Ⓐ Ⓑ Ⓒ Ⓓ Ⓔ

6. The wrestlers knew that fasting <u>could be</u>
                                        A
    dangerous, but <u>them</u> and their teammates
                        B
    were desperate <u>to</u> lose weight <u>before</u> the
                        C   D
    championship match. <u>No error</u>
                            E
    Ⓐ Ⓑ Ⓒ Ⓓ Ⓔ

7. Artifacts from Sumerian Ur, <u>though less well</u>
                                        A
    <u>known</u> <u>than</u> other archaeological discoveries,
      B   C
    <u>is</u> sophisticated in both design and execution.
    D
    <u>No error</u>
        E
    Ⓐ Ⓑ Ⓒ Ⓓ Ⓔ

8. Whenever we <u>travel</u> abroad, a <u>sense of</u>
                    A   B
    excitement and an anticipation of being

    in a foreign land <u>overtake</u> <u>you</u>. <u>No error</u>
                          C   D   E
    Ⓐ Ⓑ Ⓒ Ⓓ Ⓔ

9. My older brother and <u>me</u> <u>shared</u> a ten-speed
                            A   B
    bicycle <u>until</u> he passed <u>his</u> driver's examination
                C   D
    and received his license. <u>No error</u>
                                  E
    Ⓐ Ⓑ Ⓒ Ⓓ Ⓔ

10. The chairwoman felt that she <u>could not</u> give in
                                    A
    <u>with</u> his demands, <u>which</u> she thought were
      B   C
    <u>completely</u> unreasonable. <u>No error</u>
      D   E
    Ⓐ Ⓑ Ⓒ Ⓓ Ⓔ

11. <u>One</u> can learn more <u>about</u> new computers by
      A   B
    actually working with <u>them</u> than one can by
                            C
    <u>merely</u> reading the instruction manual.
      D
    <u>No error</u>
        E
    Ⓐ Ⓑ Ⓒ Ⓓ Ⓔ

12. To expand the newspaper's <u>coverage of</u>
                                  A
    local politics, <u>they</u> transferred a <u>popular</u>
                      B   C
    columnist <u>to</u> the City Desk. <u>No error</u>
                D   E
    Ⓐ Ⓑ Ⓒ Ⓓ Ⓔ

13. As one <u>roams</u> the <u>halls of</u> the National Gallery
              A   B
    of Art, <u>you</u> should appreciate not only the
              C
    <u>displays</u> of art, but the grandeur of the
      D
    building's architecture. <u>No error</u>
                                E
    Ⓐ Ⓑ Ⓒ Ⓓ Ⓔ

14. Before he <u>drunk</u> the poison, Socrates <u>joked</u>
                  A   B
    <u>gently</u> with his distraught and <u>grieving</u>
      C   D
    followers. <u>No error</u>
                  E
    Ⓐ Ⓑ Ⓒ Ⓓ Ⓔ

15. In <u>recently</u> constructed concert halls, there <u>is</u>
        A   B
    usually at least two <u>sets</u> of stairs at the rear <u>of</u>
                        C   D
    the balcony. <u>No error</u>
                 E

    Ⓐ Ⓑ Ⓒ Ⓓ Ⓔ

16. Many foreign electronics <u>companies</u> have
                                A
    learned <u>to build</u> machines at lower cost by
            B
    using <u>inexpensive</u> produced <u>components</u>.
              C   D
    <u>No error</u>
     E

    Ⓐ Ⓑ Ⓒ Ⓓ Ⓔ

17. Although ecological awareness is

    <u>international</u>, there are <u>few if any</u> countries
        A   B
    <u>on the rise</u> <u>in which</u> no native species are
        C   D
    endangered. <u>No error</u>
             E

    Ⓐ Ⓑ Ⓒ Ⓓ Ⓔ

18. The <u>clean</u> cars and spacious <u>stations</u> of the
        A   B
    new subway system <u>is</u> a tribute to the
                    C
    project's <u>thousands of</u> laborers. <u>No error</u>
            D   E

    Ⓐ Ⓑ Ⓒ Ⓓ Ⓔ

19. <u>Some</u> settlers move to new countries simply
     A
    <u>because of</u> the compelling <u>natural</u> beauty
        B   C
    found in <u>them</u>. <u>No error</u>
            D   E

    Ⓐ Ⓑ Ⓒ Ⓓ Ⓔ

20. The Soviet Union had <u>not hardly</u> developed a
                           A
    spaceship <u>suitable</u> for lunar <u>travel</u> when the
             B   C
    first United States astronaut <u>landed on</u> the
                              D
    moon in 1969. <u>No error</u>
                  E

    Ⓐ Ⓑ Ⓒ Ⓓ Ⓔ

21. The police officer <u>noticed</u> the wanted suspect
                     A
    only after <u>he</u> <u>removed</u> his sunglasses and
              B   C
    <u>sat down</u> at the counter. <u>No error</u>
       D   E

    Ⓐ Ⓑ Ⓒ Ⓓ Ⓔ

22. Babar <u>was created</u> over 60 years ago <u>in</u> a
            A   B
    suburb of Paris <u>but</u> is <u>the most popular</u>
                  C   D
    elephant in children's literature. <u>No error</u>
                                 E

    Ⓐ Ⓑ Ⓒ Ⓓ Ⓔ

23. Unemployment compensation <u>was developed</u> to
                                     A
    aid <u>those</u> people <u>between</u> jobs or otherwise
         B   C
    temporarily <u>without a position</u> of employment.
                      D
    <u>No error</u>
     E

    Ⓐ Ⓑ Ⓒ Ⓓ Ⓔ

24. The triathlete <u>had swam</u> three miles <u>before</u> leg
                 A   B
    cramps <u>caused</u> her to <u>withdraw from</u> the
           C   D
    competition. <u>No error</u>
              E

    Ⓐ Ⓑ Ⓒ Ⓓ Ⓔ

25. The speaker <u>whom</u> the graduating class <u>chose</u>
     A   B
<u>to deliver</u> their commencement address was
 C
an <u>imminent</u> authority on international
    D
diplomacy. <u>No error</u>
     E

       Ⓐ Ⓑ Ⓒ Ⓓ Ⓔ

26. The jazz band <u>was forced</u> <u>to return</u> the gate
        A   B
receipts after <u>they</u> had arrived at the arena one
     C
hour <u>late</u>. <u>No error</u>
   D   E

       Ⓐ Ⓑ Ⓒ Ⓓ Ⓔ

27. By the time <u>today's</u> freshmen complete <u>their</u>
      A   B
engineering degrees, the job market

<u>in their field</u> <u>has become</u> quite robust.
   C   D
<u>No error</u>
  E

       Ⓐ Ⓑ Ⓒ Ⓓ Ⓔ

28. <u>On</u> the executive board of the <u>publishing</u>
 A   B
company <u>sits</u> five women <u>and</u> four men.
    C   D
<u>No error</u>
  E

       Ⓐ Ⓑ Ⓒ Ⓓ Ⓔ

29. Today, <u>when</u> Indian leaders sue to regain
    A
<u>ancestral</u> lands, the government often <u>offered</u>
  B   C
<u>to settle</u> the disputes out of court. <u>No error</u>
  D   E

       Ⓐ Ⓑ Ⓒ Ⓓ Ⓔ

30. Borges, <u>probably</u> the most <u>innovative</u> writer of
     A   B
the twentieth century, <u>brought</u> to literature a
          C
fresh <u>concept of</u> the nature of fiction. <u>No error</u>
   D   E
       Ⓐ Ⓑ Ⓒ Ⓓ Ⓔ

Answers and Explanations

Usage Drills

Usage Drill 1

1. are 2. are 3. pass 4. correct 5. are 6. are 7. correct

Usage Drill 2

1. are 2. is 3. go 4. attracts 5. are 6. complete 7. are 8. ranks

Usage Drill 3

1. is 2. removes 3. are 4. is 5. keeps

Usage Drill 4

1. to compete 2. to increase/on increasing 3. of setting 4. to carry 5. correct 6. to triple 7. in discouraging 8. correct

Usage Drill 5

1. shrink 2. thought 3. have brought 4. was 5. correct 6. had 7. comes 8. had hit

Usage Drill 6

1. requirements 2. correct 3. reminders 4. with children 5. in college T-shirts 6. as prototypes 7. with their bank accounts 8. correct

Usage Drill 7

1. its 2. it 3. correct 4. its 5. its 6. their 7. his/her 8. their

Usage Drill 8

1. I 2. him 3. We 4. me 5. She 6. me 7. her 8. We

Usage Drill 9

1. we 2. one/she/he (stands) 3. you 4. correct 5. you (have) 6. they 7. (as infrequent flyers,) we (become) 8. one's/her/his

Usage Drill 10

1. he 2. they 3. she/her 4. they 5. they 6. he 7. they 8. they/their

Usage Drill 11

1. faulty, *Like those of many politicians* 2. faulty, *than he was as a writer and painter* 3. faulty, *than chimpanzees'* 4. faulty, *unlike Germany's Professor Heisenberg's* 5. correct 6. faulty, *than to submit to an unjust law* 7. faulty, *than the cost of a house* 8. faulty, *than they are in many countries*

Usage Drill 12

1. gradually 2. commercially 3. seriously 4. most 5. most 6. slowly 7. forcefully 8. more easily

Usage Drill 13

1. scarcely no one 2. no easy way has never been found 3. without hardly 4. had not written fiction for scarcely three years 5. correct 6. hardly no college student 7. may not be scarcely enough wheat 8. correct

Usage Practice Quiz

1. (D)—The comparison between Mt. Hood and any mountain is illogical. Mt. Hood is itself a mountain, so it cannot be contrasted with every member of its own class of things, mountains. The underlined phrase should be *any other mountain.*

2. (D)—Apparently, the plural pronoun *they* refers to the subject of this sentence. But the subject is *athlete,* a singular noun even though it represents a whole class of athletes. A singular form of the personal pronoun, *he* or *she,* corresponds to the subject in number. Of course, with a singular pronoun, the verb *begin* also changes, to *begins.*

3. (B)—*Reduce* is a plural form of the verb, *to reduce.* But the subject of this verb is *bicycling,* a gerund, and a gerund is always singular. The phrase between commas, *as well as walking and jogging,* may seem to make the subject plural. But a phrase following a subject, set off by commas, and introduced by a compound preposition like *as well as,* or *in addition to,* is not treated as part of a sentence's subject. *Bicycling* remains the singular subject requiring a singular verb, *reduces.*

4. (E)—There is no error in this sentence. The comparison here is both logical and idiomatic.

5. (C)—In this context, the adjective *concerned* requires a different preposition, *about* instead of *in.* By itself, the word *concerned* can take three different prepositions, *about, in,* or *with,* but each combination produces a different meaning.

6. (B)—*Them* is the object form of the personal pronoun that could refer to the wrestlers. But the pronoun serves as a subject in this sentence—*them . . . were desperate*—so it should be in subject form, *they.*

7. (D)—The only verb in the sentence is the singular *is.* However, the subject of the sentence is *artifacts,* a plural noun. A long phrase separating the subject and its verb makes it harder to "listen" for agreement, but the verb should be plural, *are*.

8. (D)—*We* and *you* are not interchangeable in this sentence, though either one could be grammatical. But when two pronouns within one sentence refer to the same performer of actions, the pronouns should be consistent. Here, because it's underlined, *you* can change to match *we*.

9. (A)—*Me* is part of the subject of this sentence; the position of the pronoun makes that obvious. But the form of the pronoun signals that it's an object. To be part of the subject, the pronoun should have the subject form, *I*. It's *I shared*, not *me shared*.

10. (B)—The idiomatic verb-preposition combination *give in to* means "submit to," and that is the meaning of the verb in this sentence. The preposition *with* is simply unidiomatic in this usage.

11. (E)—There is no error in this sentence. The parallel construction in this sentence balances perfectly.

12. (B)—*They* has no antecedent in this sentence. A personal pronoun cannot refer to an unstated noun.

13. (C)—*One* and *you* are not interchangeable in this sentence. Either *one* and *he*, or *you* could be used, but both *one* and *you* cannot refer to the same performer of actions within one sentence. Because *you* is underlined, it can change to be consistent with *one*.

14. (A)—This sentence requires the simple past of the verb *to drink*, that is, *drank*. The form given in this sentence is the past participle.

15. (B)—The only verb in the sentence is the singular *is*. The subject of the sentence is *sets*, a plural noun. The word *there* preceding *is* serves to delay the subject *sets*. The subject is no longer in the position where we expect to find it, before the verb. Nevertheless, the verb should be plural—*are*—to agree with the plural subject.

16. (C)—*Inexpensive* seems to modify the word *produced* and to describe how the components were produced. But adverbs describe how an action is done, so the adjective *inexpensive* needs an adverbial ending. The word needed at (C) is the adverb *inexpensively*.

17. (E)—There is no error in this sentence.

18. (C)—The only verb in the sentence is the singular *is*. But this sentence has two plural subjects, *cars* and *stations*. The verb should be plural, *are*, to correspond with the plural subjects.

19. (E)—There is no error in this sentence.

20. (A)—*Hardly* is a modifier that negates the word it modifies. In this sentence, it negates *developed*. *Not* also negates *developed* and creates a double negative construction where only one negation is intended. Such double negatives are substandard usage in modern English.

21. (B)—It is unclear to whom the pronoun *he* refers. Because the singular pronoun *he* could agree with either noun, *officer* or *suspect*, the pronoun's reference is unclear and the noun should be restated.

22. (C)—This sentence is grammatically correct, but logically faulty. The conjunction *but* expresses a contrast, but the two predicates express no contrast. Babar's great and lasting popularity is not at odds with his creation in France over 60 years ago. So, the *but* is not a logical way to link the two predicates.

23. (D)—The singular noun *position* should be the plural noun *positions*. As the phrase stands in the given sentence, *people . . . without a position of employment* seems to say that many persons lack the same position of employment, while of course, many unemployed people lack many different positions.

24. (A)—*Swam* is the simple past tense of the verb *to swim*. But the required verb tense in this sentence is the past perfect because the triathlete *had swum* before *cramps caused her to withdraw*. The past perfect is formed with an auxiliary verb, *had*, and the past participle, *swum*, not *swam*.

25. (D)—The words *imminent* and *eminent* are easily confused. *Imminent* means "likely to occur at any moment"; it is familiar and appropriate in the phrase "imminent disaster." But *eminent*, the word this sentence needs, means "highly regarded."

26. (C)—*They* seems to refer to the first subject, *jazz band*. But *jazz band* is a singular noun, although a band is made up of several musicians. The band must be singular because it acts as a unit, arriving late and disappointing the audience together. The pronoun referring to the band should be *it*.

27. (D)—The verb phrase in the second clause is *has become*, a verb in the present perfect tense. The present perfect should express recently completed, or past but continuing action: "times have changed" (and they still do). But the future time established in the first clause requires a future perfect verb in the second clause: *the job market . . . will have become*.

28. (C)—The verb *sits* is singular, but the subject of the sentence is plural, *five women and four men*. The subject appears in an unusual position following the verb. Nevertheless, the correct verb is the plural, *sit*.

29. (C)—The verb *offered* is in the past tense. But the first word of the sentence, *today*, indicates that the action takes place in the present. Therefore, the verb should be in the present tense, *offers*.

30. (E)—There is no error in this sentence.

CHAPTER 6

SENTENCE CORRECTION QUESTIONS

Sentence Correction questions are a little more involved than Usage questions, but you'll have fewer of them to answer. As we mentioned in chapter 5, you don't need to panic even if you didn't study much English grammar in school. Kaplan's careful analysis of recent Writing Tests reveals that a large majority of Sentence Correction questions relate to a surprisingly limited number of grammatical issues. In this chapter, we'll explain the grammar you need to know to get a high score on Sentence Correction questions on the Writing Test.

What Sentence Correction Questions Test

Standard written English is somewhat more formal than the average person's spoken English: Things that you're used to saying in everyday conversation may well be considered wrong on the Writing Test. Standard written English is the kind of English that you find in textbooks and the kind of English your professors will expect you to use in your college papers.

You don't have to use or define grammatical terms, so don't worry if your grasp of grammatical terminology is a little shaky. The Writing Test measures only your ability to recognize acceptable and unacceptable uses of language. It doesn't even test you on every aspect of language use. It tests you in three main areas: Basic grammar, sentence structure, and choice of words. The Writing Test doesn't test spelling or capitalization. Punctuation is tested only as a secondary matter in connection with questions of sentence structure.

How to "Fix the Mistake"

Kaplan calls Sentence Correction questions "fix-the-mistake" questions because, in addition to finding the mistake in each sentence, you have to pick the answer choice that best corrects it. In each of these questions, you're given a sentence, part or all of which is underlined. There are five answer choices: the first one reproduces the underlined part of the sentence exactly,

Relax!

To score well on the Sentence Correction sections of the Writing Test, you need to master only a relatively small number of grammar issues.

Fix the Mistakes

Sentence Corrections questions ask you only to identify and fix grammar mistakes. You don't have to explain the mistakes in formal, grammatical terms.

Be Systematic

Use the Kaplan Method for Sentence Correction questions.

and the other four rephrase the underlined portion in various ways. Here's an example.

> The Emancipation Edict freed the Russian serfs <u>in 1861; that being four years</u> before the Thirteenth Amendment abolished slavery in the United States.
>
> (A) in 1861; that being four years
>
> (B) in 1861 and is four years
>
> (C) in 1861 and this amounts to four years
>
> (D) in 1861, being four years
>
> (E) in 1861, four years

You have to pick the best choice to go in the place of the underlined portion of the sentence. The correct answer must produce a sentence that's not only grammatically correct, but also effective: It must be clear, precise, and free of awkward verbiage. Again, there's a three-step method to answering these questions.

Save Time

Don't ever waste time reading choice (A)—it's the same as the original sentence!

> ### The Kaplan Method for Sentence Correction Questions
>
> 1. Read the sentence, "listening" for a mistake.
>
> 2. Scan the choices, eliminating clearly wrong answers.
>
> 3. Plug in your choice to be sure it sounds best. Don't be afraid to pick (A).

You can probably hear that the stem sentence in the example above doesn't sound right: The semicolon and phrase *that being* seem like the wrong way of joining the two parts of the sentence. All the answer choices begin with *in 1861* and end with *four years*, so you have to look at what comes in between to see what forms the best link. Scan the choices, and you'll find that *and is* in (B), *and this amounts to* in (C), and *being*, preceded by a comma, in (D) are no better than (A). (Incidentally, answer choices that contain the word *being* are usually wrong.) Choice (E) has just a comma; is that enough? Well, if you plug (E) into the sentence, you'll find that the sentence sounds fine and makes perfect sense. Choice (E) is the best way to rewrite the underlined portion of the sentence, so (E) is the correct answer.

While the errors in the Usage questions consist of single words or short phrases, the errors in the Sentence Correction questions generally involve the structure of the sentence as a whole. And, again, not every sentence contains an error: Choice (A) is correct about one-fifth of the time. In any event, since you should begin by reading the original sentence carefully, you should never waste time reading choice (A).

The Classic Mistakes

Answering Writing Test questions correctly begins with simply reading the sentence carefully. The error, if there is one, will often be obvious to you at the first reading.

If it isn't, remember that only a rather limited range of grammar rules is tested. For this reason, we won't burden you with an exhaustive review of English grammar. What follows instead is a comprehensive survey of the grammatical problems that actually occur with some frequency on Sentence Correction questions. Rather than emphasize abstract rules of grammar, which you don't have to regurgitate on the Writing Test, we'll show you the types of grammatical errors that appear in every edition of the Writing Test. Once your inner ear has become attuned to the Writing Test's classic grammar mistakes, you'll have an easier time spotting them on test day.

On the following pages you'll find descriptions and examples of five classic Sentence Correction mistakes. You'll also find drills to give you experience spotting and fixing these typical goofs. At the end of the chapter is a drill with 18 Sentence Correction questions, the same number you'll see on test day.

Run-On Sentence

The Sentence Correction questions on the Writing Test usually include one or two run-on sentences. In a typical run-on sentence, two independent clauses, each of which could stand alone as a complete sentence, are erroneously joined together, either with no punctuation or, most often, with just a comma. Here's an example.

> The decrease in crime can be attributed to a rise in the number of police officers, more than five hundred joined the force in the last year alone.

Both clauses in the above sentence are independent; each could stand alone as a sentence. It is therefore incorrect to join them with just a comma between them. There are several ways to correct run-on sentences. One way is simply to change the inappropriate comma into a period, thereby producing two separate sentences. This method is never used on the Writing Test.

A second way is to change the comma into a semicolon. A semicolon can be described as a "weak period." It's used to indicate that two clauses are grammatically independent but that the ideas expressed are not so independent as to warrant separate sentences. Substituting a semicolon for the comma would render the above sentence correct.

Top Five

Get familiar with the five classic Sentence Correction mistakes and you'll score well on Sentence Correction questions.

The decrease in crime can be attributed to a rise in the number of police officers; more than five hundred joined the force in the last year alone.

Although inserting a semicolon for the given comma is the method used most frequently by the Writing Test writers, there are other ways to join two independent clauses. In the next example, the two clauses are independent, but one is logically subordinate to the other. To make the correction, you can convert the clause expressing the subordinate idea into a grammatically subordinate, or dependent, clause. Identify the two clauses in the sentence below.

Liquor companies are now introducing low-alcohol and alcohol-free beverages, litigation against distillers continues to increase year after year.

Although the clauses in this sentence are grammatically independent, they are not unrelated. Logically, the first clause depends on the second one; it seems to express a response to what is described in the second clause. You can logically infer that the liquor companies are introducing these products because the number of litigations against them is great. So, a good way to correct the error in this sentence would be to make the first clause grammatically dependent on the second clause, as follows.

Although liquor companies are now introducing low-alcohol and alcohol-free beverages, litigation against distillers continues to increase year after year.

A fourth way to correct a run-on sentence is simply to reduce the two independent clauses to one. This can be done in sentences in which the independent clauses have the same subject. You can compress the two clauses into one independent clause, with a compound predicate. This revision is possible in the sentence below:

The Humber Bridge in Britain was completed in 1981, it is the longest single-span suspension bridge in the world.

In this sentence, the pronoun *it*, the subject of the second clause, refers to *Humber Bridge*, the subject of the first clause. To correct this sentence, remove both the comma and the pronoun *it*, and insert the coordinating conjunction *and*. The sentence now reads:

The Humber Bridge in Britain was completed in 1981 and is the longest single-span suspension bridge in the world.

Now the sentence consists of one independent clause with a compound predicate, and only one subject.

Run-Ons

A run-on sentence is actually two complete sentences stuck together with either just a comma or no punctuation at all.

Sentence Correction Drill 1

Choose the answer that produces the most effective, clear, and exact sentence. Darken the corresponding oval in the grid next to the question. (Answers are at the end of chapter.)

1. Hockney's most arresting work has been produced at his home in <u>Los Angeles, he moved there</u> from his native Britain.

   (A) Los Angeles, he moved there
   (B) Los Angeles; he moved there
   (C) Los Angeles, but he moved there
   (D) Los Angeles and he moved there
   (E) Los Angeles he moved there

2. Banquets are frequently thrown to honor guests in a Chinese <u>home, they often feature</u> shark fin as the main dish.

   (A) home, they often feature
   (B) home; often feature
   (C) home and often feature
   (D) home and they often feature
   (E) home, these often feature

3. <u>Many well-heeled taxpayers pay</u> less than ten percent of their annual income to the Internal Revenue Service, some middle-income taxpayers pay a much larger percentage annually.

   (A) Many well-heeled taxpayers pay
   (B) However, many well-heeled taxpayers pay
   (C) With many well-heeled taxpayers which pay
   (D) Many a well-heeled taxpayer pays
   (E) Although many well-heeled taxpayers pay

One in Five

About 20 percent of your answers to Sentence Correction questions on test day should be choice (A)— the sentence is correct as is.

4. Most western European countries have decreased their consumption of fossil <u>fuels, a number of eastern European countries, however, have</u> not done so.

(A) fuels, a number of eastern European countries, however, have

(B) fuels, however a number of eastern European countries have

(C) fuels, while on the other hand a number of eastern European countries have

(D) fuels; a number of eastern European countries, however, have

(E) fuels, a number however of eastern European countries have

What's a Fragment?

A *sentence fragment* is a group of words that looks like a sentence but is grammatically incomplete because it lacks a subject or a verb; or is logically incomplete because other elements necessary for it to express a complete thought are missing.

Sentence Fragment

Sentence Correction questions on the Writing Test usually include one or two sentence fragments. Sentence fragments are parts of sentences that have no independent clauses. What looks like a sentence on the Writing Test may actually be merely a fragment. Take a look at the following example.

> While many office managers are growing more and more dependent on facsimile machines, others resisting this latest technological breakthrough.

This is a sentence fragment because it has no independent clause. The first clause begins with the subordinating conjunction *while*, and the phrase following the comma contains the incomplete verb form *resisting*. A sentence should always have at least one clause that could stand alone, and here there's none. The easiest way to repair this sentence is to insert the helping verb *are*:

> While many office managers are growing more and more dependent on facsimile machines, others are resisting this latest technological breakthrough.

Here's another sentence fragment.

> In the summertime, the kindergarten class that plays on the rope swing beneath the crooked oak tree.

Once again, this string of words includes no clause that could stand alone. Here we have a fragment not because something is missing, but because something is included that makes a clause dependent. The word *that* makes everything after the comma a dependent clause, one that cannot stand alone. Simply remove the word *that,* and look at what you get.

In the summertime, the kindergarten class plays on the rope swing beneath the crooked oak tree.

Now you have a grammatically complete sentence that is shorter than the fragment.

Sentence Correction Drill 2

Choose the answer that produces the most effective, clear, and exact sentence. Darken the corresponding oval in the grid next to the question. (Answers are at the end of the chapter.)

1. It would appear that no significant portion of the electorate <u>troubled by doubts</u> substantial enough to result in the defeat of the incumbent.

    (A) troubled by doubts
    (B) is troubled by doubts
    (C) troubled by doubts which are
    (D) are troubled with doubts, these are
    (E) being troubled with doubts that are

2. Most students enter college right after high school, <u>while a few waiting a year or two before seeking admission</u>.

    (A) while a few waiting a year or two before seeking admission
    (B) and a few, waiting a year or two before seeking admission
    (C) but a few wait a year or two before seeking admission
    (D) but a wait of a year or two is sought by a few
    (E) though a few will have begun to wait a year or two before
        seeking admission

    Ⓐ Ⓑ Ⓒ Ⓓ Ⓔ

3. Mysteriously beautiful, the Nepalese shrine <u>inlaid with semiprecious stones</u> rare enough to honor the spiritual essence of the Buddha.

    (A) inlaid with semiprecious stones
    (B) inlaid with semiprecious stones which are
    (C) being inlaid with semiprecious stones that are
    (D) is inlaid with semiprecious stones
    (E) is inlaid with semiprecious stones, these are

    Ⓐ Ⓑ Ⓒ Ⓓ Ⓔ

4. The general increase in salaries <u>surprised and delighted the employees</u>.

(A) surprised and delighted the employees
(B) surprised the employees, delighting them
(C) surprised the employees and they were delighted
(D) was a surprise and caused delight among the employees
(E) was surprising to the employees, delighting them

5. For reasons not fully understood, nearly all children on the island <u>gifted with musical ability</u> so strong they can master any instrument within hours.

(A) gifted with musical ability
(B) gifted with musical ability which is
(C) are gifted with musical ability
(D) being gifted with musical ability that is
(E) are gifted with musical abilities, these are

6. <u>That many people believe him to be</u> the most competent and well-informed of all the candidates currently listed on the ballot.

(A) That many people believe him to be
(B) That many people believe he is
(C) Because many people believe him to be
(D) Many people believe him to be
(E) That many people believe him

Out of Place

A misplaced modifier is a modifying phrase that ends up modifying the wrong part of the sentence, either because the phrase is misplaced or because the thing it's supposed to describe isn't even in the sentence.

Misplaced Modifier

A modifier is a word or group of words that gives the reader more information about some noun or verb in the sentence. To be grammatically correct, the modifier must be positioned so that it is unambiguous which word is being modified. Here is an example of a misplaced modifier like those you may see on the Writing Test:

> Flying for the first time, the roar of the jet engines intimidated the small child, and he grew frightened as the plane roared down the runway.

The modifying phrase above is found at the beginning of the sentence: *Flying for the first time.* A modifying phrase that begins a sentence should relate to the sentence's *subject*. Usually, this kind of introductory modifier is set off by a comma, and then the subject immediately follows the comma. Logically, in this example, you know that what is flying for the first time is *the small child*. But the grammatical structure of the sentence indicates that *flying for the first time* is modifying roar, which is illogical. The sentence needs to be revised to reconcile grammar and logic:

> Flying for the first time, the small child was intimidated by the roar of the jet engines and grew frightened as the plane roared down the runway.

Here's another example of a sentence with a misplaced modifying phrase.

> An advertisement was withdrawn by the producer of the local news program that was considered offensive by the city's minority communities.

Grammatically, the phrase *that was considered offensive by the city's minority communities* refers to the nearest noun: *The local news program*. Is that what the writer means? Is it the local news program or the advertisement that was offensive to these groups? Grammatically, the above sentence is correct only if it is the local news program that was considered offensive. If the writer means to say that it is the advertisement that was deemed offensive, he or she should rewrite the sentence. A revision like this would be clear.

> The producer of the local news program withdrew an advertisement that was considered offensive by the city's minority communities.

In this sentence too, a misplaced modifier conveys a confused image:

> The despondent little girl found her missing doll playing in the back yard under the swing.

The position of the modifying phrase *playing in the back yard under the swing* suggests that the phrase modifies *her missing doll*. It is more likely that the writer intended the phrase to modify *the despondent little girl*. If so, the sentence should read instead:

> Playing in the back yard under the swing, the despondent little girl found her missing doll.

Do This

Learn to recognize modifying phrases; they play an important part on the Writing Test. And keep in mind that adjectives and adverbs sometimes appear in these phrases.

Sentence Correction Drill 3

Choose the answer that produces the most effective, clear, and exact sentence. Darken the corresponding oval below the question

1. A familiar marketing strategy was reintroduced by a former client that had served the company dependably in the past.

   (A) A familiar marketing strategy was reintroduced by a former client that
   (B) By reintroducing a familiar marketing strategy, the former client that
   (C) Reintroduced by a former client, a familiar marketing strategy that
   (D) A former client reintroduced a familiar marketing strategy that
   (E) A former client, by reintroducing a familiar marketing strategy

   Ⓐ Ⓑ Ⓒ Ⓓ Ⓔ

2. After practicing for months, auditions went much more smoothly for the young actor.

   (A) After practicing for months, auditions went much more smoothly for the young actor.
   (B) Auditions, after practicing for months, went much more smoothly for the young actor.
   (C) The young actor having practiced for auditions for months, auditions went much more smoothly for him.
   (D) The young actor presenting auditions after months of practice, they went much more smoothly.
   (E) The young actor presented auditions much more smoothly after practicing for months.

   Ⓐ Ⓑ Ⓒ Ⓓ Ⓔ

3. To ensure that a novel will sell well, it should appeal to currently popular tastes.

   (A) it should appeal to currently popular tastes
   (B) a novel should be appealing to currently popular tastes
   (C) a writer should appeal to currently popular tastes
   (D) currently popular tastes should be appealed to
   (E) currently popular tastes should be appealed to by the novel

   Ⓐ Ⓑ Ⓒ Ⓓ Ⓔ

4. Hoping to receive a promotion, <u>the letter he received instead informed the employee</u> that he had been fired.

    (A) the letter he received instead informed the employee
    (B) the letter having been received, instead informing the employee
    (C) the employee instead received a letter informing him
    (D) information from the received letter instead told the employee
    (E) the employee, instead informed by the letter he received

Be Suspicious

When the entire sentence is underlined, suspect an error in modification.

5. <u>A cornerstone of the community since 1925, the fund-raising drive did not generate enough revenue to keep the recreational center operating another year.</u>

    (A) A cornerstone of the community since 1925, the fund-raising drive did not generate enough revenue to keep the recreational center operating another year.
    (B) The fund-raising drive did not generate enough revenue to keep the recreational center, a cornerstone of the community since 1925, operating another year.
    (C) The fund-raising drive did not generate enough revenue, a cornerstone of the community since 1925, to keep the recreational center operating another year.
    (D) A cornerstone of the community since 1925, the recreational center did not generate enough revenue to keep the fund-raising drive operating another year.
    (E) The fund-raising drive, a cornerstone of the community since 1925, did not generate enough revenue to keep the recreational center operating another year.

Signal

One sign that words or groups of words are doing the same job in a sentence is that the words or groups are linked together by a coordinating conjunction: *and*, *but*, *or*, or *nor*.

Faulty Parallelism

This class of errors found on the Writing Test covers a wide range of faulty sentence constructions. Certain sets of words in a sentence, or the general design of a sentence often requires a parallel construction. If this construction is off-balance, then parallelism in the sentence is faulty.

There are generally two situations in which the Writing Test writers present errors in parallel construction. The first occurs in sentences with pairs of connective words that require parallelism. On the following page is a list of connective words that demand parallel constructions.

neither . . . nor

either . . . or

both . . . and

the better . . . the better

the more . . . the more (or *less*)

not only . . . but also

In the sentence below, look at that first pair of words, neither . . . nor, and the phrases that follow both words.

Nineteenth-century nihilists were concerned with neither the origins of philosophical thought nor how societal laws developed.

The phrases following the words *neither* and *nor* must be parallel in grammatical structure. That is, if a noun phrase follows *neither*, then a noun phrase must follow *nor*, too. If the phrase after a first paired connective word is adverbial, the phrase after the second connective word must also be adverbial. In this sentence, the words that follow *neither* are *the origins of philosophical thought*; this is a noun phrase, composed of a noun followed by a prepositional phrase. But what follows *nor* is *how societal laws developed*, a dependent clause. These two parts of the sentence are not grammatically parallel. Since the dependent clause is the underlined part of the sentence, it must be changed to be parallel to the first phrase; it must be revised into a noun phrase. The underlined phrase can be rewritten as *nor the development of societal laws*. In this revision, both phrases following the connective words consist of a noun followed by a prepositional phrase; in other words, both are noun phrases, so the sentence now has a proper parallel construction.

Another situation that demands the use of parallel grammatical structure occurs when a sentence consists of a list of two or more items. That list can comprise two or more nouns or noun phrases, verbs or verb phrases, or dependent clauses. Any kind of list calls for grammatically parallel items. Look for the faulty parallelism in the sentence below:

To run for a seat in the United States Senate, a candidate must be an adult at least thirty years of age, a citizen of the United States, and is to reside in the state to be represented.

This sentence consists of an introductory infinitive phrase and an independent clause that ends with three listed phrases. The first two phrases in the list, *an adult at least thirty years of age* and *a citizen of the United States*, are both nouns modified by prepositional phrases. *Is to reside in the state* is the third phrase in the list. This is a verbal phrase including the present tense form *is* plus the infinitive form *to reside*. Because the first two items in the list are noun phrases, and the last item is a verbal phrase, parallelism is faulty in this sentence. To correct this error, you should transform the underlined verbal phrase into a noun phrase. If a person *is to live in a state* in order to be elected to the Senate, he or she must be a resident *of the state*. The corrected noun form of the underlined phrase is *a resident of the state*.

Sentence Correction Drill 4

Choose the answer that produces the most effective, clear, and exact sentence. Darken the corresponding oval in the grid next to the question. (Answers are at the end of the chapter.)

Parallels

Make sure that parallel parts of a sentence are in parallel form.

1. The great wastes of the southeast quadrant of Saudi Arabia are at once forbiddingly empty, climatically harsh, <u>and the beauty of them is haunting</u>.

   (A) and the beauty of them is haunting
   (B) with haunting beauties
   (C) while their beauties are haunting
   (D) and hauntingly beautiful
   (E) but their beauty is haunting

2. When the artist first began sketching, she discovered that it is important both <u>to be attentive to the line of the figure and studying</u> the relationship of one volume to another.

   (A) to be attentive to the line of the figure and studying
   (B) being attentive to the line of the figure, and studying
   (C) be attentive to the line of the figure as well as studying
   (D) being attentive to the line of the figure and that one study
   (E) to be attentive to the line of the figure and to study

3. After the doctor warned her that she was in poor health, the chairwoman resolved to go on a diet, stop smoking, <u>and exercising every day</u>.

   (A) and exercising every day
   (B) and exercise every day
   (C) and be exercising every day
   (D) and therefore exercise every day
   (E) as well as exercising every day

Faulty Coordination/Subordination

This category includes two forms of faulty sentence structure that appear on the Writing Test. Both kinds of error occur when clauses are joined incorrectly in sentences with more than one clause. Faulty coordination and faulty subordination are closely related, but they require separate explanations.

Coordination between two clauses is faulty if it doesn't express the logical relation between the clauses. Often, this error involves a misused conjunction. A conjunction is a connective word joining two clauses or phrases in one sentence; the most common conjunctions are *and*, *but*, *because*, and *however*. Identify the conjunction in the following sentence. Why does it fail to connect the clauses logically?

> Ben Franklin was a respected and talented statesman, and he was most famous for his discovery of electricity.

To identify and correct the faulty coordination, determine what the relation between the sentence's two clauses really is. Does the simple additive connective word *and* adequately express the relation? In the sentence above, the writer states two facts about Ben Franklin: He was a talented statesman, and he discovered electricity. Although these two facts are quite distinct, the writer joins the two ideas with the conjunction *and*, which normally expresses a consistency between two equally emphasized facts. This is an error in coordination. A better way to coordinate these two contrasting ideas would be to use the conjunction *but*, which indicates some contrast between the two clauses. In this sentence, *but* points to a common expectation. An individual usually distinguishes herself or himself in one field of accomplishment: in politics *or* in science, *but* not in both. So Franklin's distinction in two diverse fields seems to contradict common expectations, and calls for a *but*.

Faulty subordination is most commonly found on the Writing Test in a group of words which contains two or more subordinate, or dependent clauses, but no independent clause. Look at the group of words below and identify the faulty subordination.

> Since the small electronics industry is one of the world's fastest growing sectors, because demand for the computer chip continues to be high.

Since, *because*, *so that*, *if*, and *although* are connective words which, when introducing a sentence or clause, always indicate that the phrase which follows is dependent, or subordinate. Whenever a dependent clause begins a sentence, an independent clause must follow somewhere in the sentence. In the group of words above, *since* indicates that the first clause in the group of words is subordinate, and needs to be followed by an independent clause. But *because* in the second clause indicates that the second clause is also subordinate. The "sentence" is faulty because there is no independent clause to make the group of words grammatically complete. The second connective word, *because*, should be eliminated to make the group of words a complete and logical sentence. With this revision, the *since-* clause expresses a cause, and the independent clause expresses an effect or result.

Sentence Correction Drill 5

Choose the answer that produces the most effective, clear, and exact sentence. Darken the corresponding oval in the grid next to the question. (Answers are at the end of the chapter.)

1. Although her first business, a health food store, went bankrupt, <u>but she eventually launched a successful mail-order</u> business.

   (A) but she eventually launched a successful mail-order business
   (B) a successful mail-order business was eventually launched
   (C) and eventually launched a successful mail-order business
   (D) a successful mail-order business, successfully launched
   (E) she eventually launched a successful mail-order business

2. Because the carpenter would not do the work exactly as Jane wanted it done, <u>so she refused</u> to pay him.

   (A) so she refused
   (B) but she was refusing
   (C) she refused
   (D) and this led to her refusing
   (E) and she refused

   Ⓐ Ⓑ Ⓒ Ⓓ Ⓔ

3. <u>Because her sons believed in the power of print advertising,</u> pictures of Lydia Pinkham appeared with her vegetable compound in newspapers across America in the late nineteenth century.

   (A) Because her sons believed in the power of print advertising
   (B) Her sons believed that print advertising was powerful
   (C) Being as her sons believed in the power of print advertising
   (D) That her sons believed in the power of print advertising, they put
   (E) Although her sons believed that print advertising was powerful

   Ⓐ Ⓑ Ⓒ Ⓓ Ⓔ

4. Yeats eventually created a unique voice in his <u>poetry, but he was</u> able to shake off the restricting influences of the British literary tradition.

   (A) poetry, but he was
   (B) poetry; however, he was
   (C) poetry because he was
   (D) poetry that was
   (E) poetry only while being

   Ⓐ Ⓑ Ⓒ Ⓓ Ⓔ

Sentence Correction Practice Quiz

18 Questions (10 minutes)

Directions: The following sentences test accuracy and effectiveness of expression. In selecting answers, follow the rules of standard written English; in other words, consider grammar, choice of words, sentence construction, and punctuation.

In each of the following sentences, a portion or all of the sentence is underlined. Under each sentence you will find five ways of phrasing the underlined portion. Choice A repeats the original underlined portion; the other four choices provide alternative phrasings.

Select the choice that best expresses the meaning of the original sentence. If the original sentence is better than any of the alternative phrasings, choose A; otherwise select one of the alternatives. Your selection should construct the most effective sentence—clear and precise, with no awkwardness or ambiguity.

SAMPLE QUESTION

Wanting to reward her assistant for loyalty,
Sheila gave a bonus to him as large as his paycheck.

SAMPLE ANSWER

Ⓐ Ⓑ Ⓒ ⬤ Ⓔ

(A) Sheila gave a bonus to him as
large as his paycheck
(B) given to him by Sheila was a
bonus as large as his paycheck
(C) he was given a bonus as large
as his paycheck by Sheila
(D) Sheila gave him a bonus as
large as his paycheck
(E) Sheila gave him a paycheck
to him as large as his bonus

---

1. Although the candidate received crucial votes
from rural precincts, <u>but he was defeated by</u> his
opponent's broad base of political support.

    (A) but he was defeated by
    (B) defeating him by
    (C) and what made his defeat possible
    (D) he was defeated by
    (E) and he was defeated by

    Ⓐ Ⓑ Ⓒ Ⓓ Ⓔ

2. Most wholesale dealers are reluctant to reveal
either how much they pay for their goods or
<u>their profit margin per item sold</u>.

    (A) their profit margin per item sold
    (B) how great a profit margin per item sold
    (C) how great a profit they receive per item
    sold
    (D) if their profit margin per item sold
    (E) how great the margin of profit

    Ⓐ Ⓑ Ⓒ Ⓓ Ⓔ

3. Exposed to the extremely long and severe cold spell, <u>frost soon killed the buds of the citrus trees and they did not produce fruit that season</u>.

   (A) frost soon killed the buds of the citrus trees and they did not produce fruit that season
   (B) soon the buds of the citrus trees were killed by frost, and therefore not producing fruit that season
   (C) the buds of the citrus trees were soon killed by frost, they did not produce fruit that season
   (D) fruit was not produced by the citrus trees that season because their buds had been killed by frost
   (E) the buds of the citrus trees were soon killed by frost, and the trees did not produce fruit that season

   Ⓐ Ⓑ Ⓒ Ⓓ Ⓔ

4. This group of artists, masters of the short brush stroke developed by the Impressionists in the nineteenth century, did not believe in selling works of art; however, <u>some giving paintings away</u>.

   (A) some giving paintings away
   (B) giving some paintings away
   (C) paintings were given away by some of them
   (D) some having given paintings away
   (E) some gave paintings away

   Ⓐ Ⓑ Ⓒ Ⓓ Ⓔ

5. <u>Credulous people believe</u> in the existence of extraterrestrial beings, most scientists and other informed students of nature do not.

   (A) Credulous people believe
   (B) While credulous people believe
   (C) Credulous people are always believing
   (D) Since credulous people believe
   (E) Credulous people tend to believe

   Ⓐ Ⓑ Ⓒ Ⓓ Ⓔ

6. In the closing decades of the eighteenth century, it was believed that young women should not only <u>be obedient and soft-spoken but also master</u> such skills as needlepoint.

   (A) be obedient and soft-spoken but also master
   (B) being obedient and soft-spoken but also mastering
   (C) obey and speak softly but also to master
   (D) be obedient and soft-spoken but also to master
   (E) obeying and speaking softly but also mastering

   Ⓐ Ⓑ Ⓒ Ⓓ Ⓔ

7. Few of us have seen war, but <u>most of us fearing it</u>.

   (A) most of us fearing it
   (B) most of us fear it
   (C) it is feared by most of us
   (D) it has been feared
   (E) it is being feared by most of us

   Ⓐ Ⓑ Ⓒ Ⓓ Ⓔ

8. Learning the rules of musical harmony is one <u>thing, but applying</u> them with inspired, creative zest is another.

   (A) thing, but applying
   (B) thing and applying
   (C) thing; to apply
   (D) thing, but to apply
   (E) thing, that you apply

9. Saint Bernard dogs are fabled to have rescued many a stranded <u>traveler, such displays of valor</u> have endeared these dogs to many pet owners.

   (A) traveler, such displays of valor
   (B) traveler, displays of such valor
   (C) traveler and therefore, such displays of valor
   (D) traveler; such displays of valor
   (E) traveler but such displays of valor

10. Environmental scientists are very concerned <u>about dangerous fluorocarbons, found in pressurized aerosol cans which quicken the erosion of the ozone layer cans which quicken the erosion of the ozone layer.</u>

    (A) About dangerous fuorocarbons, found in pressurized aerosol cans which quicken the erosion of the ozone layer
    (B) that, while emitting dangerous fluorocarbons, pressurized aerosol cans quicken the erosion of the ozone layer
    (C) about the erosion of the ozone layer caused by pressurized aerosol cans emitting dangerous fluorocarbons
    (D) that pressurized aerosol cans emit dangerous fluorocarbons, which quicken the erosion of the ozone layer
    (E) when, quickening the erosion of the ozone layer, pressurized aerosol cans emit dangerous fluorocarbons

11. Last of the world's leaders to do so, the Prime Minister admits that terrorist threats <u>credible enough to warrant</u> the imposition of stringent security measures.

    (A) credible enough to warrant
    (B) credible enough warrant
    (C) are credible enough to warrant
    (D) credible enough, warranting
    (E) are credible enough to be warranted

12. The characteristics of a typical Avery canvas are a purposely limited palette, a distinctive use of color for perspective, <u>and it employs obvious brush strokes for effect</u>.

    (A) and it employs obvious brush strokes for effect
    (B) and an employment of obvious brush strokes for effect
    (C) but it employs obvious brush strokes for effect
    (D) whereby, for effect, it employs obvious brush strokes
    (E) it employs obvious brush strokes for effect

13. According to Aristotle, a catastrophe <u>is when the action of a tragic drama turns toward its disastrous conclusion</u>.

    (A) is when the action of a tragic drama turns towards its disastrous conclusion
    (B) is where a tragic drama turns the action toward its disastrous conclusion
    (C) occurs where, towards its disastrous conclusion, the action of a tragic drama is turning
    (D) approaches when the action of a tragic drama has turned toward its disastrous conclusion
    (E) is the turning point at which the action of a tragic drama approaches its disastrous conclusion

14. Abhorring rampant commercialism, the neighborhood theater group has always attempted to try to produce original work by worthy, if unknown, playwrights.

    (A) has always attempted to try to
    (B) has always tried to
    (C) tries and attempts to
    (D) makes an attempt at
    (E) attempts to try to

    Ⓐ Ⓑ Ⓒ Ⓓ Ⓔ

15. Emerging from the jungle to surrender decades after the war ended, the last Japanese soldier still in World War II uniform was hailed as a symbol of steadfastness.

    (A) the last Japanese soldier still in World War II uniform was hailed as
    (B) they called the last Japanese soldier still in World War II uniform
    (C) was the last Japanese soldier still in World War II uniform hailed as
    (D) the last Japanese soldier still in World War II uniform hailed as
    (E) popular opinion refers to the Japanese soldier still in World War II uniform as

    Ⓐ Ⓑ Ⓒ Ⓓ Ⓔ

16. Women are not rejecting the idea of raising children, but many taking jobs as well.

    (A) many taking jobs
    (B) many are taking jobs
    (C) jobs are taken by many of them
    (D) jobs are being taken
    (E) many having taken jobs

    Ⓐ Ⓑ Ⓒ Ⓓ Ⓔ

17. Changing over from a military to a peacetime economy means producing tractors rather than tanks, radios rather than rifles, and to producing running shoes rather than combat boots.

    (A) to producing running shoes rather than combat boots
    (B) to the production of running shoes rather than combat boots
    (C) running shoes rather than combat boots
    (D) replacing combat boots with running shoes
    (E) to running shoes rather combat boots

    Ⓐ Ⓑ Ⓒ Ⓓ Ⓔ

18. The protest movement's impact will depend on both how many people it touches and its durability.

    (A) its durability
    (B) is it going to endure
    (C) if it has durability
    (D) how long it endures
    (E) the movement's ability to endure

    Ⓐ Ⓑ Ⓒ Ⓓ Ⓔ

Answers and Explanations

Sentence Correction Drill 1

1. *B*   2. *C*   3. *E*   4. *D*

Sentence Correction Drill 2

1. *B*   2. *C*   3. *D*   4. *A*   5. *C*   6. *D*

Sentence Correction Drill 3

1. *D*   2. *E*   3. *C*   4. *C*   5. *B*

Sentence Correction Drill 4

1. *D*   2. *E*   3. *B*

Sentence Correction Drill 5

1. *E*   2. *C*   3. *A*   4. *C*

Sentence Correction Practice Quiz

1. **(D)**—The original sentence contains both a dependent and an independent clause, but it uses two connecting words when only one is needed. Choice (D) creates an independent clause with no unnecessary connecting word joining the two clauses.

2. **(C)**—The given sentence has faulty parallelism. With coordinating words like *either . . . or*, word order and sentence structure following the two coordinating words should be parallel. Here, a dependent clause follows the word *either: how much they pay for their goods*. Choice (C) contains a dependent clause and makes the wording after *or* parallel to the wording after *either*.

3. **(E)**—This sentence contains a misplaced modifier. The introductory phrase should modify the noun immediately following the comma. In choices (E) and (C), the modified noun, *the buds*, is in the correct position following the introductory modifying phrase. But notice that choice (C) introduces a new error when it links the second clause to the first with only a comma. Only choice (E) corrects the original problem without adding a new one.

4. **(E)**—The semicolon require an independent clause. Choice (C) is an independent clause, but the passive verb, *were given (away)*, makes it wordy. Only choice (E) gives the proper grammatical structure concisely.

5. **(B)**—The given sentence is a run-on; two independent clauses are joined only by a comma, with no proper conjunction. The run-on can be corrected by turning the first clause into a dependent clause. Only choice (B) creates a clause, which solves the run-on problem and expresses the logical relation of the two clauses.

6. (A)—The sentence is correct as given. Word order is parallel after the correlative words *not only . . . but also.*

7. (B)—The phrase following the comma should be a second clause with word order parallel to that of the first clause. Choice (B) correctly supplies a main or indicative verb, *fear,* for the subject, *most of us,* and converts the phrase to a clause. The word order and active verb of this second clause also follow the active construction of the first clause.

8. (A)—The sentence is correct as given. The subjects of the two clauses, *learning* and *applying,* are in parallel gerund form.

9. (D)—This is another run-on sentence. The semicolon of choice (D) correctly separates the two independent clauses.

10. (D)—This sentence contains a misplaced modifier, *which quicken the erosion of the ozone layer.* Choice (D) correctly places the modifier immediately following the noun it modifies, that is, *fluorocarbons.*

11. (C)—The second clause of the given sentence lacks a main verb. Choice (C) provides the verb *are* for the subject *threats* so that the second, dependent clause is complete, and the sentence is correct.

12. (B)—This sentence has faulty parallelism. The underlined portion of the sentence is a clause. But to be parallel with the two preceding noun phrases, the underlined part should also be a noun phrase.

13. (E)—The problem with this sentence is faulty logic, rather than grammatical error. A *catastrophe,* a noun, cannot actually *be when* . . . , though it could *occur when* . . . . Only choice (E) solves the original problem without introducing a new one. A *catastrophe can be,* and *is,* a *turning point.*

14. (B)—The underlined phrase contains a redundant verb because *to attempt* and *to try to* are synonymous. Choice (B) simply removes one of the two synonyms from an otherwise grammatically correct sentence.

15. (A)—This sentence is correct as given.

16. (B)—This sentence uses a *not . . . but . . .* word pair, so it requires parallel blocks of words around each half of the pair. The first block is *are not rejecting* so the second block must be *are taking.* Don't be misled because *are* and *rejecting* are separated by the word *not. Are* is still a helping verb that works together with *rejecting.*

17. (C)—This sentence presents a list of comparisons. All items in a list must have parallel construction. Only choice (C) gives the last comparison an appearance parallel to the previous two comparisons. The word *producing* could have been repeated in all three comparisons. But since it wasn't repeated in the second comparison, it can't be repeated in the third one either.

18. (D)—This sentence uses a *both . . . and . . .* pair, so it requires parallel blocks of words following each half of the pair. Only choice (D) has a second block of words—*how long it endures*—similar to the first block—*how many people it touches.*

CHAPTER 7

PARAGRAPH CORRECTION QUESTIONS

In this chapter, we'll discuss the third multiple-choice question type on the SAT II: Writing Test. As in the chapter on Usage and the chapter on Sentence Correction, we'll include lots of sample questions and practice drills in this chapter. After working through this chapter, you'll have a good idea of what to expect on the Paragraph Correction section of the Writing Test.

The Basics

If you remember chapter 2, you'll recall that Paragraph Correction questions are based on short "student" essays. The main thing to bear in mind when working on these questions is the importance of *context*. Most Paragraph Correction questions will ask you to revise or combine sentences. Specifically, you'll be asked to clean up awkward or ambiguous sentences. That's where context comes in. You can't determine the best way to repair poor or unclear sentences without knowing what comes before and after them.

A few Paragraph Correction questions will ask you about the overall organization of the essays. Again, context is critical. You can't, for example, decide which of five possible sentences best concludes an essay without having a strong sense of what the essay is all about.

Big Picture

To answer Paragraph Correction questions, you've got to grasp the bigger picture—the context.

Kaplan's Three-Step Method for Paragraph Correction Questions

You'll find that Kaplan's three-step method works equally well for every kind of Paragraph Correction question.

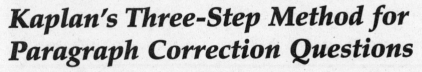

The Kaplan Method for Paragraph Correction Questions

1. Read the essay.

2. Read the question stem.

3. Reread the relevant portion of the essay.

Be Systematic

Follow the Kaplan three-step method for handling Paragraph Correction questions whether you're asked about a single word in one sentence or the entire passage.

Avoid Impulse Shopping

When working on Paragraph Correction questions, always anticipate what the correct answer should look like before shopping among the answer choices. Many of the choices will look very similar, and you may be confused by them if you don't have a general idea of what to look for.

Step 1: Read the Essay

Read the entire essay slowly and carefully. It'll be very short, so it won't take more than one minute to get through it. Get a sense of the essay's overall main idea, as well as the main idea of each paragraph (an essay will generally have three to five brief paragraphs). This knowledge will come in handy when you're asked to answer questions about the essay as a unified entity.

Step 2: Read the Question Stem

Read the question stem closely. Make sure that you understand exactly what you're asked to do. Questions that require you to revise or combine sentences will supply the sentence numbers to you. Questions that ask about the entire essay generally won't refer to specific sentences.

Step 3: Reread the Relevant Portion of the Essay

Once the question stem has guided you to a particular sentence or two, go back and reread that sentence or two. But don't stop there. Also reread the sentences before and after the affected sentence(s). Rereading the lines around the affected sentence(s) will provide you with a sense of context. This sense of context, in turn, will help you to choose the best construction from among the answer choices. For those questions that concern the essay as a whole, you may want to skim quickly over the entire essay to refamiliarize yourself with its contents.

Handling the Questions

There are three basic types of Paragraph Correction questions:

- Revising sentences questions

- Combining sentences questions

- General organization questions

Read on and get familiar with all three types and how to handle them.

Revising Sentences

Take a look at the following paragraph and question. The question focuses on a single word in one sentence but in order to answer this typical example of a revision question you'll need to reread the entire paragraph.

(1) The Spanish-American War was one of the shortest and most decisive wars ever fought. (2) The postwar settlement, the Treaty of Paris, reflected the results of the fighting. (3) Under its terms, Spain was compelled to cede large territories in North America and the Pacific. (4) The United States gained control over some of these territories, including Puerto Rico and Guam. (5) It was reduced in status from a major to a minor power. (6) The United States, in contrast, emerged from the war as a world power, and would soon go on to become a major participant in Asian and European affairs.

In context, which is the best version of the underlined part of sentence 5?

It was reduced in status from a major to a minor power.

(A) (As it is now)
(B) Spain was reduced
(C) The war caused Spain to be reduced
(D) As a result of the war, it had been reduced
(E) It had now been reduced

Sentence 5 refers to Spain's status. That much should have been clear to you by reading sentences 2, 3, 4, and 6. The pronoun *it*, however, makes sentence 5 ambiguous. What does it refer to? To make this sentence less ambiguous, *it* should be changed to the noun *Spain*. That leaves (B) and (C) as possible correct answers. Since (B) is a more concise and less awkward construction than (C), (B) is correct.

Paragraph Correction Drill 1

For each question, pick the choice that creates the clearest sentence in the context of the paragraph. Darken the oval in the grid next to the question. (Answers appear at the end of the chapter.)

(1) Marine mammals like seals, sea lions, and whales would be in danger of freezing to death if not for their natural defenses against the cold. (2) Their principal defense consists of several types of insulation. (3) Body hair traps air, which is then heated by the body, creating a warm air mass around the animal. (4) More important than hair is a layer of body fat (or blubber) that lies between the skin and muscle. (5) Commonly known as blubber, it has a freezing temperature well below that of water. (6) Thus, it prevents the body's heat from flowing into colder surroundings.

In a Nutshell

Your basic task in revision questions is to pick the construction that creates the clearest sentence possible in the context of the essay.

1. In context, which is the best version of sentence 5?

    Commonly known as blubber, it has a freezing temperature well below that of water.

    (A) (As it is now)
    (B) Known as blubber, it has a freezing temperature well below that of water.
    (C) It has a freezing temperature well below that of water.
    (D) Water has a freezing temperature well below that of blubber.
    (E) The freezing temperature of blubber is well below that of water.

(1) The archaeopteryx, a prehistoric bird that lived in the Jurassic period 150 million years ago, is a perfect example of a transitional form in the evolution of modern birds from reptiles. (2) Despite its birdlike appearance, the bone structure of archaeopteryx suggests that it could not fly particularly well. (3) The absence of a sternum indicates that it had not fully developed the strong pectoral muscles that modern birds require for flight.

2. In context, which is the best version of the underlined part of sentence 2?

    Despite its birdlike appearance, the bone structure of archaeopteryx suggests that it could not fly particularly well.

    (A) (As it is now)
    (B) Because of its birdlike appearance
    (C) Due to its birdlike appearance
    (D) In spite of archaeopteryx's birdlike appearance
    (E) In contrast to its birdlike appearance

(1) The earliest colonists in America were not very concerned with creating a formal legal system. (2) Solutions to problems were based on common sense rather than abstract principles. (3) Once England strengthened its hold over the American colonies, however, this informal system was gradually displaced by a formal legal system of laws, courts, and judges. (4) Even though it eventually rejected its political domination, its legal system rests heavily on the English model.

3. In context, which is the best version of the underlined part of sentence 4?

    Even though it eventually rejected its political domination, *its legal system rests heavily on the English model.*

    (A) (As it is now)
    (B) Despite its rejection of its political domination
    (C) Although America rejected its political domination
    (D) Its rejection of its political domination notwithstanding
    (E) Even though the United States eventually rejected English
       political domination

    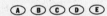

You Must Understand Punctuation. Period.

To combine sentences in a clear and concise manner, you must have a firm grasp of the rules of punctuation. If you haven't already done so, now would be a good time to review the rules discussed in chapter 4.

Combining Sentences

Take a look at the following paragraph and question.

(6) Albert Einstein was a great physicist. (7) He won a Nobel Prize in Physics. (8) He got the prize for his research into the photoelectric effect. (9) Later physicists demonstrated the validity of Einstein's ideas.

Which of the following is the best way to combine sentences 7 and 8?

He won a Nobel Prize in Physics. He got the prize for his research into the photoelectric effect.

(A) The Nobel Prize in Physics that he won was for his research
   into the photoelectric effect.
(B) Having researched the photoelectric effect, he won a Nobel
   Prize in Physics.
(C) He won a Nobel Prize in Physics for his research into the pho-
   toelectric effect.
(D) He got the prize in physics, the Noble Prize in Physics, for his
   research into the photoelectric effect.
(E) Because of his research into the photoelectric effect he got the
   Nobel Prize in Physics.

Did you choose (C)? It's the best written and most economical of the choices. Whether you're asked to revise or combine sentences, the correct answer will often (but by no means always) be the shortest answer. Good writing, after all, is concise.

What to Expect

Only one or two questions per essay will test your grasp of the essay as a whole.

Sound Familiar?

General organization questions are very similar to SAT I Critical Reading questions—they test your understanding of what the author's thinking and doing in the essay.

Paragraph Correction Drill 2

Combine each pair of sentences into a single sentence that conforms to the rules of standard written English. Use the line below the sentences to write your new sentence. (Suggested answers appear at the end of the chapter.)

1. *Marsha went to the grocery store. At the grocery store, she bought cheese, eggs, and milk.*

    _____

    _____

2. *I attended a lecture at the university. My wife, on the other hand, decided to watch a movie.*

    _____

    _____

3. *Napoleon won many great military victories. Despite these military victories, he was eventually defeated and dethroned.*

    _____

    _____

4. *Interstellar travel is far beyond the limits of today's rockets. Their engines are not powerful enough to reach even the closest star.*

    _____

    _____

5. *The first function of tariffs is to protect local industry. And the second function of tariffs is to raise money for the national government.*

    _____

    _____

Suggested answers appear at the end of the chapter. While there is no single correct way to combine the sentences above, try to make your sentences as concise and straightforward as our sentences.

General Organization Questions

If you've got a firm grasp of the essay after you first read through it, you should jump right to the general organization questions. Do these questions while the essay is fresh in your mind. On the other hand, if your grasp of the essay is a bit shaky at first, it's best to work on general organization questions last. Start with questions that ask you to revise or combine sentences: Doing so should improve your grasp of the overall essay, making it easier for you to tackle the general organization questions. Try the following drill.

Paragraph Correction Drill 3

Read the following essay excerpt and answer the questions that follow. For each question, pick the best answer choice among those given. Darken the corresponding oval in the grid next to the question. (Answers appear at the end of the chapter.)

(1) At the Battle of Gettysburg in July 1863, 75,000 Confederate troops faced 90,000 Union soldiers in one of the largest battles of the American Civil War. (2) For two days, both armies suffered heavy casualties in constant fighting, without either gaining a clear advantage. (3) On the third and final day of the battle, Confederate forces mounted one last effort to penetrate Union lines. (4) But the attempt ended in complete failure, forcing Confederate troops to withdraw to the south.

(5) Gettysburg was a turning point in the Civil War. (6) Before the battle, Confederate forces had defeated their Union counterparts in a string of major engagements. (7) After the battle, however, Union forces took the initiative, finally defeating the Confederacy less than two years later. (8) By invading Union territory, the Confederate leadership sought to shatter the Union's will to continue the war and to convince European nations to recognize the Confederacy as an independent nation.

1. Which sentence most appropriately follows sentence 8?

   (A) The Confederacy lost the war because it lacked the industrial capacity of the Union.
   (B) Gettysburg is considered by military experts to be the bloodiest battle of the Civil War.
   (C) France and Great Britain refused to provide the Confederacy with military assistance.
   (D) When President Lincoln issued the Emancipation Proclamation, which ended slavery in the United States, the Confederacy's international position was weakened.
   (E) Instead, the Union's willingness to fight was strengthened and the Confederacy squandered its last chance for foreign support.

   Ⓐ Ⓑ Ⓒ Ⓓ Ⓔ

2. In the essay, the author does all of the following EXCEPT

   (A) describe a specific example
   (B) criticize an opposing viewpoint
   (C) explain the importance of an event
   (D) analyze the results of a historical event
   (E) discuss what happened on a particular day

   Ⓐ Ⓑ Ⓒ Ⓓ Ⓔ

Paragraph Correction Practice Quiz

12 Questions (8 Minutes)

Directions: The following passages are first drafts of student essays. Portions of the essays have to be rewritten.

Read the essays and answer the questions that follow them. Some of the questions concern particular sentences or fragments of sentences and require you to make choices about sentence structure, word choice, and usage. Other questions pertain to the entire essay or pieces of the essay and require you to think about organization, development, and appropriateness of language. Pick the answer that most effectively conveys the meaning and follows the rules of standard written English. Once you have chosen an answer, fill in the corresponding oval in the grid next to the question.

Questions 1–6 are based on the following essay.

(1) When I was younger, I thought to myself, "Why do baseball players get paid so much for swinging a bat?" (2) Baseball, basketball, or football games they would have seemed like a real waste of money to me. (3) I would watch a game for about ten minutes without seeing a single hit and wonder why these athletes got so much money.

(4) I recently joined the Little-League home-team. (5) Before this time, sports was just recreation to me like wiffleball with my friends. (6) Once I began Little League, though, I went through all sorts of drills, like catch and batting practice. (7) I started to understand what it felt like to become an athlete. (8) Sure, natural talent helped. (9) I realized hard work and practice were just as important. (10) Because of my experience, I was able to appreciate professional sports more because I finally understood the strong commitment to the game that every professional athlete has to have.

(11) There is only a small group of great athletes. (12) Because of intense competition, hardly any of them in this group make it to the pros. (13) And the ones who want to make it have to dedicate all their energies to perfecting their skills so they can be the best. (14) People feel that professional athletes get paid too much for too little. (15) I'm convinced our sports heroes are receiving a fair salary for displaying and maintaining their hard-won skills.

1. Which of the following revisions of the underlined portion of sentence 2 (reproduced below) is clearest?

   Baseball, basketball, or football games they would have seemed like a real waste of money to me.

   (A) (As it is now)
   (B) Baseball, basketball, or football games seemed
   (C) Baseball, basketball, or football games will have seemed
   (D) Games of baseball, basketball, or football would have seemed
   (E) Games of baseball, basketball, or, football would be seeming

   Ⓐ Ⓑ Ⓒ Ⓓ Ⓔ

2. Which sentence listed below, if placed after sentence 3, would best tie in the first paragraph with the rest of the essay?

   (A) I have kept my point of view about the salaries of sports stars for a long time.
   (B) Still, my school coaches defended the excessive salaries of their favorite players.
   (C) My friends could never convince me to go to a local sporting event with them.
   (D) However, I ended up changing my mind about whether famous athletes deserve all the money they make.
   (E) Usually, sports personalities don't even work a full year.

   Ⓐ Ⓑ Ⓒ Ⓓ Ⓔ

3. Which of the following options is the best edit for the underlined portions of sentences 8 and 9 (reproduced below) so that the two sentences are combined into one?

Sure, natural talent helped. I realized hard work and practice were just as important.

(A) helped, and I realized
(B) helped, so I realized
(C) helped, so I was realizing
(D) helped, but I realize
(E) helped, but I realized

4. Which of the following words or phrases best replaces *"And"* at the beginning of sentence 13 (reproduced below)?

And the ones who want to make it have to dedicate all their energies to perfecting their skills so they can be the best.

(A) Therefore,
(B) Besides this,
(C) Nevertheless,
(D) Moreover,
(E) Including this,

5. In the context of the preceding paragraphs, which of the following would be the best way to combine the underlined portions of sentences 14 and 15 (reproduced below)?

People feel that professional athletes get paid too much for too little. I'm convinced our sports heroes are receiving a fair salary for displaying and maintaining their hard-won skills.

(A) While some people feel that professional athletes get paid too much for too little, I've been convinced that our sports heroes are receiving
(B) In relation to people who feel that professional athletes get paid too much for too little, I will be convinced that they receive
(C) Unlike some people, who feel that professional athletes get paid too much for too little, I'm now convinced our sports heroes are receiving
(D) People feel that professional athletes get paid too much for too little and I am different because I'm convinced our sports heroes receive
(E) People were feeling that professional athletes get paid too much for too little, I was convinced our sports heroes were receiving

6. All of the following strategies are used by the writer of the passage EXCEPT

(A) referring to personal experience in order to illustrate an idea
(B) quoting those whose opinions concur with his
(C) using a narrative to develop a point
(D) articulating a change of opinion from an original position stated in the first paragraph
(E) supporting conclusions by evidence or example

Questions 7–12 are based on the following essay.

(1) Recently a report came out in a science magazine that claimed the earth's protective ozone layer was being steadily depleted. (2) It named several companies that produced chemicals responsible for this situation, and consumers were advised by it to boycott these businesses. (3) An editorial in a business magazine insisted that this report was faulty. (4) It stated that there could be other, less dangerous reasons for the changes in climate that we've been experiencing. (5) However, I believe that the scientists are right, we should all consider the effect we can have on making sure the ozone layer is not harmed more than it already has been.

(6) In the past few decades, the ozone layer has been steadily depleted. (7) This means harmful ultraviolet rays get through to our atmosphere. (8) People who do these bad things which contribute to this situation should know that their actions could harm future generations. (9) Not buying products that are harmful to the ozone layer means our children's children will be more secure. (10) Consumers can choose to purchase any kind of product they desire. (11) They should be aware of what happens when they make their choices. (12) If they don't boycott companies that produce harmful substances, our atmosphere will steadily worsen.

7. Considering the essay as a whole, which is the best edit for the underlined section of sentence 2 (reproduced below)?

It named several companies that produced chemicals responsible for this situation, and consumers were advised by it to boycott these businesses.

(A) (As it is now)
(B) It names several companies that produced chemicals responsible for this situation and advises consumers
(C) Naming several companies that produce chemicals responsible for this situation, consumers are advised by the report
(D) It is naming several companies that produce chemicals responsible for this situation and advising consumers
(E) The report named several companies that produced chemicals responsible for this situation, and advised consumers

8. Considering the essay as a whole, which is the best way to edit and link the underlined portions of sentences 3 and 4 (reproduced below)?

An editorial in a business magazine insisted that this report was faulty. It stated that there could be other, less dangerous reasons for the changes in climate that we've been experiencing.

(A) The report was faulty, an editorial in a business magazine insisted, it stated
(B) An editorial in a business magazine insisted that this report was faulty, stating
(C) In an editorial in a business magazine was the insistence that the report was faulty and
(D) The editorial in a business magazine insists that the consumers were faulty,
(E) Insisting that the report was faulty, an editorial in a business magazine states

KAPLAN

9. The phrase *do these bad things* in sentence 8 can be made clearer in relation to the content of the essay if it is edited as

   (A) exacerbate the situations
   (B) don't participate in events
   (C) are in need of services
   (D) use the types of chemicals
   (E) consider options

   (A) (B) (C) (D) (E)

10. Which is the best version of the underlined portions of sentences 10 and 11 (reproduced below)?

    Consumers can choose to purchase any kind of product they desire. They should be aware of what happens when they make their choices.

    (A) (As it is now)
    (B) Evidently, consumers can choose to purchase any kind of product they desire. If they would just be aware
    (C) Consumers can definitely choose to purchase any kind of product they desire, in spite
    (D) Consumers can definitely choose to purchase any kind of product they desire, but they should be aware
    (E) While consumers can choose to purchase any kind of product they desire, they are also aware

    (A) (B) (C) (D) (E)

11. Which of the following words or phrases best replaces the word *"they"* in sentence 12?

    (A) workers
    (B) future generations
    (C) consumers
    (D) chemical industries
    (E) editors

    (A) (B) (C) (D) (E)

12. What sentence most clearly represents the main idea of the writer?

    (A) I understand now how the scientists who wrote the report are right.
    (B) From now on, consumers must refuse to buy products that threaten the ozone layer and the health and safety of us all.
    (C) In conclusion, we all have to watch out for each other.
    (D) All of us have to find ways to maintain integrity in our economic choices.
    (E) Businesses are responsible for the safety of their products.

    (A) (B) (C) (D) (E)

Answers and Explanations
Paragraph Correction

Drill 1

1. (C)—Since the layer of body fat is identified as *blubber* in sentence 4, there's no need to identify it again in sentence 5. Thus, the sentence in (C) is clearly the best fit in the context of the paragraph.

2. (A)—This choice creates the necessary contrast with the second part of sentence 2. (D), too, creates the necessary contrast, but it isn't as concise and smooth as (A).

3. (E)—What do *it* and *its* in sentence 4 refer to? The antecedents of these pronouns aren't clear from the larger context. Choice (E)'s substitution of *the United States* for *it* and *English* for *its* clarifies the sentence's meaning in the larger context of the paragraph.

Drill 2

1. Marsha bought cheese, eggs, and milk at the grocery store.

2. While I attended a lecture at the university, my wife watched a movie.

3. Although Napoleon won many great military victories, he was eventually defeated and dethroned.

4. Interstellar travel is far beyond the limits of today's rockets, whose engines are not powerful enough to reach even the closest star.

5. Tariffs have two functions: to protect local industry and raise money for the national government.

Drill 3

1. (E)—The second paragraph of the essay assesses the results of Gettysburg. Collectively, sentences 5–7 indicate that the Confederacy's fortunes went downhill after the battle. Sentence 8 reveals what the Confederacy sought to gain from the battle. Hence, the following sentence should contrast the Confederacy's high hopes with reality. (E) does exactly that by pointing out that Gettysburg both strengthened the Union's will to fight and ended the Confederacy's chances for international recognition. (A), (B), and (D) raise issues that aren't even addressed in the essay. While (C) touches on the results of Gettysburg, it's a much less convincing choice than (E).

2. (B)—What opposing viewpoint? This essay provides only the author's perspective on Gettysburg. The first paragraph describes the Battle of Gettysburg, including what happened on specific days, while the second paragraph evaluates the importance of the battle to the final outcome of the Civil War. Thus, choices (A), (C), (D), and (E) are eliminated.

Paragraph Correction Practice Quiz

1. (B)—Choice (B) is the only one that is consistent in tense with the rest of the paragraph. Also, *they* in the original sentence is unnecessary.

2. (D)—This choice introduces the idea of a change of opinion that is articulated and explained in the remainder of the essay.

3. (E)—The coordinating conjunction *but* emphasizes how the author's thoughts developed from seeing the role of *natural talent* as important to recognizing that *hard work and practice were just as important*. The word *and* in choice (A) lacks the emphasis which shows development in thought. The tense in choice (D) is inconsistent with the rest of the sentence.

4. (A)—*Therefore* logically introduces the idea that *because of* intense competition, the *ones who want to make it have to dedicate all their energies to perfecting their skills so they can be the best.*

5. (C)—*Unlike* contrasts the author with the people who feel athletes are overpaid. Additionally, the phrase *I'm now* indicates how the author's original position has changed from the position stated in the first paragraph. The phrase *I've been* in choice (A) is more ambiguous than choice (C)—that is, the author might have been convinced in the past but it is not clear that he is convinced *now*. Choice (D) is grammatically awkward and its tense is inconsistent with the rest of the paragraph.

6. (B)—The author does not actually quote anyone else's opinion in this essay, though he does refer to other people.

7. (E)—The word *It* does not clearly refer to the report, so choices (A), (B), and (D) are incorrect. Only choice (E) includes the phrase *The report*; furthermore, the rest of this sentence is grammatically consistent with the paragraph as a whole.

8. (B)—Choices (B) and (E) are the only ones that clearly maintain that the *editorial*, as opposed to the magazine itself, was *stating that there could be other, less dangerous reasons for the changes in climate that we've been experiencing*. However, choice (E) is in the present tense, whereas the rest of the information surrounding the discussion of the report and the editorial is in the past tense. Therefore, choice (B) is correct.

9. (D)—The types of products that contribute to the destruction of the ozone layer are certain types of *chemicals*; therefore, choice (D) is the most logical and specific answer.

10. (D)—The essay serves as an entreaty to desist from using harmful chemicals. Therefore, the word *but* following the first independent clause in choice (D)—*Consumers can definitely choose to purchase any kind of product they desire*—consistently carries on the tone and meaning of the essay by suggesting that consumers should be aware of the results of their choices.

11. (C)—Since the author is talking about the choices that *consumers* make and how their choices affect the ozone layer, choice (C) is best.

12. (B)—Again, the essay tends to focus on the responsibility consumers have in regard to the condition of the ozone layer, so choice (B) is best. Choices (C) and (D) are too vague in terms of the people and actions they refer to. Though the author would agree with choice (A), this is not the main idea of the essay.

SECTION FOUR:
Ready, Set, Go!

CHAPTER 8

STRESS MANAGEMENT™

The countdown has begun. Your date with THE TEST is looming on the horizon. Anxiety is on the rise. The butterflies in your stomach have gone ballistic. Perhaps you feel as if the last thing you ate has turned into a lead ball. Your thinking is getting cloudy. Maybe you think you won't be ready. Maybe you already know your stuff, but you're going into panic mode anyway. Worst of all, you're not sure of what to do about it.

Don't freak! It is possible to tame that anxiety and stress—before and during the test. We'll show you how. You won't believe how quickly and easily you can deal with that killer anxiety.

Make the Most of Your Prep Time

Lack of control is one of the prime causes of stress. A ton of research shows that if you don't have a sense of control over what's happening in your life, you can easily end up feeling helpless and hopeless. So, just having concrete things to do and to think about—taking control—will help reduce your stress. This section shows you how to take control during the days leading up to taking the test.

Identify the Sources of Stress

In the space provided, jot down anything you identify as a source of your test-related stress. The idea is to pin down that free-floating anxiety so that you can take control of it. Here are some common examples to get you started:

- I always freeze up on tests.

- I'm nervous about the Essay (or Usage Questions, or Paragraph Corrections, etcetera).

- I need a good/great score to go to Acme College.

- My older brother/sister/best friend/girl- or boyfriend did really well. I must match their scores or do better.

Avoid Must-y Thinking

Let go of "must-y" thoughts, those notions that you must do something in a certain way—for example, "I must get a great score, or else!" or "I must meet Mom and Dad's expectations."

Don't Do It in Bed

Don't study on your bed, especially if you have problems with insomnia. Your mind might start to associate the bed with work, and make it even harder for you to fall asleep.

Think Good Thoughts

Create a set of positive but brief affirmations and mentally repeat them to yourself just before you fall asleep at night. (That's when your mind is very open to suggestion.) You'll find yourself feeling a lot more positive in the morning. Periodically repeating your affirmations during the day makes them more effective.

- My parents, who are paying for school, will be really disappointed if I don't test well.

- I'm afraid of losing my focus and concentration.

- I'm afraid I'm not spending enough time preparing.

- I study like crazy, but nothing seems to stick in my mind.

- I always run out of time and get panicky.

- I feel as though thinking is becoming like wading through thick mud.

Sources of Stress

_____ _____

_____ _____

_____ _____

_____ _____

Take a few minutes to think about the things you've just written down. Then rewrite them in some sort of order. List the statements you most associate with your stress and anxiety first, and put the least disturbing items last. Chances are, the top of the list is a fairly accurate description of exactly how you react to test anxiety, both physically and mentally. The later items usually describe your fears (disappointing Mom and Dad, looking bad, etcetera). As you write the list, you're forming a hierarchy of items so you can deal first with the anxiety provokers that bug you most. Very often, taking care of the major items from the top of the list goes a long way toward relieving overall testing anxiety. You probably won't have to bother with the stuff you placed last.

Strengths and Weaknesses

Take one minute to list the areas of the test that you are good at. They can be general ("grammar") or specific ("Sentence Correction"). Put down as many as you can think of, and if possible, time yourself. Write for the entire time; don't stop writing until you've reached the one-minute stopping point.

Strong Test Subjects

_____   _____

_____   _____

_____   _____

_____   _____

Next, take one minute to list areas of the test you're not so good at, just plain bad at, have failed at, or keep failing at. Again, keep it to one minute, and continue writing until you reach the cutoff. Don't be afraid to identify and write down your weak spots! In all probability, as you do both lists, you'll find you are strong in some areas and not so strong in others. Taking stock of your assets and liabilities lets you know the areas you don't have to worry about, and the ones that will demand extra attention and effort.

Weak Test Subjects

_____   _____

_____   _____

_____   _____

_____   _____

Facing your weak spots gives you some distinct advantages. It helps a lot to find out where you need to spend extra effort. Increased exposure to tough material makes it more familiar and less intimidating. (After all, we mostly fear what we don't know and are probably afraid to face.) You'll feel better about yourself because you're dealing directly with areas of the test that bring on your anxiety. You can't help feeling more confident when you know you're actively strengthening your chances of earning a higher overall test score.

Now, go back to the "good" list, and expand it for two minutes. Take the general items on that first list and make them more specific; take the specific items and expand them into more general conclusions. Naturally, if anything new comes to mind, jot it down. Focus all of your attention and effort on your strengths. Don't underestimate yourself or your abilities. Give yourself full credit. At the same time, don't list strengths you don't really have; you'll only be fooling yourself.

Very Superstitious

Stress expert Stephen Sideroff, Ph.D., tells of a client who always stressed out before, during, and even after taking tests. Yet, she always got outstanding scores. It became obvious that she was thinking superstitiously—subconsciously believing that the great scores were a result of her worrying. She didn't trust herself, and believed that if she didn't worry she wouldn't study hard enough. Sideroff convinced her to take a risk and work on relaxing before her next test. She did, and her test results were still as good as ever—which broke her cycle of superstitious thinking.

Get It Together

Don't work in a messy or cramped area. Before you sit down to study, clear yourself a nice, open space. And, make sure you have books, paper, pencils—whatever tools you will need—within easy reach before you sit down to study.

Expanding from general to specific might go as follows. If you listed "grammar" as a broad topic you feel strong in, you would then narrow your focus to include areas of this subject about which you are particularly knowledgeable. Your areas of strength might include a good ear for idiomatic English, a strong sense of logical construction, ability to spot faulty verb forms, etc.

Whatever you know comfortably goes on your "good" list. Okay. You've got the picture. Now, get ready, check your starting time, and start writing down items on your expanded "good" list.

Strong Test Subjects: An Expanded List

_____   _____

_____   _____

_____   _____

_____   _____

After you've stopped, check your time. Did you find yourself going beyond the two minutes allotted? Did you write down more things than you thought you knew? Is it possible you know more than you've given yourself credit for? Could that mean you've found a number of areas in which you feel strong?

You just took an active step toward helping yourself. Notice any increased feelings of confidence? Enjoy them.

Here's another way to think about your writing exercise. Every area of strength and confidence you can identify is much like having a reserve of solid gold at Fort Knox. You'll be able to draw on your reserves as you need them. You can use your reserves to solve difficult questions, maintain confidence, and keep test stress and anxiety at a distance. The encouraging thing is that every time you recognize another area of strength, succeed at coming up with a solution, or get a good score on a test, you increase your reserves. And, there is absolutely no limit to how much self-confidence you can have or how good you can feel about yourself.

Imagine Yourself Succeeding

This next little group of exercises is both physical and mental. It's a natural follow-up to what you've just accomplished with your lists.

First, get yourself into a comfortable sitting position in a quiet setting. Wear loose clothes. If you wear glasses, take them off. Then, close your eyes and breathe in a deep, satisfying breath of air. Really fill your lungs until your rib cage is fully expanded and you can't take in any more. Then, exhale the air completely. Imagine you're blowing out a candle with your last little puff of air. Do this two or three more times, filling your lungs to their maximum and emptying them totally. Keep your eyes closed, comfortably but not tightly. Let your body sink deeper into the chair as you become even more comfortable.

With your eyes shut you can notice something very interesting. You're no longer dealing with the worrisome stuff going on in the world outside of you. Now you can concentrate on what happens *inside* you. The more you recognize your own physical reactions to stress and anxiety, the more you can do about them. You might not realize it, but you've begun to regain a sense of being in control.

Let images begin to form on the "viewing screens" on the back of your eyelids. You're experiencing visualizations from the place in your mind that makes pictures. Allow the images to come easily and naturally; don't force them. Imagine yourself in a relaxing situation. It might be in a special place you've visited before or one you've read about. It can be a fictional location that you create in your imagination, but a real-life memory of a place or situation you know is usually better. Make it as detailed as possible, and notice as much as you can.

Stay focused on the images as you sink farther back into your chair. Breathe easily and naturally. You might have the sensations of any stress or tension draining from your muscles and flowing downward, out your feet and away from you.

Take a moment to check how you're feeling. Notice how comfortable you've become. Imagine how much easier it would be if you could take the test feeling this relaxed and in this state of ease. You've coupled the images of your special place with sensations of comfort and relaxation. You've also found a way to become relaxed simply by visualizing your own safe, special place.

Now, close your eyes and start remembering a real-life situation in which you did well on a test. If you can't come up with one, remember a situation in which you did something (academic or otherwise) that you were really proud of—a genuine accomplishment. Make the memory as detailed as possible. Think about the sights, the sounds, the smells, even the tastes associated with this remembered experience. Remember how confident you felt as you accomplished your goal. Now start thinking about the upcoming test. Keep your thoughts and feelings in line with that successful experience. Don't make comparisons between them. Just imagine taking the upcoming test with the same feelings of confidence and relaxed control.

This exercise is a great way to bring the test down to Earth. You should practice this exercise often, especially when the prospect of taking the exam

Ocean Dumping

Visualize a beautiful beach, with white sand, blue skies, sparkling water, a warm sun, and seagulls. See yourself walking on the beach, carrying a small plastic pail. Stop at a good spot and put your worries and whatever may be bugging you into the pail. Drop it at the water's edge and watch it drift out to sea. When the pail is out of sight, walk on.

Counseling

Don't forget that your school probably has counseling available. If you can't conquer test stress on your own, make an appointment at the counseling center. That's what counselors are there for.

Nutrition and Stress: The Dos and Don'ts

Do eat:

- Fruits and vegetables (raw is best, or just lightly steamed or nuked)
- Low-fat protein such as fish, skinless poultry, beans, and legumes (like lentils)
- Whole grains such as brown rice, whole wheat bread, and pastas (no bleached flour)

Don't eat:

- Refined sugar; sweet, high-fat snacks (simple carbohydrates like sugar make stress worse, and fatty foods lower your immunity)
- Salty foods (they can deplete potassium, which you need for nerve functions)

Play the Music

If you want to play music, keep it low and in the background. Music with a regular, mathematical rhythm—reggae, for example—aids the learning process. A recording of ocean waves is also soothing.

---

starts to bum you out. The more you practice it, the more effective the exercise will be for you.

Exercise Your Frustrations Away

Whether it is jogging, walking, biking, mild aerobics, pushups, or a pickup basketball game, physical exercise is a very effective way to stimulate both your mind and body and to improve your ability to think and concentrate. A surprising number of students get out of the habit of regular exercise, ironically because they're spending so much time prepping for exams. Also, sedentary people—this is a medical fact—get less oxygen to the blood and hence to the head than active people. You can live fine with a little less oxygen; you just can't think as well.

Any big test is a bit like a race. Thinking clearly at the end is just as important as having a quick mind early on. If you can't sustain your energy level in the last sections of the exam, there's too good a chance you could blow it. You need a fit body that can weather the demands any big exam puts on you. Along with a good diet and adequate sleep, exercise is an important part of keeping yourself in fighting shape and thinking clearly for the long haul.

There's another thing that happens when students don't make exercise an integral part of their test preparation. Like any organism in nature, you operate best if all your "energy systems" are in balance. Studying uses a lot of energy, but it's all mental. When you take a study break, do something active instead of raiding the fridge or vegging out in front of the TV. Take a 5- to 10-minute activity break for every 50 or 60 minutes that you study. The physical exertion gets your body into the act, which helps to keep your mind and body in sync. Then, when you finish studying for the night and hit the sack, you won't lie there, tense and unable to sleep because your head is overtired and your body wants to pump iron or run a marathon.

One warning about exercise, however: It's not a good idea to exercise vigorously right before you go to bed. This could easily cause sleep onset problems. For the same reason, it's also not a good idea to study right up to bedtime. Make time for a "buffer period" before you go to bed: For 30 to 60 minutes, just take a hot shower, meditate, simply veg out.

The Dangers of Drugs

Using drugs (prescription or recreational) specifically to prepare for and take a big test is definitely self-defeating. (And if they're illegal drugs, you can end up with a bigger problem than the SAT II Writing test on your hands.) Except for the drugs that occur naturally in your brain, every drug has major drawbacks—and a false sense of security is only one of them.

You may have heard that popping uppers helps you study by keeping you alert. If they're illegal, definitely forget about it. They wouldn't really work anyway, since amphetamines make it hard to retain information. Mild stimulants, such as coffee, cola, or over-the-counter caffeine pills can sometimes help as you study, since they keep you alert. On the down side, they can also lead to agitation, restlessness, and insomnia. Some people can drink a pot of high-octane coffee and sleep like a baby. Others have one cup and start to vibrate. It all depends on your tolerance for caffeine. Remember, a little anxiety is a good thing. The adrenaline that gets pumped into your bloodstream helps you stay alert and think more clearly. But, too much anxiety and you can't think straight at all.

Instead, go for endorphins—the "natural morphine." Endorphins have no side effects and they're free—you've already got them in your brain. It just takes some exercise to release them. Running around on the basketball court, bicycling, swimming, aerobics, power walking—these activities cause endorphins to occupy certain spots in your brain's neural synapses. In addition, exercise develops staying power and increases the oxygen transfer to your brain. Go into the test naturally.

Take a Deep Breath . . .

Here's another natural route to relaxation and invigoration. It's a classic isometric exercise that you can do whenever you get stressed out—just before the test begins, even *during* the test. It's very simple and takes just a few minutes.

Close your eyes. Starting with your eyes and—without holding your breath—gradually tighten every muscle in your body (but not to the point of pain) in the following sequence:

1. Close your eyes tightly.

2. Squeeze your nose and mouth together so that your whole face is scrunched up. (If it makes you self-conscious to do this in the test room, skip the face-scrunching part.)

3. Pull your chin into your chest, and pull your shoulders together.

4. Tighten your arms to your body, then clench your hands into tight fists.

5. Pull in your stomach.

6. Squeeze your thighs and buttocks together, and tighten your calves.

7. Stretch your feet, then curl your toes (watch out for cramping in this part).

Cyberstress

If you spend a lot of time in cyberspace anyway, do a search for the phrase "stress management." There's a ton of stress advice on the Net, including material specifically for students.

Take a Hike, Pal

When you're in the middle of studying and hit a wall, take a short, brisk walk. Breathe deeply and swing your arms as you walk. Clear your mind. (And, don't forget to look for flowers that grow in the cracks of the sidewalk.)

Enlightenment

A lamp with a 75-watt bulb is optimal for studying. But don't put it so close to your study material that you create a glare.

The Relaxation Paradox

Forcing relaxation is like asking yourself to flap your arms and fly. You can't do it, and every push and prod only gets you more frustrated. Relaxation is something you don't work at. You simply let it happen. Think about it. When was the last time you tried to force yourself to go to sleep, and it worked?

At this point, every muscle should be tightened. Now, relax your body, one part at a time, *in reverse order*, starting with your toes. Let the tension drop out of each muscle. The entire process might take five minutes from start to finish (maybe a couple of minutes during the test). This clenching and unclenching exercise should help you to feel very relaxed.

And Keep Breathing

Conscious attention to breathing is an excellent way of managing test stress (or any stress, for that matter). The majority of people who get into trouble during tests take shallow breaths. They breathe using only their upper chests and shoulder muscles, and may even hold their breath for long periods of time. Conversely, the test taker who by accident or design keeps breathing normally and rhythmically is likely to be more relaxed and in better control during the entire test experience.

So, now is the time to get into the habit of relaxed breathing. Do the next exercise to learn to breathe in a natural, easy rhythm. By the way, this is another technique you can use during the test to collect your thoughts and ward off excess stress. The entire exercise should take no more than three to five minutes.

With your eyes still closed, breathe in slowly and *deeply* through your nose. Hold the breath for a bit, and then release it through your mouth. The key is to breathe slowly and deeply by using your diaphragm (the big band of muscle that spans your body just above your waist) to draw air in and out naturally and effortlessly. Breathing with your diaphragm encourages relaxation and helps minimize tension. Try it and notice how relaxed and comfortable you feel.

CHAPTER 9

THE FINAL COUNTDOWN

Quick Tips for the Days Just Before the Exam

- The best test takers do less and less as the test approaches. Taper off your study schedule and take it easy on yourself. You want to be relaxed and ready on the day of the test. Give yourself time off, especially the evening before the exam. By then, if you've studied well, everything you need to know is firmly stored in your memory banks.

- Positive self-talk can be extremely liberating and invigorating, especially as the test looms closer. Tell yourself things such as, "I choose to take this test" rather than "I have to"; "I will do well" rather than "I hope things go well"; "I can" rather than "I cannot." Be aware of negative, self-defeating thoughts and images and immediately counter any you become aware of. Replace them with affirming statements that encourage your self-esteem and confidence. Create and practice visualizations that build on your positive statements.

- Get your act together sooner rather than later. Have everything (including choice of clothing) laid out days in advance. Most important, know where the test will be held and the easiest, quickest way to get there. You will gain great peace of mind if you know that all the little details—gas in the car, directions, etcetera—are firmly in your control before the day of the test.

- Experience the test site a few days in advance. This is very helpful if you are especially anxious. If at all possible, find out what room your part of the alphabet is assigned to, and try to sit there (by yourself) for a while. Better yet, bring some practice material and do at least a section or two, if not an entire practice test, in that room. In this situation, familiarity doesn't breed contempt, it generates comfort and confidence.

Dress for Success

On the day of the test, wear loose layers. That way, you'll be prepared no matter what the temperature of the room is. (An uncomfortable temperature will just distract you from the job at hand.) And, if you have an item of clothing that you tend to feel "lucky" or confident in—a shirt, a pair of jeans, whatever—wear it. A little totem couldn't hurt.

What Are "Signs of a Winner," Alex?

Here's some advice from a Kaplan instructor who won big on *Jeopardy!*™ In the green room before the show, he noticed that the contestants who were quiet and "within themselves" were the ones who did great on the show. The contestants who did not perform as well were the ones who were fact-cramming, talking a lot, and generally being manic before the show. Lesson: Spend the final hours leading up to the test getting sleep, meditating, and generally relaxing.

• Forego any practice on the day before the test. It's in your best interest to marshal your physical and psychological resources for 24 hours or so. Even race horses are kept in the paddock and treated like princes the day before a race. Keep the upcoming test out of your consciousness; go to a movie, take a pleasant hike, or just relax. Don't eat junk food or tons of sugar. And—of course—get plenty of rest the night before. Just don't go to bed too early. It's hard to fall asleep earlier than you're used to, and you don't want to lie there thinking about the test.

Handling Stress During the Test

The biggest stress monster will be the test itself. Fear not; there are methods of quelling your stress during the test.

• Keep moving forward instead of getting bogged down in a difficult question. You don't have to get everything right to achieve a fine score. The best test takers skip difficult material temporarily in search of the easier stuff. They mark the ones that require extra time and thought. This strategy buys time and builds confidence so you can handle the tough stuff later.

• Don't be thrown if other test takers seem to be working more furiously than you are. Continue to spend your time patiently thinking through your answers; it's going to lead to better results. Don't mistake the other people's sheer activity as signs of progress and higher scores.

• *Keep breathing!* Weak test takers tend to forget to breathe properly as the test proceeds. They start holding their breath without realizing it, or they breathe erratically or arrhythmically. Improper breathing interferes with clear thinking.

• Some quick isometrics during the test—especially if concentration is wandering or energy is waning—can help. Try this: Put your palms together and press intensely for a few seconds. Concentrate on the tension you feel through your palms, wrists, forearms, and up into your biceps and shoulders. Then, quickly release the pressure. Feel the difference as you let go. Focus on the warm relaxation that floods through the muscles. Now you're ready to return to the task.

• Here's another isometric that will relieve tension in both your neck and eye muscles. Slowly rotate your head from side to side, turning your head and eyes to look as far back over each shoulder as you can. Feel the muscles stretch on one side of your neck as they contract on the other. Repeat five times in each direction.

With what you've just learned here, you're armed and ready to do battle with the test. This book and your studies will give you the information you'll need to answer the questions. It's all firmly planted in your mind. You also know how to deal with any excess tension that might come along, both when you're studying for and taking the exam. You've experienced everything you need to tame your test anxiety and stress. You're going to get a great score.

SECTION FIVE:
Kaplan Practice Tests

ANSWER SHEET
FOR PRACTICE TEST 1

1 (A)(B)(C)(D)(E)	16 (A)(B)(C)(D)(E)	31 (A)(B)(C)(D)(E)	46 (A)(B)(C)(D)(E)
2 (A)(B)(C)(D)(E)	17 (A)(B)(C)(D)(E)	32 (A)(B)(C)(D)(E)	47 (A)(B)(C)(D)(E)
3 (A)(B)(C)(D)(E)	18 (A)(B)(C)(D)(E)	33 (A)(B)(C)(D)(E)	48 (A)(B)(C)(D)(E)
4 (A)(B)(C)(D)(E)	19 (A)(B)(C)(D)(E)	34 (A)(B)(C)(D)(E)	49 (A)(B)(C)(D)(E)
5 (A)(B)(C)(D)(E)	20 (A)(B)(C)(D)(E)	35 (A)(B)(C)(D)(E)	50 (A)(B)(C)(D)(E)
6 (A)(B)(C)(D)(E)	21 (A)(B)(C)(D)(E)	36 (A)(B)(C)(D)(E)	51 (A)(B)(C)(D)(E)
7 (A)(B)(C)(D)(E)	22 (A)(B)(C)(D)(E)	37 (A)(B)(C)(D)(E)	52 (A)(B)(C)(D)(E)
8 (A)(B)(C)(D)(E)	23 (A)(B)(C)(D)(E)	38 (A)(B)(C)(D)(E)	53 (A)(B)(C)(D)(E)
9 (A)(B)(C)(D)(E)	24 (A)(B)(C)(D)(E)	39 (A)(B)(C)(D)(E)	54 (A)(B)(C)(D)(E)
10 (A)(B)(C)(D)(E)	25 (A)(B)(C)(D)(E)	40 (A)(B)(C)(D)(E)	55 (A)(B)(C)(D)(E)
11 (A)(B)(C)(D)(E)	26 (A)(B)(C)(D)(E)	41 (A)(B)(C)(D)(E)	56 (A)(B)(C)(D)(E)
12 (A)(B)(C)(D)(E)	27 (A)(B)(C)(D)(E)	42 (A)(B)(C)(D)(E)	57 (A)(B)(C)(D)(E)
13 (A)(B)(C)(D)(E)	28 (A)(B)(C)(D)(E)	43 (A)(B)(C)(D)(E)	58 (A)(B)(C)(D)(E)
14 (A)(B)(C)(D)(E)	29 (A)(B)(C)(D)(E)	44 (A)(B)(C)(D)(E)	59 (A)(B)(C)(D)(E)
15 (A)(B)(C)(D)(E)	30 (A)(B)(C)(D)(E)	45 (A)(B)(C)(D)(E)	60 (A)(B)(C)(D)(E)

right

wrong

Use the answer key following the test to count up the number of questions you got right and the number you got wrong. (Remember not to count omitted questions as wrong.) The "Compute Your Score" section at the back of the book will show you how to find your score.

ANSWER SHEET
FOR PRACTICE TEST 1

Part A (ESSAY). Begin your composition on this side. If you need more space, you may continue on the reverse side.

_____

_____

_____

_____

_____

_____

_____

_____

_____

_____

_____

_____

_____

_____

_____

_____

_____

_____

_____

_____

_____

_____

_____

_____

ANSWER SHEET
FOR PRACTICE TEST 1

Continuation of Part A (ESSAY) from reverse side. Write below if you need more space.

_____

_____

_____

_____

_____

_____

_____

_____

_____

_____

_____

_____

_____

_____

_____

_____

_____

_____

_____

_____

_____

_____

PART A
Time—20 Minutes (1 Question)

You have 20 minutes to write an essay on the following topic. DO NOT WRITE AN ESSAY ON ANY OTHER TOPIC. AN ESSAY ON A DIFFERENT TOPIC IS UNACCEPTABLE.

This essay provides you with an opportunity to demonstrate how well you write. Therefore, you should express your ideas clearly and effectively. How much you write is much less important than how well you write; but to express your thoughts on the topic adequately you may want to write more than a single paragraph. Your essay should be specific.

Your essay must be written in the lines provided on your answer sheet. No other paper will be given to you. There is enough space to write your essay on the answer sheet if you write on every line, avoid wide margins, and keep your handwriting to a reasonable size.

Consider the following statement and assignment. Then write an essay as directed.

"The greatest griefs are those we cause ourselves."

Assignment: Choose one example from personal experience, current events, or history, literature, or any other discipline and use this example to write an essay in which you agree or disagree with the statement above. Your essay should be specific.

WHEN THE PROCTOR ANNOUNCES THAT 20 MINUTES HAVE PASSED, YOU MUST STOP WRITING AND GO ON TO PART B OF THE TEST. IF YOU FINISH YOUR ESSAY BEFORE 20 MINUTES PASS, YOU MAY GO ON TO PART B.

YOU MAY MAKE NOTES ON THIS PAGE AND THE FOLLOWING ONE, BUT YOU MUST WRITE YOUR ESSAY ON THE ANSWER SHEET.

TURN TO THE NEXT PAGE.

You may use this page to outline your essay or make other notes as you plan your essay. Don't write your essay here, though. Your essay must be written on the lined pages of the answer sheet at the beginning of this answer section.

TURN TO THE NEXT PAGE.

PART B
Time—40 Minutes (60 Questions)

For each of the following questions, choose the best answer from the given choices and darken the corresponding oval on the answer sheet.

Directions: The following sentences contain problems in grammar, usage, diction (choice of words), and idiom.

Some of the sentences are correct.
None of the sentences contains more than one error.

The error, if there is one in the sentence, is underlined and lettered. Parts of the sentence that are not underlined are correct and cannot be changed. In selecting answers, follow the requirements of standard written English.

If there is an error, choose the <u>one underlined part</u> that must be changed to make the sentence correct and fill in the corresponding oval on your answer grid.

If there is no error, fill in oval E.

SAMPLE QUESTION

<u>Even though</u> he <u>had to</u> supervise a large
    A   B

staff, his salary <u>was no greater</u> than <u>a clerk.</u>
               C   D

<u>No error</u>
  E

SAMPLE ANSWER

Ⓐ Ⓑ Ⓒ ● Ⓔ

---

1. Before <u>the advent of</u> modern surgical
           A

   techniques, <u>bleeding patients</u> with leeches
              B

   <u>were considered</u> <u>therapeutically effective.</u>
        C   D

   <u>No error</u>
     E

2. The <u>recent</u> establishment <u>of</u> "Crime Busters,"
        A   B

   officially sanctioned neighborhood block-

   watching groups, <u>have</u> dramatically improved
             C

   relations <u>between</u> citizens and police. <u>No error</u>
          D   E

3. The masterpiece auctioned so <u>successfully</u>
                         A

   today depicts a Biblical <u>scene in which</u> the
                    B

   king is on his throne with his <u>counselors</u>
                           C

   standing <u>respectively</u> below. <u>No error</u>
         D   E

TURN TO THE NEXT PAGE.

4. During the election campaign, the major

   political parties agreed that minorities must be

   given the opportunity <u>to advance</u>, <u>to seek</u>
                             A   B
   justice, and <u>to the kinds</u> of special treatment
                       C
   that might compensate <u>in part</u> for historical
                                D
   inequities. <u>No error</u>
                    E

5. Most of the delegates <u>which</u> attended the
                             A
   convention <u>felt</u> the resolution was <u>too strongly</u>
                  B   C
   worded, and the majority voted <u>against</u> it.
                                        D
   <u>No error</u>
       E

6. <u>Lost in the forest</u> on a cold night, the hunters
       A
   <u>built</u> a fire <u>to keep themselves</u> warm and
     B   C
   <u>to frighten away</u> the wolves. <u>No error</u>
          D   E

7. The effort <u>to create appropriate</u> theatrical
                       A
   effects <u>often result</u> in settings that cannot be
              B
   <u>effective</u> without an imaginative <u>lighting</u> crew.
       C   D
   <u>No error</u>
       E

8. Every one of the shops in the town <u>were closed</u>
                                            A
   on Thursday <u>because</u> of the <u>ten-inch</u> rainfall
                    B   C
   that <u>had fallen</u> during the day. <u>No error</u>
              D   E

9. <u>According</u> to the directions on the package, the
       A
   contents <u>are</u> intended for external use <u>only</u> and
                B   C
   <u>should not be</u> swallowed, even in small
       D
   quantities. <u>No error</u>
                    E

10. <u>The late president's numerous memoirs</u> now
                        A
    <u>about to be published</u> <u>promises</u> to be of special
              B   C
    <u>historical</u> interest. <u>No error</u>
        D   E

11. Mr. Webster's paper is <u>highly imaginary</u> and
                                    A
    <u>very creative</u>, <u>but</u> <u>lacking in</u> cogency. <u>No error</u>
          B   C   D   E

12. The point at issue <u>was whether</u> the dock
                            A
    workers, <u>which</u> were <u>an extremely vocal group</u>,
                B   C
    <u>would decide to return</u> to work. <u>No error</u>
              D   E

13. <u>Raising</u> living costs, <u>together</u> with escalating
        A   B
    taxes, <u>have</u> proved to be a burden for
              C
    everyone. <u>No error</u>
                  D   E

14. A number of <u>harried</u> department store
                    A
    employees <u>were congregating</u> <u>around</u> the
                    B   C
    water cooler <u>to compare and discuss</u> their
                        D
    grievances. <u>No error</u>
                    E

TURN TO THE NEXT PAGE.

15. The deep-sea diver <u>considered himself</u> not
                              A
    only a <u>competent</u> barnacle scraper but also
                B
    <u>capable of collecting</u> interesting <u>specimens of</u>
            C   D
    seashells. <u>No error</u>
                  E

16. A round robin <u>is where</u> each team <u>must</u>
                      A   B
    compete <u>against</u> every <u>other</u> team. <u>No error</u>
                C   D   E

17. The voters were <u>dismayed</u> at <u>him retiring</u> from
                        A   B
    <u>elected</u> office at such an early age, seemingly
      C
    <u>at the outset of</u> a brilliant career. <u>No error</u>
            D   E

18. <u>Having a reasonable amount of</u> intelligence
                    A
    and <u>steady persistence</u> <u>assure one</u> of acquitting
              B   C
    oneself <u>creditably</u> in any undertaking. <u>No error</u>
                D   E

19. If the current rate of progress <u>in raising</u> school
                                        A
    standards <u>is to be</u> accelerated, every pupil,
                  B
    <u>teacher, and parent</u> in the neighborhood must
              C
    assume <u>their share</u> of the responsibility.
                D
    <u>No error</u>
      E

20. "Elementary, my dear Watson," <u>was</u> a <u>frequent</u>
                                      A   B
    observation <u>of</u> the <u>imminent</u> Sherlock Holmes.
                    C   D
    <u>No error</u>
      E

TURN TO THE NEXT PAGE.

For each of the following questions, choose the best answer from the given choices and darken the corresponding oval on the answer sheet.

Directions: The following sentences test accuracy and effectiveness of expression. In selecting answers, follow the rules of standard written English; in other words, consider grammar, choice of words, sentence construction, and punctuation.

In each of the following sentences, a portion or all of the sentence is underlined. Under each sentence you will find five ways of phrasing the underlined portion. Choice A repeats the original underlined portion; the other four choices provide alternative phrasings.

Select the choice that best expresses the meaning of the original sentence. If the original sentence is better than any of the alternative phrasings, choose A; otherwise select one of the alternatives. Your selection should construct the most effective sentence—clear and precise with no awkwardness or ambiguity.

SAMPLE QUESTION

Wanting to reward her assistant for loyalty,
Sheila gave a bonus to him as large as his paycheck.

(A) Sheila gave a bonus to him as large as his paycheck
(B) given to him by Sheila was a bonus as large as his paycheck
(C) he was given a bonus as large as his paycheck by Sheila
(D) Sheila gave him a bonus as large as his paycheck
(E) Sheila gave him a paycheck to him as large as his bonus

SAMPLE ANSWER

---

21. After depositing and burying her eggs, the female sea turtle returns to the water, never to view or nurture the offspring that she is leaving behind.

   (A) never to view or nurture the offspring that she is leaving behind
   (B) never to view or nurture the offspring which she had left behind
   (C) never to view nor nurture the offspring that are being left behind
   (D) never to view or nurture the offspring she has left behind
   (E) never to view or nurture the offspring who she has left behind

22. Congress was in no doubt about who would take credit for winning the war on inflation.

   (A) about who would take credit
   (B) about who takes credit
   (C) about whom would take credit
   (D) of who would take credit
   (E) over who would take credit

23. In *War and Peace*, Tolstoy presented his theories on history and illustrated them with a slanted account of actual historical events.

   (A) illustrated them
   (B) also illustrating them
   (C) he also was illustrating these ideas
   (D) then illustrated the theories also
   (E) then he went about illustrating them

TURN TO THE NEXT PAGE.

24. Laval, the first bishop of Quebec, exemplified aristocratic vigor and concern <u>on account of his giving up his substantial inheritance to become an ecclesiastic</u> and to help shape Canadian politics and education.

    (A) on account of his giving up his substantial inheritance to become an ecclesiastic
    (B) since he gave up his substantial inheritance to become an ecclesiastic
    (C) since giving up his substantial inheritance to become an ecclesiastic
    (D) because of his having given up his substantial inheritance for the purpose of becoming an ecclesiastic
    (E) as a result of becoming an ecclesiastic through giving up his substantial inheritance

25. In the United States, an increasing number of commuters <u>that believe their families to be</u> immune from the perils of city life.

    (A) that believe their families to be
    (B) that believe their families are
    (C) believes their families are
    (D) who believe their families to be
    (E) believe their families to be

26. <u>Developed by a scientific team at his university</u>, the president informed the reporters that the new process would facilitate the diagnosing of certain congenital diseases.

    (A) Developed by a scientific team at his university
    (B) Having been developed by a scientific team at his university
    (C) Speaking of the discovery made by a scientific team at his university
    (D) Describing the developments of a scientific team at his university
    (E) As it had been developed by a scientific team at his university

27. The Equal Rights Amendment to Islandia's constitution is dying a lingering political death, <u>many dedicated groups and individuals have attempted</u> to prevent its demise.

    (A) many dedicated groups and individuals have attempted
    (B) although many dedicated groups and individuals have attempted
    (C) many dedicated groups and persons has attempted
    (D) despite many dedications of groups and individuals to attempt
    (E) however, many dedicated groups and individuals have attempted

28. One ecological rule of thumb states that there is opportunity for the accumulation of underground water reservoirs <u>but in regions where vegetation remains undisturbed</u>.

    (A) but in regions where vegetation remains undisturbed
    (B) unless vegetation being left undisturbed in some regions
    (C) only where undisturbed vegetation is in regions
    (D) except for vegetation remaining undisturbed in some regions
    (E) only in regions where vegetation remains undisturbed

TURN TO THE NEXT PAGE.

29. The ancient Chinese were convinced that air was composed of two kinds of particles, <u>one inactive and one active, the latter of which they called yin and which we today call oxygen</u>.

    (A) one inactive and one active, the latter of which they called yin and which we today call oxygen

    (B) an inactive and an active one called yin, now known as oxygen

    (C) an inactive type and the active type they called yin we now know to be oxygen

    (D) inactive and active; while they called the active type yin, today we call it oxygen

    (E) contrasting the inactive type with the active ones they named yin and we call oxygen

30. There are several rules <u>which must be followed by whomever</u> wants to be admitted to this academy.

    (A) which must be followed by whomever

    (B) that must be followed by whomever

    (C) which must get followed by whom

    (D) that must be followed by whoever

    (E) which must be followed by those who

31. Developing a suitable environment for house plants <u>is in many ways like when you are managing</u> soil fertilization for city parks.

    (A) is in many ways like when you are managing

    (B is in many ways similar to when you are managing

    (C) in many ways is on a par with managing your

    (D) is in many ways similar to the managing of

    (E) is in many ways like managing

32. Most students would probably get better grades if <u>writing were to be studied by them</u>.

    (A) writing were to be studied by them

    (B) they studied writing

    (C) writing was studied by them

    (D) they would have studied writing

    (E) they were to have studied writing

33. <u>If they do not go into bankruptcy</u>, the company will probably survive its recent setbacks.

    (A) If they do not go into bankruptcy

    (B) Unless bankruptcy cannot be avoided

    (C) If they can avoid bankruptcy

    (D) If bankruptcy will be avoided

    (E) Unless it goes bankrupt

34. Having read the works of both Henry and William James, I'm convinced that Henry is <u>the best psychologist and William the best writer</u>.

    (A) the best psychologist and William the best writer

    (B) a better psychologist, William is the best writer

    (C) the best as a psychologist, William the best as a writer

    (D) the best psychologist, William the better writer

    (E) the better psychologist and William the better writer

TURN TO THE NEXT PAGE.

35. When he arrived at the hospital, the doctor found that <u>several emergency cases had been admitted before</u> he went on duty.

    (A) several emergency cases had been admitted before
    (B) there were several emergency cases admitted prior to
    (C) two emergency cases were being admitted before
    (D) a couple of emergency cases were admitted before
    (E) several emergency cases was admitted before

36. The variety of Scandinavian health care services offered to residents at reduced cost <u>far exceeds low-cost health programs</u> available in the United States.

    (A) far exceeds low-cost health programs
    (B) far exceeds the number of low-cost health programs
    (C) tends to be greater than low-cost programs
    (D) far exceed the number of low-cost health programs
    (E) are greater than comparable low-cost health programs

37. <u>Recently, scientists concerned about the growing popularity of astrologers have begun to speak out against them.</u>

    (A) Recently, scientists concerned about the growing popularity of astrologers have begun to speak out against them.
    (B) Recently, scientists who are concerned about the growing popularity of astrologers have begun to speak out against such things.
    (C) Recently, scientists, concerned about the growing popularity of astrologers, are beginning to speak out against them.
    (D) Recently, scientists concerned with the growing popularity of astrologers have begun to speak out about it.
    (E) Recently, scientists concerned about the growing popularity of astrologers have begun to speak out against what they will be doing.

38. The politician is benefiting from behavioral <u>research, there are new techniques for them</u> to utilize and new broadcasting methods to experiment with.

    (A) research, there are new techniques for them
    (B) research; he has new techniques
    (C) research; there are new techniques for them
    (D) research, there are new techniques for him
    (E) research; they have new techniques

TURN TO THE NEXT PAGE.

Directions: The following passages are first drafts of student essays. Some portions of the essays have to be rewritten.

Read the essays and answer the questions that follow them. Some of the questions concern particular sentences or fragments of sentences and require you to make choices about sentence structure, word choice, and usage. Other questions pertain to the entire essay or pieces of the essay and require you to think about organization, development, and appropriateness of language. Pick the answer that most effectively conveys the meaning and follows the rules of standard written English. Once you have chosen an answer, fill in the corresponding oval on your answer sheet.

Questions 39–44 are based on the following essay.

(1) Many young people think there is no point in studying liberal arts anymore. (2) They think this because with the kinds of jobs out there today, it's hard to see the relevance of them. (3) They say, "What's the point of reading Shakespeare if it's not going to help me get any sort of job?" (4) I thought things like this too.

(5) Not long ago, my English teacher asked me if I wanted to compete in a school-wide quiz show, and I said yes. (6) I did well on the show. (7) I was invited to join the school Trivia Team. (8) We were competing at high schools across the state. (9) It was a lot of fun and we won prize money. (10) Then came the championship game. (11) Nervous, my palms sweating, it was time for the tie-breaker question. (12) The host pulled the card from the envelope. (13) "What is the name of the wife of the jealous Moor in Shakespeare's Othello?" (14) I knew the answer. (15) I just read that play in my English class. (16) My hand hit the buzzer. (17) "Desdemona!" I shouted. (18) My teammates cheered and everyone hugged me. (19) We won!

(20) The next time I hear someone say there's no point in reading Shakespeare, I'll tell that person my story. (21) Who knows, maybe I'll appear on Jeopardy!™ some day.

39. Which of the following best replaces the word *"them"* in sentence 2?

    (A) many young people
    (B) liberal arts
    (C) jobs
    (D) Shakespeare's plays
    (E) things like this

40. Which of the following sentences, if added after sentence 4, would best link the first paragraph with the rest of the essay?

    (A) It's hard to see the point of reading Shakespeare when people with Ph.D.'s are out of work.
    (B) With so much television everywhere, hardly anyone reads anymore.
    (C) It was becoming more and more difficult for me to complete my school assignments.
    (D) However, I recently had an experience that caused me to change my mind.
    (E) My parents and teachers tried to convince me otherwise, to no avail.

TURN TO THE NEXT PAGE.

41. Which of the following is the best way to revise and combine sentences 6 and 7 (reproduced below)?

    I did well on the show. I was invited to join the school Trivia Team.

    (A) After doing well on the show, I was invited to join the school Trivia Team.
    (B) In order to be invited to join the school Trivia Team, I first had to do well on the show.
    (C) Doing well on the show and being invited to join the school Trivia Team were the next two things that happened to me.
    (D) Joining the school Trivia Team, I did well on the show.
    (E) Because I was doing well on the show, I was being invited to join the school Trivia Team.

42. In context, which of the following is the best way to revise sentence 11 (reproduced below)?

    Nervous, my palms sweating, it was time for the tie-breaker question.

    (A) (As it is now)
    (B) Nervous, my palms sweating, the tie-breaker question arrived.
    (C) Nervous and sweating, my palms waited for the arrival of the tie-breaker question.
    (D) Nervous, my palms sweating, I waited for the tie-breaker question.
    (E) Being nervous and having sweating palms, I was waiting for the arrival of the tie-breaker question.

43. To vary the pattern of short, choppy sentences in the second paragraph, which of the following would be the best way to revise and combine sentences 14 and 15 (reproduced below)?

    I knew the answer. I just read that play in my English class.

    (A) I knew the answer, I just read that play in my English class.
    (B) Although I just read that play in my English class, I knew the answer.
    (C) Having just read that play in my English class, I knew the answer.
    (D) I have known the answer to that question ever since I had been reading that play in my English class.
    (E) In my English class, where I was reading that play, I knew the answer.

44. All of the following strategies are used by the writer of the passage EXCEPT

    (A) refuting the assertion put forth in the first paragraph
    (B) recounting a personal anecdote in order to make a point
    (C) creating suspense by making references to the passage of time
    (D) providing specific details
    (E) including examples of jobs that require knowledge of liberal arts

TURN TO THE NEXT PAGE.

Questions 45–50 are based on the following essay, which is a response to an assignment to write about an economic issue facing the United States.

(1) Last year, my social studies class attended a talk given by a young woman who worked in a factory in Central America making shirts for a popular U.S. retail chain. (2) The working conditions she described were horrific. (3) She spoke of being forced to work 14-hour days and even longer on weekends. (4) The supervisors often hit her and the other women, most of whom were teenagers, to get them to work faster. (5) They gave them contaminated water to drink and were only allowed to go to the bathroom twice a day. (6) She urged us to boycott the retail chain and to inform consumers about the conditions in their factories.

(7) A group of us decided to meet with a representative of the chain and we would discuss our concerns and would announce our plans to boycott. (8) The representative said that low wages were necessary to keep costs down. (9) And she claimed a boycott would never work because it would be impossible to stop people from shopping at such a popular store. (10) "Nobody is going to listen to a bunch of teenagers," she said. (11) We decided to prove her wrong.

(12) First, we calculated that the workers' wages accounted for less than one percent of the price people paid for the shirts in the United States. (13) We argued that if the chain were willing to make slightly lower profits, it could afford to pay the workers more without raising prices. (14) And when we began informing people about the conditions under which the shirts they bought were made, they were horrified. (15) Many were agreeing to shop there no longer, they even wrote letters to the president of the chain in which he was urged to do something about the conditions in the factories. (16) Even local politicians got involved. (17) The winner of that year's City Council election pledged to change the conditions in the factories or shut the store down once and for all. (18) Finally, with business almost at a standstill, the store agreed to consumers' demands.

45. In context, which is the best version of the underlined portion of sentence 5 (reproduced below)?

    They gave them contaminated water to drink and were only allowed to go to the bathroom twice a day.

    (A) (As it is now)
    (B) and were only allowing them to go
    (C) and only allowed them to go
    (D) and they were only given permission to go
    (E) and were allowed to only go

46. In context, which of the following best replaces the word *"their"* in sentence 6?

    (A) the consumers'
    (B) its
    (C) the workers'
    (D) the supervisors'
    (E) the students'

47. Which of the following versions of the underlined portion of sentence 7 (reproduced below) is best?

    A group of us decided to meet with a representative of the chain and we would discuss our concerns and would announce our plans to boycott.

    (A) (As it is now)
    (B) to discuss our concerns and announce
    (C) for the purpose of discussing our concerns and announcing
    (D) where we would discuss our concerns and announce
    (E) with whom we would be discussing our concerns and to whom we would announce

TURN TO THE NEXT PAGE.

48. Which of the following would be the best replacement for the word *"And"* at the beginning of sentence 9?

    (A) Moreover,
    (B) Rather,
    (C) However,
    (D) Even so,
    (E) Instead,

49. In context, which of the following is the best way to revise the underlined portion of sentence 15 (reproduced below)?

    Many were agreeing to shop there no longer, they even wrote letters to the president of the chain in which he was urged to do something about the conditions in the factories.

    (A) (As it is now)
    (B) Many were agreeing to no longer shop there and even writing letters to the president of the chain in order that he be urged
    (C) Agreeing to shop there no longer, many even wrote letters to the president of the chain urging him
    (D) Many agreed to no longer shop there and also to urge the president of the chain by writing letters in which they asked him
    (E) Shopping there no longer, many agreed to write letters to the president of the chain and also to urge him

50. Which sentence would most appropriately follow sentence 18?

    (A) Despite the boycott, people were not willing to pay more for clothing.
    (B) Unfortunately, people rarely do things for selfless reasons.
    (C) Simply informing others is not enough; a plan of action must be devised.
    (D) We should have listened to the young factory worker in the first place.
    (E) We had proven the representative wrong; people had listened to "a bunch of teenagers."

TURN TO THE NEXT PAGE.

For each of the following questions, choose the best answer from the given choices and darken the corresponding oval on the answer sheet.

Directions: The following sentences contain problems in grammar, usage, diction (choice of words), and idiom.

Some of the sentences are correct.

None of the sentences contains more than one error.

The error, if there is one in the sentence, is underlined and lettered. Parts of the sentence that are not underlined are correct and cannot be changed. In selecting answers, follow the requirements of standard written English.

If there is an error, choose the <u>one underlined part</u> that must be changed to make the sentence correct and fill in the corresponding oval on your answer grid.

If there is no error, fill in oval E.

SAMPLE QUESTION

<u>Even though</u> he <u>had to</u> supervise a large
    A   B

staff, his salary <u>was no greater</u> than <u>a clerk</u>.
             C   D

<u>No error</u>
  E

SAMPLE ANSWER

Ⓐ Ⓑ Ⓒ ● Ⓔ

---

51. The more scientists learn about subatomic

    particles, <u>the more closely</u> they come
            A

    <u>to being able</u> to describe <u>the ways in which</u> the
        B   C

    universe <u>operates</u>. <u>No error</u>
           D   E

52. To have <u>reached a verdict</u> <u>so quickly</u>, the
             A   B

    members of the <u>jury would have to make up</u>
                 C

    <u>their minds</u> before leaving the courtroom.
        D

    <u>No error</u>
      E

53. <u>Drinking carbonated beverages</u> and eating
              A

    food <u>that</u> <u>contain</u> chemical preservatives can
         B   C

    be unhealthy <u>when indulged in to excess</u>.
                       D

    <u>No error</u>
      E

54. Albert Schweitzer <u>was</u> not only
               A

    an <u>accomplished doctor</u> but also
           B

    a <u>talented musician</u> <u>as well</u>. <u>No error</u>
        C   D   E

TURN TO THE NEXT PAGE.

55. Harley Goodsleuth, private detective, <u>found</u>
                                            A
    the <u>incriminating</u> evidence <u>where</u> the murderer
             B   C
    <u>had left</u> it. <u>No error</u>
       D   E

56. When the tall, cloaked figure had finished his

    bleak <u>pronouncement about</u> <u>the strange destiny</u>
                  A   B
    of the twins, <u>he vanished</u> <u>without hardly</u> a
                       C   D

    trace. <u>No error</u>
              E

57. <u>Many people feel</u> that a large defense budget
        A
    <u>is necessary</u> <u>in order to</u> make the United States
        B   C
    <u>stronger than any country in the world.</u>
                        D

    <u>No error</u>
       E

58. <u>Drawn</u> by the large crowd <u>gathered</u> outside
        A   B
    the tent, <u>the small boy</u> <u>standing</u> listening to the
                    C   D

    hoarse conversation of the circus barker.

    <u>No error</u>
       E

59. Not only <u>the poorest residents</u> of the city,
                     A
    <u>but also</u> the wealthiest man in town <u>eat at</u>
        B   C
    the <u>popular</u> cafeteria. <u>No error</u>
            D   E

60. Typhoid fever is a <u>bacterial</u> infection <u>that is</u>
                            A   B
    <u>transmitted by</u> contaminated water, milk,
        C
    shellfish, or <u>eating other foods</u>. <u>No error</u>
                        D   E

STOP!

END OF TEST. DO NOT TURN THE PAGE UNTIL
YOU ARE READY TO CHECK YOUR ANSWERS.

PRACTICE TEST 1 ANSWERS AND EXPLANATIONS

The Essay Section

This section contains sample essays for the essay topic in Practice Test 1. Use these sample essays as benchmarks to help you grade your own essay on the same topic. Does your essay sound more like the grade 5 essay or the grade 3 essay?

Sample Grade 5 Essay

It was a crisp weekend morning in early spring. The sun shone through the still chilly air and the crocus buds were pushing their way through the thawing earth. My teammates and I had just arrived at Dellville High's lacrosse field, where the final game of the season would be played. Tension hung heavy in the air: we were tied for first place in Girls' Division 3.

But no one felt tenser than me. Our team had never done as well as it was doing that season, and as captain of the team our success had earned me the admiration of my classmates. Everyone envied me and wanted to be my friend. Little did they know how much pressure I was under, how much I feared a fall from grace.

Dellville turned out to be a worthy opponent. With only five minutes left, we were tied 4-4. My chest ached from running and my legs were sore. Suddenly, one of my teammates passed the ball to me. Like a dog trained to respond unthinkingly to certain stimuli, I began charging down the field, and with my aching arms I flung the hard rubber sphere into the goalie's cage. Instead of the cheers I expected, there was nothing but silence. I looked around me and with horror realized I had scored a goal for the other team!

On the bus ride home, I sat alone. No one would talk to me. But the rejection by others did not wound nearly as much as my own overwhelming feeling that I had done this and that I had no one to blame but myself. This is why I agree with the statement, "The greatest griefs are those we cause ourselves." The grief one feels is compounded by an awful sense of guilt; knowing you could have prevented your unhappiness emphasizes it even more.

Grader's comments: This essay solidly fulfills the writing assignment. It is logically organized, uses vocabulary well, and mixes sentence structure well. The evidence provided clearly supports the writer's ideas. There are occasional flaws ("no one felt tenser than me," and "as captain of the team our success . . . "), but they do not detract from the overall effectiveness of the writing.

Sample Grade 3 Essay

Someone once said that "The greatest griefs are those we cause ourselves," but I for one do not agree. I think that if your greif results from some tragedy you did not cause, it can be even worse because you feel no sense of control over your life. My cousin dying of cancer when she was only 28 was this way. We did not cause her cancer, but we felt great greif. Can you say that our greif would of been greater if we had caused her to die?

Likewise, in The Scarlet Letter Hester Prynne is made to suffer and were an A on her chest because of having a baby out of wedlock. So she suffers, but Hawthorn makes it clear his heroin did not cause her own suffering. It is Puritannical society which is hypocritical and punishes Hester while letting the minister that's the father of her baby get off. So Hester does not cause her greif, it is the society she lived in who caused it. If they didn't have such a repressive attitude about sex outside of marriage, she wouldn't have suffered as much. On the other hand, you could say Hester caused her own suffering because she got involved with a minister, which she must have known was not such a good idea back in her day and age. But the minister is responsable too, so shouldn't he take some of the blame?

Grader's comments: This essay demonstrates limited competence. There are numerous errors in grammar, diction, and sentence structure that detract from its quality. Moreover, the essay's organization is inadequate. Although the evidence about the cousin supports the writer's argument, the evidence from *The Scarlet Letter* is confused. The writer makes conflicting statements about Hester Prynne's innocence or guilt, and seems unsure as to the overall point being made.

Sample Grade 1 Essay

I agree with the statement, "The greatest greifs are those we cause ourselves." If I do something to myself, it's much worse. Like the time my dog got run over because I didn't leave him tied up in the yard. It is true I didn't drive the car (it was Mrs. Savini from next door), but I could of prevented the acident so I felt really bad. Of course it depends on the situatian. When my grandfather died I had nothing to do with it but I still got sad from his deth. I guess I would of felt worse if I had made him die. So in general I agree but their may be excepitons to the rule. Trying to make up your mind about something like this is tough to do when you only have 20 minutes total for thinking about it and

Grader's comments: This essay is deficient. First, it's very poorly organized. Second, its ideas are inadequately developed. Finally, the many and serious errors in usage and syntax somewhat obscure the writer's intended meaning.

The Multiple-Choice Section

This section contains an answer key and explanations for the Multiple-Choice section in Practice Test 1. Use the scoring conversion table in the back of the book to see how you've done on this section. Pay careful attention to the explanations for the multiple-choice questions you got wrong.

Answer Key

1. C	11. A	21. D	31. E	41. A	51. A
2. C	12. B	22. A	32. B	42. D	52. C
3. D	13. A	23. A	33. E	43. C	53. C
4. C	14. E	24. B	34. E	44. E	54. D
5. A	15. C	25. E	35. A	45. C	55. E
6. E	16. A	26. C	36. B	46. B	56. D
7. B	17. B	27. B	37. A	47. B	57. D
8. A	18. C	28. E	38. B	48. A	58. D
9. E	19. D	29. D	39. B	49. C	59. C
10. C	20. D	30. D	40. D	50. E	60. D

Answers and Explanations

1. (C)—Note that *patients* is not the subject of this sentence: *bleeding* is (it's a gerund, the *-ing* form of a verb used as a noun). *Bleeding* is singular, so *were* should be changed to *was*.

2. (C)—The subject of the sentence is *establishment*, which is singular; so the main verb should be *has*, not *have*.

3. (D)—*Respectively* means "with respect to each in order." One might say, "Their names were John, Paul, and George, respectively." *Respectively* doesn't make any sense in this context. The word that's probably intended is *respectfully*.

4. (C)—Items in a list should always be in parallel grammatical form. *To advance* and *to seek* are infinitive verbs. But *to the kinds* is a noun preceded by a preposition. It should be changed to something like *to get the kinds*.

5. (A)—The word *which* should not be used to refer to people. In this sentence, it needs to be corrected to *who*.

6. (E)—There is no error in this sentence.

7. (B)—The subject of this sentence is the singular noun *effort*. The main verb should therefore be *results*, rather than the plural *result*.

8. (A)—*Every one* is singular. *Were closed* is plural: It should be corrected to *was closed*.

9. (E)—There is no error in this sentence.

10. (C)—The subject of the sentence is *memoirs*, which is plural. The main verb is *promises*, which is singular: It should be *promise*.

11. (A)—If the paper were *imaginary*, it wouldn't exist. The correct word is *imaginative*, an approximate synonym of *creative*.

12. (B)—The pronoun *which* should never be used to refer to people. *Which* should be changed to *who*.

13. (A)—*Raise* is a transitive verb: One thing *raises* another thing, but something that is getting higher on its own, with no specified cause, isn't described as *raising*. The correct word here is *rising*.

14. (E)—There is no error in this sentence.

15. (C)—The items linked by *not only* and *but also* should be in parallel form. *A competent barnacle scraper* is a noun phrase, but *capable of collecting interesting specimens of seashells* is an adjectival phrase. The second item should be changed to something like *a collector of* or *someone capable of collecting*.

16. (A)—*Where* should be used only to refer to a place, and a *round robin* is not a place. The phrase *is where* should be replaced with *is a tournament in which*.

17. (B)—*Him* should be replaced with *his*: They were dismayed at *his* act of retiring.

18. (C)—The subject of this sentence is *having* (*amount* and *persistence* are the objects of this participle). Since *having* is singular, *assure* should be changed to *assures*.

19. (D)—*Every* is singular: The plural pronoun *their* should be corrected to *his* or *her*.

20. (D)—*Imminent* means "near, close," which doesn't make sense in this context. The context of the sentence demands *eminent*, which means "famous, important."

21. (D)—The present perfect *has left* makes the sequence of events clearer than the present progressive *is leaving*. Note that *nor* in (C) is wrong.

22. (A)—The original sentence is best.

23. (A)—The original sentence is best.

24. (B)—*Since he gave up* is clearer and more concise than *on account of his giving up* or any of the other choices. Note also that *to help shape* must be paired with another infinitive.

25. (E)—In the original form of the sentence, the word *that* forms a dependent clause and leaves the sentence without a main verb. The main verb should be *believe*, which is plural because its subject is *commuters*.

26. (C)—The introductory clause has to describe the nearest noun, *the president*. This is not the case in the original sentence. (C) is preferable to (D) because *the discovery made by a scientific team* is clearer than *the developments of a scientific team*.

27. (B)—This sentence contains a comma splice: two independent clauses joined only by a comma. Choice (B) corrects the sentence by the adding the conjunction *although*.

28. (E)—*But* is used incorrectly in this sentence; the correct word to use here is *only*.

29. (D)—This sentence contains a great deal of information. Choice (D) is the most successful in conveying that information clearly and logically.

30. (D)—*Whomever* is the subject of the verb *wants*, so it should be in the subjective form, *whoever*. Choice (E) uses the right case, but the wrong number: *wants* is singular, but *those* is plural.

31. (E)—Things being compared should be in the same grammatical form; *developing* should be compared with *managing*. (E) is the simplest and clearest choice.

32. (B)—The original sentence and choice (C) use the passive voice unnecessarily. Choices (D) and (E) use the perfect tense incorrectly.

33. (E)—*Company* is singular, so it should be represented by the pronoun *it*. (E) is the clearest and most concise of the answer choices.

34. (E)—*Best* should be used only when comparing three or more things. *Better* is correct when comparing two things.

35. (A)—The original sentence is best. The past perfect tense is used correctly.

36. (B)—The original sentence illogically compares a variety of services with programs themselves, rather than with the number of programs, as in (B).

37. (A)—The original sentence is best. Choice (B) refers to *astrologers*—people—as *things*. Choice (C) sets up a confusing array of modifying phrases. Choice (D) uses the neuter plural pronoun *it* to refer to *astrologers*. Choice (E) uses the future progressive tense for no reason.

38. (B)—This sentence contains a comma splice: two independent clauses joined only by a comma. Also, there is no clear antecedent for *them*. (B) replaces the comma with a semicolon, and uses *he* to make it clear that the pronoun refers to the *politician*.

39. (B)—Within the context of the sentence, *them* has no clear antecedent. However, it is clear from the first sentence that *them* refers to liberal arts, so (B) is correct.

40. (D)—Since the second paragraph refutes the idea stated in the first paragraph, a sentence that sets up this contrast, as (D) does, best links the two paragraphs. (A), (B), and (E) elaborate on why liberal arts are irrelevant and therefore do not logically lead to the second paragraph, which debunks this notion. (C) comes out of nowhere: The passage concerns the value of studying liberal arts, not the writer's struggles with schoolwork.

41. (A)—Although there is nothing grammatically wrong with sentences 6 and 7, the essay flows better if they are combined into one sentence. (A) connects them in the most logical and straightforward manner. (B) and (D) illogically reverse the sequence of events. (C) is awkwardly phrased and unnecessarily changes the meaning of the sentence from an active idea to a passive one. In (E), the tense used is inconsistent with the rest of the paragraph.

42. (D)—The sentence contains a dangling modifier and must be recast so that it is clear that it is the writer who is *nervous*, her *palms sweating*. Only (D) and (E) correct this problem, and (E)'s tense shift is both inconsistent with the rest of the paragraph and unnecessarily wordy. Therefore (D) is correct.

43. (C)—Choice (C) provides a smooth and effective variation in sentence structure by transforming the second sentence into a clause modifying the first sentence. (A) incorrectly strings two claus-

es together with a comma. (B)'s use of *although* is illogical. (D) is unnecessarily wordy and contains an error in tense. (E) is awkwardly worded and is incorrect in the context of the paragraph because it changes the meaning of the original sentence.

44. (E)—In the second paragraph, the writer recounts a personal anecdote that refutes the first paragraph's claim that studying liberal arts is a waste of time. She includes many specific details and creates suspense as she tells the story (" . . . it was time for the tie-breaker question. The host pulled the card from the envelope."). She does not, however, list jobs that require knowledge of liberal arts, so (E) is correct.

45. (C)—In sentence 5, the shift to the passive voice makes it sound as if it was the supervisors whose bathroom visits were restricted. Only (C) fixes this error. In addition to the other choices' incorrect use of the passive voice, (B) is inconsistent in tense, (D) is unnecessarily wordy and needlessly substitutes *given permission* for *allowed*, and (E) splits an infinitive.

46. (B)—From the context, it is clear that the author means that the factories belong to the retail chain, but the use of the word *their* incorrectly conveys the idea that they belong to the consumers. Substituting *its* for *their* fixes this problem.

47. (B)—The sentence as written is not consistent: The tense shifts from the infinitive ("to meet") to the conditional ("would discuss . . . would announce"). Choice (B) makes the tenses consistent. (C) is grammatically correct but excessively wordy and awkwardly phrased. In (D), there is no antecedent for *where*; moreover, (D) is inconsistent in tense. (E) is even more inconsistent in tense and unnecessarily wordy.

48. (A)—In sentences 8 and 9, the retail chain representative presents arguments against the students' plan to boycott. Since sentence 9 is essentially a continuation of the idea expressed in sentence 8 (i.e., that the representative disagrees with the students), the best replacement is *Moreover*. All of the other choices provide a sense of contrast rather than continuation, and are therefore inappropriate in the context of the sentence.

49. (C)—As written, the sentence incorrectly connects two clauses with a comma and is inconsistent in tense; it also contains a misplaced modifier (*which* appears to refer to the chain when it should refer to the letter) and an unnecessary shift to the passive voice (*he was urged*). (C) fixes these errors. (B) is incorrect in context; the use of the past progressive (*were agreeing*) changes the meaning of the sentence. (D), too, changes the meaning: Consumers agreed to stop patronizing the store, not to write letters to the president. (E) likewise changes the original meaning and is repetitive and awkward.

50. (E)—Choice (E) works well as a concluding sentence because it provides a nice summary of the author's main point and ties the second and third paragraphs together with the reference to "a bunch of teenagers." (A) does not logically follow from the essay; it is never stated whether consumers were willing to pay more. (B) comes out of left field, and (C) and (D) are just wrong: The students *did* devise a plan of action (boycotting) and they *did* listen to the factory worker.

51. (A)—Since the word *closely* modifies *they*, not *come*, it should be in the adjectival form, *close*. The comparative form of *close* is *closer*.

52. (C)—The sentence forms the conditional mood incorrectly. Instead, it should read *would have to have made up . . . .*

53. (C)—The subject of *contain* is *food*, which is singular. So, the sentence should say *contains*.

54. (D)—To say both *also* and *as well* is redundant. Since *as well* is underlined, it should be deleted.

55. (E)—With *found* in the past tense, *had left* is correct, indicating that the leaving took place before the finding.

56. (D)—*Without hardly* is a double negative. It should be *with hardly*.

57. (D)—The United States can't be *stronger than any country in the world*, because it's one of the countries in the world, and it can't be *stronger* than itself. *Any country* should be changed to *any other country*.

58. (D)—The sentence as it stands has no main verb. *Standing* should be changed to *stood*.

59. (C)—This sentence uses the *not only . . . but also* formula. Of the items linked by the formula, the one closer to the verb is singular. Therefore, *eat* should be changed to *eats*.

60. (D)—The items in a list should all be in the same grammatical form. Since the other items in the list in this sentence are expressed as nouns, the final item should be simply *other foods*.

ANSWER SHEET
FOR PRACTICE TEST 2

1 (A) (B) (C) (D) (E)	16 (A) (B) (C) (D) (E)	31 (A) (B) (C) (D) (E)	46 (A) (B) (C) (D) (E)
2 (A) (B) (C) (D) (E)	17 (A) (B) (C) (D) (E)	32 (A) (B) (C) (D) (E)	47 (A) (B) (C) (D) (E)
3 (A) (B) (C) (D) (E)	18 (A) (B) (C) (D) (E)	33 (A) (B) (C) (D) (E)	48 (A) (B) (C) (D) (E)
4 (A) (B) (C) (D) (E)	19 (A) (B) (C) (D) (E)	34 (A) (B) (C) (D) (E)	49 (A) (B) (C) (D) (E)
5 (A) (B) (C) (D) (E)	20 (A) (B) (C) (D) (E)	35 (A) (B) (C) (D) (E)	50 (A) (B) (C) (D) (E)
6 (A) (B) (C) (D) (E)	21 (A) (B) (C) (D) (E)	36 (A) (B) (C) (D) (E)	51 (A) (B) (C) (D) (E)
7 (A) (B) (C) (D) (E)	22 (A) (B) (C) (D) (E)	37 (A) (B) (C) (D) (E)	52 (A) (B) (C) (D) (E)
8 (A) (B) (C) (D) (E)	23 (A) (B) (C) (D) (E)	38 (A) (B) (C) (D) (E)	53 (A) (B) (C) (D) (E)
9 (A) (B) (C) (D) (E)	24 (A) (B) (C) (D) (E)	39 (A) (B) (C) (D) (E)	54 (A) (B) (C) (D) (E)
10 (A) (B) (C) (D) (E)	25 (A) (B) (C) (D) (E)	40 (A) (B) (C) (D) (E)	55 (A) (B) (C) (D) (E)
11 (A) (B) (C) (D) (E)	26 (A) (B) (C) (D) (E)	41 (A) (B) (C) (D) (E)	56 (A) (B) (C) (D) (E)
12 (A) (B) (C) (D) (E)	27 (A) (B) (C) (D) (E)	42 (A) (B) (C) (D) (E)	57 (A) (B) (C) (D) (E)
13 (A) (B) (C) (D) (E)	28 (A) (B) (C) (D) (E)	43 (A) (B) (C) (D) (E)	58 (A) (B) (C) (D) (E)
14 (A) (B) (C) (D) (E)	29 (A) (B) (C) (D) (E)	44 (A) (B) (C) (D) (E)	59 (A) (B) (C) (D) (E)
15 (A) (B) (C) (D) (E)	30 (A) (B) (C) (D) (E)	45 (A) (B) (C) (D) (E)	60 (A) (B) (C) (D) (E)

right

wrong

Use the answer key following the test to count up the number of questions you got right and the number you got wrong. (Remember not to count omitted questions as wrong.) The "Compute Your Score" section at the back of the book will show you how to find your score.

ANSWER SHEET
FOR PRACTICE TEST 2

Part A (ESSAY). Begin your composition on this side. If you need more space, you may continue on the reverse side.

_____

_____

_____

_____

_____

_____

_____

_____

_____

_____

_____

_____

_____

_____

_____

_____

_____

_____

_____

_____

_____

ANSWER SHEET
FOR PRACTICE TEST 2

Continuation of Part A (ESSAY) from reverse side. Write below if you need more space.

_____

_____

_____

_____

_____

_____

_____

_____

_____

_____

_____

_____

_____

_____

_____

_____

_____

_____

PART A
Time—20 Minutes (1 Question)

You have 20 minutes to write an essay on the following topic. DO NOT WRITE AN ESSAY ON ANY OTHER TOPIC. AN ESSAY ON A DIFFERENT TOPIC IS UNACCEPTABLE.

This essay provides you with an opportunity to demonstrate how well you write. Therefore, you should express your ideas clearly and effectively. How much you write is much less important than how well you write; but to express your thoughts on the topic adequately you may want to write more than a single paragraph. Your essay should be specific.

Your essay must be written in the lines provided on your answer sheet. No other paper will be given to you. There is enough space to write your essay on the answer sheet if you write on every line, avoid wide margins, and keep your handwriting to a reasonable size.

Consider the following statement and assignment. Then write an essay as directed.

> **"My life has been filled with good days, bad days, and days I no longer can remember, but one day I will never forget is _____."**

Assignment: Write an essay that completes the statement above. Explain the reasons behind your choice.

WHEN THE PROCTOR ANNOUNCES THAT 20 MINUTES HAVE PASSED, YOU MUST STOP WRITING AND GO ON TO PART B OF THE TEST. IF YOU FINISH YOUR ESSAY BEFORE 20 MINUTES PASS, YOU MAY GO ON TO PART B.

YOU MAY MAKE NOTES ON THIS PAGE AND THE FOLLOWING ONE, BUT YOU MUST WRITE YOUR ESSAY ON THE ANSWER SHEET.

TURN TO THE NEXT PAGE.

You may use this page to outline your essay or make other notes as you plan your essay. Don't write your essay here, though. Your essay must be written on the lined pages of the answer sheet at the beginning of this answer section.

TURN TO THE NEXT PAGE.

PART B
Time—40 Minutes (60 Questions)

For each of the following questions, choose the best answer from the given choices and darken the corresponding oval on the answer sheet.

Directions: The following sentences contain problems in grammar, usage, diction (choice of words), and idiom.

Some of the sentences are correct.

None of the sentences contains more than one error.

The error, if there is one in the sentence, is underlined and lettered. Parts of the sentence that are not underlined are correct and cannot be changed. In selecting answers, follow the requirements of standard written English.

If there is an error, choose the <u>one underlined part</u> that must be changed to make the sentence correct and fill in the corresponding oval on your answer grid.

If there is no error, fill in oval E.

SAMPLE QUESTION	SAMPLE ANSWER

<u>Even though</u> he <u>had to</u> supervise a large
    A   B

staff, his salary <u>was no greater</u> than <u>a clerk</u>.
                C   D

<u>No error</u>
 E

---

1. <u>Virtually</u> all of the members <u>who</u> attended the
    A   B
   meeting <u>agreed to</u> the president's viewpoint on
            C
   <u>the issue</u> of budgetary restraints. <u>No error</u>
     D   E

2. <u>Fewer</u> U.S. citizens are visiting
    A
   Europe <u>as</u> American currency dwindles in
        B
   exchange value and prices <u>raise</u> <u>in</u> several
                       C D
   European countries. <u>No error</u>
                E

3. The first public school in North America,

   Boston Latin School, <u>begun teaching</u> <u>its</u>
                   A   B
   classical curriculum in 1635, one year <u>before</u>
                               C
   Harvard University <u>was founded</u>. <u>No error</u>
                D   E

4. <u>Of all</u> the disasters that occurred during the
    A
   movie's production, the death of the two stars

   <u>who</u> performed their own stunts <u>were</u> surely
    B   C
   <u>the worst</u>. <u>No error</u>
    D   E

TURN TO THE NEXT PAGE.

5. There is no sense <u>in continuing</u> the research,
   A
   now that the assumptions <u>on which</u> it
   B
   <u>was based</u> <u>had been</u> disproved. <u>No error</u>
   C   D   E

6. The councilwoman could not understand how

   the mayor <u>could declare</u> that the city
   A
   <u>is thriving</u> <u>when</u> the number of firms declaring
   B   C
   bankruptcy <u>increase</u> every month. <u>No error</u>
   D   E

7. Arthur Rubinstein was long ranked <u>among</u> the
   A
   world's finest pianists, <u>although</u> he was some-
   B
   times known <u>as playing</u> several wrong notes
   C
   <u>in a single</u> performance. <u>No error</u>
   D   E

8. The new office complex is beautiful, but <u>fully</u>
   A
   two hundred longtime residents <u>were forced</u>
   B
   to move when <u>they</u> <u>tore down</u> the old
   C   D
   apartment buildings. <u>No error</u>
   E

9. Neither the singers <u>on stage</u> <u>or</u> the announcer
   A   B
   in the wings <u>could be heard</u> <u>over</u> the noise of
   C   D
   the crowd. <u>No error</u>
   E

10. The delegates <u>among which</u> the candidates
    A
    circulated <u>became</u> <u>gradually less</u> receptive and
    B   C
    more determined <u>to elicit</u> candid responses.
    D
    <u>No error</u>
    E

11. None of this injury <u>to life</u> and damage to prop-
    A
    erty <u>wouldn't have</u> happened if the amateur
    B
    pilot <u>had only</u> heeded the weather forecasts
    C
    and <u>stayed</u> on the ground. <u>No error</u>
    D   E

12. The doctor recommended that young athletes

    <u>with a history</u> of severe asthma take <u>particular</u>
    A   B   C
    care <u>not to exercise</u> alone. <u>No error</u>
    D   E

13. The piano, although <u>considerably less</u> capable
    A
    of expressive nuance <u>than many other</u> musical
    B
    instruments, <u>are</u> <u>marvelously dramatic.</u>
    C   D
    <u>No error</u>
    E

14. <u>Of</u> the respondents surveyed, <u>more</u> European
    A   B
    travelers preferred taking the train <u>to flying,</u>
    C
    <u>even</u> for long trips. <u>No error</u>
    D   E

TURN TO THE NEXT PAGE.

15. By the time World War I <u>broke out</u>, there <u>was</u>
                          A   B
    <u>scarcely any</u> region of the world that <u>had not</u>
        C   D
    been colonized by the Western powers.

    <u>No error</u>
        E

16. <u>When in Rome</u>, we <u>should do</u> <u>as the Romans</u>
         A   B   C
    do, but in English-speaking countries, <u>they call</u>
                                              D
    the Italian city Livorno "Leghorn." <u>No error</u>
                                             E

17. <u>Before</u> Ms. Winchester <u>spoke to</u> the assembled
        A   B
    crowd, she quietly called her bodyguards'

    attention <u>to</u> a man who <u>seemed to be carrying</u>
              C   D
    a weapon. <u>No error</u>
                  E

18. The document, written by the local burghers in

    1757, <u>shows</u> <u>little</u> concern <u>in</u> law's
              A   B   C
    <u>effects on</u> their constituents. <u>No error</u>
        D   E

19. <u>Despite</u> the Preservation Society's efforts
        A
    <u>at saving</u> the old mill, the <u>overwhelming</u>
        B   C
    majority of city council members voted

    <u>to raze</u> it. <u>No error</u>
        D   E

20. A Midwesterner <u>who</u> relocates to the urban
                      A
    northeast <u>may find</u> his new colleagues unso-
                  B
    ciable <u>if they</u> pass him in the workplace
               C
    <u>without hardly</u> a word. <u>No error</u>
        D   E

TURN TO THE NEXT PAGE.

For each of the following questions, choose the best answer from the given choices and darken the corresponding oval on the answer sheet.

Directions: The following sentences test accuracy and effectiveness of expression. In selecting answers, follow the rules of standard written English; in other words, consider grammar, choice of words, sentence construction, and punctuation.

In each of the following sentences, a portion or all of the sentence is underlined. Under each sentence you will find five ways of phrasing the underlined portion. Choice A repeats the original underlined portion; the other four choices provide alternative phrasings.

Select the choice that best expresses the meaning of the original sentence. If the original sentence is better than any of the alternative phrasings, choose A; otherwise select one of the alternatives. Your selection should construct the most effective sentence—clear and precise with no awkwardness or ambiguity.

SAMPLE QUESTION

Wanting to reward her assistant for loyalty,
<u>Sheila gave a bonus to him as large as his paycheck.</u>

(A) Sheila gave a bonus to him as large as his paycheck
(B) given to him by Sheila was a bonus as large as his paycheck
(C) he was given a bonus as large as his paycheck by Sheila
(D) Sheila gave him a bonus as large as his paycheck
(E) Sheila gave him a paycheck to him as large as his bonus

SAMPLE ANSWER

---

21. Mary Cassatt, an American painter strongly influenced by French <u>impressionism, she also responded</u> to Japanese paintings exhibited in Paris in the 1890s.

    (A) impressionism, she also responded
    (B) impressionism, also responded
    (C) impressionism, also responding
    (D) impressionism, nevertheless, she responded
    (E) impressionism before responding

22. The choreographer Katherine Dunham <u>having trained as an anthropologist, she studied</u> dance in Jamaica, Haiti, and Senegal and developed a distinctive dance method.

    (A) having trained as an anthropologist, she studied
    (B) was also a trained anthropologist, having studied
    (C) was also a trained anthropologist and a student of
    (D) was also a trained anthropologist who studied
    (E) training as an anthropologist, she studied

TURN TO THE NEXT PAGE.

23. The few surviving writings of Greek philosophers before Plato <u>are not only brief and obscure, but also figurative</u> at times.

   (A) are not only brief and obscure, but also figurative
   (B) are not only brief and obscure, they can be figurative too,
   (C) not only are brief and obscure, but also figurative
   (D) while not only brief and obscure, they also are figurative
   (E) being not only brief and obscure, are also figurative

24. <u>Because its glazed finish resembles a seashell's surface is why porcelain china derives its name from the French word for the cowrie shell.</u>

   (A) Because its glazed finish resembles a seashell's surface is why porcelain china derives its name from the French word for the cowrie shell.
   (B) Its glazed finish resembling a seashell's surface, therefore, porcelain china derives its name from the French word for the cowrie shell.
   (C) Resembling a seashell's surface in its glazed finish, that is why porcelain china derives its name from the French word for the cowrie shell.
   (D) The French word for the cowrie shell gives its name to porcelain china because, with its glazed finish, its resemblance to a seashell's surface.
   (E) Because its glazed finish resembles a seashell's surface, porcelain china derives its name from the French word for the cowrie shell.

25. <u>In 1891, the Chace Copyright Act began protecting British authors, until then</u> American publishers could reprint British books without paying their writers.

   (A) In 1891, the Chace Copyright Act began protecting British authors, until then
   (B) The Chace Copyright Act began, in 1891, protecting British authors, whom, until then
   (C) Although the Chace Copyright Act began to protect British authors in 1891, until which time
   (D) Before 1891, when the Chace Copyright Act began protecting British authors,
   (E) Finally, the Chace Copyright Act began protecting British authors in 1891, however, until then

26. Theorists of extraterrestrial intelligence depend on astronomical observations, chemical research, <u>and they draw inferences about non-human biology</u>.

   (A) and they draw inferences about nonhuman biology
   (B) while they infer biologically about nonhuman life
   (C) and biologically infer about nonhuman life
   (D) as well as drawing inferences biologically about nonhuman life
   (E) and biological inferences about nonhuman life

TURN TO THE NEXT PAGE.

27. Even after becoming blind, <u>the poet John Milton's daughters took dictation of his epic poem *Paradise Lost*</u>.

    (A) the poet John Milton's daughters took dictation of his epic poem *Paradise Lost*
    (B) the poet John Milton's daughters taking dictation, his epic poem *Paradise Lost* was written
    (C) the epic poem *Paradise Lost* was dictated by the poet John Milton to his daughters
    (D) the epic poem *Paradise Lost* was dictated to his daughters by the poet John Milton
    (E) the poet John Milton dictated his epic poem *Paradise Lost* to his daughters

28. Initiated in 1975, <u>sandhill cranes must unwittingly cooperate in the conservationists' project to raise</u> endangered whooping crane chicks.

    (A) sandhill cranes must unwittingly cooperate in the conservationists' project to raise
    (B) sandhill cranes' unwitting cooperation is required in the conservationists' project to raise
    (C) the conservationists require that sandhill cranes unwittingly cooperate in their project of raising
    (D) the conservationists require sandhill cranes to cooperate unwittingly in their project to raise
    (E) the conservationists' project requires the unwitting cooperation of sandhill cranes in raising

29. <u>The journalist lived and conversed with the guerrilla rebels and he</u> was finally accepted as an informed interpreter of their cause.

    (A) The journalist lived and conversed with the guerrilla rebels and he
    (B) The journalist living and conversing with the guerrilla rebels, and he
    (C) The journalist, who lived and conversed with the guerrilla rebels,
    (D) The journalist's having lived and conversed with the guerrilla rebels,
    (E) While living and conversing with the guerrilla rebels, the journalist

30. Modern dance and classical ballet help strengthen concentration, tone muscles, <u>and for creating a sense of poise</u>.

    (A) and for creating a sense of poise
    (B) thereby creating a sense of poise
    (C) and the creation of a sense of poise
    (D) and create a sense of poise
    (E) so that a sense of poise is created

31. Historians of literacy encounter a fundamental <u>obstacle, no one can know for certain</u> how many people could read in earlier centuries.

    (A) obstacle, no one can know for certain
    (B) obstacle; no one can know for certain
    (C) obstacle; no one being able to know for certain
    (D) obstacle; none of whom can know with certainty
    (E) obstacle and no one can know for certain

TURN TO THE NEXT PAGE.

32. With his plays, George Bernard Shaw tested the limits of British censorship; the purpose being to make audiences aware of social inequities.
    (A) censorship; the purpose being to
    (B) censorship and the purpose was to
    (C) censorship, with the purpose to
    (D) censorship; so that he could
    (E censorship to

33. Beethoven bridged two musical eras, in that his earlier works are essentially Classical; his later ones, Romantic.

    (A) his earlier works are essentially Classical; his later ones, Romantic
    (B) his earlier works are essentially Classical, nevertheless, his later ones are Romantic
    (C) his earlier works being essentially Classical; his later are Romantic
    (D) whereas essentially, his earlier works are Classical, his later ones would be Romantic
    (E) despite his earlier works' being essentially Classical; his later are more Romantic

34. The method of printing fabric called *batik* originated in Southeast Asia; wax is applied to patterned areas, then boiled off after dyeing.
    (A) then boiled off after dyeing
    (B) then, after dyeing, it is boiled off
    (C) later it is boiled off after dyeing
    (D) after which, dyers boil it off
    (E) but then it is boiled off after dyeing

35. In the grip of intense anxiety, tears swept over the actress who actually seemed to live her role.

    (A) tears swept over the actress who
    (B) tears provoked the actress who
    (C) the actress was swept by tears as she
    (D) the actress' tears fell as she
    (E) the actress was crying tears who

36. Delighted by the positive response to his address, the candidate instructed his speechwriter to only concentrate on similar themes for the remainder of the campaign.

    (A) the candidate instructed his speechwriter to only concentrate on similar themes
    (B) the candidate gave instructions to his speechwriter to concentrate on similar themes only
    (C) the candidate's speechwriter was instructed to concentrate only on similar themes
    (D) the candidate told the speechwriter to only concentrate on similar themes
    (E) the candidate instructed his speechwriter to concentrate only on similar themes

37. None of the hysterical bystanders was clear-sighted enough to remain calm or offer assistance to the victim.

    (A) was clear-sighted enough to remain calm or offer assistance
    (B) were clear-sighted enough to remain calm or offer assistance
    (C) were clear-sighted enough to remain calm or offering assistance
    (D) was clear-sighted enough to have remained calm or offer assistance
    (E) was clear-sighted enough to be remaining calm or offering assistance

38. Bearing an uncanny resemblance to the famous man was no handicap for the ambitious entertainer.

    (A) Bearing an uncanny resemblance to the famous man
    (B) His uncanny resemblance to the famous man
    (C) Resembling uncannily the famous man
    (D) Having an uncanny resemblance upon the famous man
    (E) It was found by him that bearing an uncanny resemblance to the famous man

---

TURN TO THE NEXT PAGE.

Directions: The following passages are first drafts of student essays. Some portions of the essays have to be rewritten.

Read the essays and answer the questions that follow them. Some of the questions concern particular sentences or fragments of sentences and require you to make choices about sentence structure, word choice, and usage. Other questions pertain to the entire essay or pieces of the essay and require you to think about organization, development, and appropriateness of language. Pick the answer that most effectively conveys the meaning and follows the rules of standard written English. Once you have chosen an answer, fill in the corresponding oval on your answer sheet.

Questions 39–44 are based on the following essay, which was written in response to an assignment to write a letter to the editor of a local newspaper.

(1) I agree with the school board's recent decision to require high school students to complete a community service requirement before graduating. (2) As a student who has both worked and volunteered, my volunteer experience has truly enriched me as a person. (3) When I worked at a hamburger joint all I was caring about was the money. (4) Tutoring disadvantaged children taught me to appreciate how much I have.

(5) Volunteering teaches you different lessons than working for pay does. (6) Your paycheck is not your motivation but something higher. (7) In today's consumer-oriented society, it is especially important that students learn to value something other than material things. (8) Taking care of elderly patients at a hospital can teach them respect for age. (9) Getting together with a non-profit group to clean up abandoned neighborhoods can teach them the importance of teamwork and of doing good for others. (10) There is simply no way they can get so many good lessons out of the types of paying jobs available to them. (11) This is why I support the school board's decision. (12) Furthermore, it is feasible for low-income students, despite what critics have said.

39. Which of the following is the best way to revise the underlined portion of sentence 2 (reproduced below)?

As a student who has both worked and volunteered, my volunteer experience has truly enriched me as a person.

(A) my experience as a volunteer has been the thing that has truly enriched me as a person

(B) I have truly been enriched by my volunteer experience

(C) it is by volunteering that I have truly become an enriched person

(D) I will have truly been enriched by my volunteer experience

(E) that which has truly enriched me as a person is my volunteer experience

TURN TO THE NEXT PAGE.

40. In context, which is the best way to revise and combine the underlined portions of sentences 3 and 4 (reproduced below)?

    When I worked at a hamburger joint all I was caring about was the money. Tutoring disadvantaged children taught me to appreciate how much I have.

    (A) Working at a hamburger joint, it was only the money that mattered to me, and tutoring disadvantaged children
    (B) While working at a hamburger joint all I was caring about was the money, until tutoring disadvantaged children
    (C) Although the money was the only thing that mattered to me while working at a hamburger joint, when I tutored disadvantaged children
    (D) Despite working at the hamburger joint, where all I was caring about was the money, by contrast when I was tutoring disadvantaged children
    (E) When I worked at a hamburger joint all I cared about was the money, but tutoring disadvantaged children

41. In context, which version of sentence 6 (reproduced below) is the clearest?

    Your paycheck is not your motivation but something higher.

    (A) (As it is now)
    (B) Your paycheck is not what motivates you but it is something higher.
    (C) You are motivated not by your paycheck but by something higher.
    (D) Your paycheck is not what you are being motivated by but something higher.
    (E) Not your paycheck, something higher, is your motivation.

42. Which of the following best replaces the word "*they*" in sentence 10?

    (A) students
    (B) paying jobs
    (C) material things
    (D) others
    (E) neighborhoods

43. Of the following, the most accurate criticism of sentence 11 is that it

    (A) fails to mention the writer's own views
    (B) is grammatically incorrect
    (C) ignores drawbacks to the requirement
    (D) is redundant, reiterating an idea already expressed
    (E) does not follow from the rest of the essay

44. The author could best improve sentence 12 by

    (A) explaining how the requirement is feasible for low-income students
    (B) including a definition of "low income"
    (C) outlining other criticisms of the proposal
    (D) providing examples of volunteer opportunities
    (E) acknowledging the opinions of high school students

TURN TO THE NEXT PAGE.

Questions 45–50 are based on the following essay.

(1) I used to be sure that I would never really win anything great whenever I entered a piano competition: that always happened to other people. (2) Maybe I'd get a plaque. (3) I wouldn't win anything that would change my life.

(4) I'm not your average teenager. (5) My friends spend their weekends playing sports. (6) I play the piano. (7) One day my music teacher told me about a piano competition with the first prize of a free trip to Europe! (8) I'm always happy to perform in public, whether it's in a competition or just for fun. (9) Anyway, I decided to apply for a spot in the competition.

(10) I pretty much forgot about the whole thing. (11) Then the notice from the music judges came to my house a few weeks later telling me when the competition would be held. (12) I was a little nervous. (13) But instead of getting scared and rejecting the whole idea, I just started practicing. (14) After about a month, the day of the recital competition came. (15) I played really well, but I assumed I'd never hear from the recital committee again. (16) That is, until just a few days after the event, when I got a call from one of the judges. (17) She began by saying "I have some good news for you . . . . " (18) I had actually won something, an all-expenses paid trip to Europe.

45. Which of the following is the best edit of the underlined portions of sentences 2 and 3 (reproduced below) so that the two are combined into one sentence?

Maybe I'd get <u>a plaque. I wouldn't win</u> anything that would change my life.

(A) a plaque, so I do win
(B) a plaque, while there was no winning
(C) a plaque, but I wouldn't win
(D) a plaque, but wouldn't be winning
(E) a plaque, and I couldn't win

46. Which sentence listed below, if placed after sentence 3, would best tie in the first paragraph with the rest of the essay?

(A) After all, the competitions were usually too difficult for me.
(B) However, something happened to me recently that made me reconsider my pessimistic attitude.
(C) I never really wanted to take part in piano competitions anyway, since the pressure was too great.
(D) Sometimes I'd take part in these recitals and win, but the prizes were never very impressive.
(E) My parents encouraged me to try out for competitions with better prizes.

TURN TO THE NEXT PAGE.

47. Which is the best way to combine sentences 5 and 6 (reproduced below) into one sentence?

    My friends spend their weekends playing sports. I play the piano.

    (A) Unlike my friends, who spend their weekends playing sports, I play the piano.
    (B) Although my friends spend their weekends playing sports, I play the piano.
    (C) My friends spend their weekends playing sports and I play the piano.
    (D) When my friends spend their weekends playing sports, I play the piano.
    (E) My friends are spending their weekends playing sports and I am playing the piano.

48. Which of the following versions of sentence 7 (reproduced below) is clearest?

    One day my music teacher told me about a piano competition with the first prize of a free trip to Europe!

    (A) My music teacher was telling me about a piano competition that had featured a free trip to Europe as its first prize!
    (B) My music teacher one day told me about a piano competition having a first prize of a free trip to Europe!
    (C) One day my music teacher is telling me about a piano competition with the first prize being a free trip to Europe!
    (D) One day my music teacher told me about a piano competition that was having as its first prize a free trip to Europe!
    (E) One day my music teacher told me about a piano competition featuring a free trip to Europe as its first prize!

49. Which of the following, in light of the information in the essay, is a more appropriate replacement for "*Anyway,*" beginning sentence 9 (reproduced below)?

    Anyway, I decided to apply for a spot in the competition.

    (A) Finally,
    (B) That's why
    (C) Eventually,
    (D) Despite this,
    (E) Apparently,

50. Which is the best version of the underlined portions of sentences 16 and 17 (reproduced below)?

    That is, until just a few days after the event, when I got a call from one of the judges. She began by saying "I have some good news for you . . . ."

    (A) (As it is now)
    (B) That is, until just a few days after the event, having been called by one of the judges, who began by saying
    (C) Until, that is, just a few days after the event, being called by one of the judges. She began by saying
    (D) That is, until just a few days after the event, being called from one of the judges. She began by saying
    (E) That is, when I got a call from one of the judges, who began by saying

TURN TO THE NEXT PAGE.

For each of the following questions, choose the best answer from the given choices and darken the corresponding oval on the answer sheet.

Directions: The following sentences contain problems in grammar, usage, diction (choice of words), and idiom.

Some of the sentences are correct.

None of the sentences contains more than one error.

The error, if there is one in the sentence, is underlined and lettered. Parts of the sentence that are not underlined are correct and cannot be changed. In selecting answers, follow the requirements of standard written English.

If there is an error, choose the <u>one underlined part</u> that must be changed to make the sentence correct and fill in the corresponding oval on your answer grid.

If there is no error, fill in oval E.

SAMPLE QUESTION

<u>Even though</u> he <u>had to</u> supervise a large
     A   B

staff, his salary <u>was no greater</u> than <u>a clerk</u>.
              C   D

<u>No error</u>
  E

SAMPLE ANSWER

Ⓐ Ⓑ Ⓒ ● Ⓔ

---

51. <u>Fewer buildings</u> with granite facades are
      A

    <u>being erected</u> as skilled stonecarvers die out
       B

    and <u>as</u> the cost of granite <u>will soar</u>. <u>No error</u>
        C   D   E

52. We <u>expect</u> this election <u>to be hotly contested</u>,
      A   B

    <u>since already</u> both the incumbent and her chal-
      C

    lenger <u>have complained</u> of negative campaign-
          D

    ing. <u>No error</u>
       E

53. However strong the desires for freedom and

    independence, there <u>are</u> <u>invariably</u> a conflict-
             A   B

    ing urge <u>towards</u> security, <u>as well as</u> an emo-
          C   D

    tional need for stability. <u>No error</u>
               E

54. Hiking along mountain trails <u>is</u> a less expen-
                     A

    sive but <u>considerably</u> <u>more demanding</u>
          B   C

    vacation activity than <u>to cruise</u> in the Bahamas.
                  D

    <u>No error</u>
      E

TURN TO THE NEXT PAGE.

55. <u>Among</u> divergent schools of psychology, dif-
    A
ferences of opinion <u>about</u> human motivation
               B
<u>have led</u> to <u>widely different</u> methods of treat-
 C   D
ment and research. <u>No error</u>
             E

56. Even though <u>their</u> commissions <u>are paid</u> by the
          A   B
musicians, the <u>typical</u> booking agent repre-
         C
sents the interests <u>of</u> the nightclub owners and
           D
managers. <u>No error</u>
      E

57. Even students <u>who know</u> about the grant
        A
rarely apply for it, because <u>you</u> hate <u>to fill out</u>
            B   C
<u>so many</u> forms. <u>No error</u>
 D   E

58. The Haitian religious cult of voodoo combines

<u>elements of</u> Roman Catholic ritual <u>beside</u> reli-
  A   B
gious and magical practices <u>that</u> <u>originated in</u>
             C   D
the African nation of Dahomey. <u>No error</u>
                 E

59. Daniel Defoe wrote successful fictional mem-

oirs <u>like</u> *Robinson Crusoe* in the early 1700s, but
   A
Samuel Richardson <u>is judged</u> by some
          B
<u>to introduce</u> the modern novel twenty years
  C
later. <u>No error</u>
 D   E

60. Not the cotton gin <u>that made</u> him famous, but
             A
<u>his</u> <u>concept of</u> interchangeable machine parts
 B   C
<u>were</u> Eli Whitney's greatest contribution to
 D
U.S. industry. <u>No error</u>
        E

STOP!
END OF TEST. DO NOT TURN THE PAGE UNTIL YOU ARE READY TO CHECK YOUR ANSWERS.

PRACTICE TEST 2 ANSWERS AND EXPLANATIONS

The Essay Section

This section contains sample essays for the essay topic in Practice Test 2. Use these sample essays as benchmarks to help you grade your own essay on the same topic. Does your essay sound more like the grade 6 essay or the grade 4 essay?

Sample Grade 6 Essay

People often complain that our generation is politically apathetic. Just 25 years ago, it was common for students to join in strikes and antiwar protests, but nowadays, the stereotype goes, young people are more likely to be found watching MTV or shopping at the mall. I certainly was no different. Appallingly ignorant of current events, I never read a paper or watched the news, but I knew all about the personal lives of popular TV and movie stars. Then something happened to change my outlook forever.

In my social studies class, we had an assignment to interview an older person about the changes he or she had witnessed in his or her lifetime. I decided to interview my neighbor, Mrs. Fletcher. Since she had never spoken to me much before, I figured she would have little to say and I could complete the assignment quickly. Instead she started telling me all about life in our town before the civil rights movement. I was astonished to learn that in the 1950s, blacks went to separate schools, rode at the backs of buses, and were prevented from living in white neighborhoods. As Mrs. Fletcher talked about how she and other African Americans helped break the color barrier by insisting on being served at white-only lunch counters, I became filled with shame at my own ignorance. How could I have been so unaware?

From that moment onward, politics and history became my passions. In school we had been taught that there was no society freer than the United States, but that was only part of the story. By reading about the political struggles of minorities, women, blue-collar workers, and others, I learned that freedom is not something you're given, it's something you have to fight for. And once you win it, you have to make sure no one tries to take it away again. This is why I can say that my life has been filled with good days, bad days, and days I no longer remember, but one day I will never forget is the day I became politically aware.

Grader's comments: This essay is outstanding. Its ideas are well developed, well organized, and supported by appropriate evidence. Furthermore, the writing flows nicely as a result of the varied sentence structure and vocabulary.

Sample Grade 4 Essay

My life has been filled with good days, bad days, and days I no longer remember but one day I will never forget is the day my father got laid off from work. I was about 12 at the time and I selfishly wanted a new bike. When I got home from school, my father was already home. This surprised me for a minute but I plunged on: "Daddy, can I have a new bike? All the other kids have ten-speed mountain bikes and I don't even have a three-speed. Please Daddy?" He looked down at me and I saw there were tears in his eyes. "I'm sorry but we can't afford it. I was just laid off." I didn't understand what that meant yet but over the next few months I would learn. It meant school shopping at thrift shops instead of department stores. It meant no steak, only chicken or spaghetti. It meant no eating out on weekends. And no new bike.

But the good thing was it taught me to be more self reliant. My parents couldn't afford to give me my allowence any more so I got a paper route. This taught me the disipline of getting up early, getting a job done, plus saving money and not just spending it *all at once. I guess you could say every cloud has a silver lining. My dad got laid off and was*

out of work for several months and then had to take a much lower paying one. But the good

part was becoming more independant. One thing for sure: I'll never forget that day.

Grader's comments: This essay demonstrates adequate competence. Although it displays some grammatical errors and some lapses in quality, the essay's overall organization and development are clear, and its ideas are supported with appropriate evidence.

Sample Grade 2 Essay

My life has been filled with alot of good days. For instance, the day I passed my

math test was a good day. My life has also been filled with many bad days. Like, the day

when I was a kid and I fell down and broke my arm. That was certainly a day you could

classify as "bad". Then there are the days I don't remember, which covers most of them

because how often is it that something truely memorible happens in a day? Most days

you just get up, go to school, come home, do chores or homework, eat dinner, watch a

little TV and go to bed so you can get up and do it all over again. But one day I'll never,

ever, ever forget is the day I met my best friend Jill. She lived down the street from me

but we went to differant schools so we didn't see much of each other. Anyway it was

summer vacation so we both happened to be around. I was going to the local swimming

pool and my mother said why don't we invite Jill from down the street. So I did. We had

such a good time that day, standing on our hands on the bottom of the pool, seeing

who could hold their breathe the longest, jumping off the high diving board, etc. We made

so much noise the life guard had to tell us to be quiet! I never liked her much, she was

always so stuck up. We spent the whole day together. Then I asked my mother if Jill

could come over for dinner and she said "YES". She even spent the night! I'd never had

a slumber party before. From then on we were inseperable. So that was really I day I

won't ever forget, as long as I live I'll remember it.

Grader's comments: This essay is flawed. It's poorly organized, tends to ramble, is repetitive, and strays from the assigned topic. Development is thin at best and ideas are not especially well supported. Errors in grammar, diction, and sentence structure are very numerous.

The Multiple-Choice Section

This section contains an answer key and explanations for the Multiple-Choice section in Practice Test 2. Use the scoring conversion table in the back of the book to see how you've done on this section. Pay careful attention to the explanations for the multiple-choice questions you got wrong.

1. C	11. B	21. B	31. B	41. C	51. D
2. C	12. A	22. D	32. E	42. A	52. E
3. A	13. C	23. A	33. A	43. D	53. A
4. C	14. E	24. E	34. A	44. A	54. D
5. D	15. E	25. D	35. C	45. C	55. E
6. D	16. D	26. E	36. E	46. B	56. A
7. C	17. E	27. E	37. B	47. A	57. B
8. C	18. C	28. E	38. C	48. E	58. B
9. B	19. B	29. C	39. B	49. B	59. C
10. A	20. D	30. D	40. E	50. A	60. D

Answers and Explanations

1. **(C)**—*Agreed to* and *agreed with* are both perfectly good idioms, but they mean different things. This context calls for *agreed with*.

2. **(C)**—Unlike *rise*, *raise* requires a direct object. Prices can't *raise* by themselves; something or someone has to raise them.

3. **(A)**—Even if you didn't know that a past participle can't stand alone, *begun* should still have "sounded" wrong to you.

4. **(C)**—The subject isn't *stunts*, *stars*, or *disasters*, but *death*, a singular noun. Therefore, the verb must be singular. *Was* is correct here.

5. **(D)**—Temporarily ignoring the clause *on which it was based*, the phrase *now that* strongly suggests that the disproving has happened relatively recently. The verb should be *have been*: the present perfect, used to represent a present state as the outcome of recent past events, or to express actions occurring in the past and continuing in the present.

6. **(D)**—The subject of the clause is *number*, not *firms*. Thus, a singular verb, *increases*, is needed.

7. **(C)**—The correct answer is *to play*.

8. **(C)**—Who tore down the old buildings? Surely not the *longtime residents*. The antecedent—some group such as "landlords" or "developers"—is missing.

9. **(B)**—*Neither* calls for *nor*.

10. **(A)**—*Which* can't refer to people; *that* or *who* or *whom* should be used instead.

11. **(B)**—To see the double negative more easily, remove the intervening words: *None of this . . . wouldn't have happened*. The correct phrase should say *would have*.

12. **(A)**—In this sentence, the plural noun *athletes* is modified by the prepositional phrase *with a history of severe asthma*. But the athletes don't have a collective medical history; each athlete has his or her own. The sentence should read either *young athletes with histories of severe asthma* or *a young athlete with a history of severe asthma*. Since the prepositional phrase is underlined, it must be changed.

13. **(C)**—The subject of this sentence, *piano*, is singular. Thus, the main verb must also be singular: *is* instead of *are*.

14. (E)—This sentence contains no error.

15. (E)—This sentence contains no errors, though the negative phrasing may have made it a bit hard to read.

16. (D)—This sentence lacks an appropriate antecedent for *they*.

17. (E)—This sentence contains no error.

18. (C)—The idiom should be *concern for* or *about*, not *concern in*.

19. (B)—The correct phrase should read *efforts to save the old mill*.

20. (D)—*Not, no one, never*, and *nowhere* aren't the only negative words in English. There are also less obvious negatives: *without, scarcely, barely*, and *cannot but*. *Without hardly* is a double negative. The corrected sentence would read *with hardly a word* or *without so much as a word*.

21. (B)—The subject of the sentence is *Mary Cassatt*; the noun phrase *an American painter strongly influenced by French impressionism* is an appositive. The pronoun *she* is therefore an extra subject, completely superfluous in (A) and (D). (B) correctly omits this pronoun. (C) and (E) also omit the pronoun, but they change the present tense verb into a present participle, which can't act as a verb all by itself.

22. (D)—The original sentence turns the whole first part of the sentence into an elliptical clause. It's awkward, and the chronology becomes muddled. (B), (C), and (E) all start the same, but then diverge after *anthropologist*. (B) implies that Dunham's development of *a distinctive dance method* was part of her training as an anthropologist, but that's not very likely. (C) links so many ideas with *and* that it's hard to tell what goes with what. (E) totally muddies the chronological and other links among various parts of the sentence.

23. (A)—The original sentence is best. The parallelism of the construction *not only . . . but also . . .* goes awry in the revisions.

24. (E)—If you eliminate all of the clutter, the original sentence boils down to *Because . . . is why . . .*, a grammatically and idiomatically unacceptable construction. The original sentence is also wordy and convoluted. (E) is the best available sentence.

25. (D)—(A) and (E) are comma splices. *Whom* is unnecessary in (B). (C) is a fragment.

26. (E)—Items in a list joined by *and* or *or* should be grammatically parallel. This sentence lists two noun phrases and an independent clause. (E) provides a third noun phrase.

27. (E)—*John Milton* has to be the subject of the sentence. The introductory phrase in this sentence can't modify anything else.

28. (E)—An introductory modifying phrase must modify the subject of the sentence. Since the introductory phrase isn't underlined, the subject must be changed. It's the *project*, not the *cranes* or the *conservationists*, that was initiated in 1975. (E) gets it right.

29. (C)—The original sentence is a run-on, in which two independent clauses are improperly coordinated without linking punctuation. (C) corrects this problem by transforming one clause into a dependent clause.

30. (D)—Items in a list must be parallel. In this sentence, neither of the first two items is underlined. Each is a predicate consisting of a verb and direct object, so the third item must also be a predicate, not a prepositional phrase.

31. (B)—A semicolon separates two complete, but related, sentences.

32. (E)—The preposition *to* conveys the meaning of *purpose* perfectly well.

33. (A)—The original sentence is best. (B) is a comma splice. (C) removes the parallelism and the verb of the *that* clause. (D) is wordy and misuses the conditional. (E) turns *works* into a possessive adjective modifying the gerund *being*, so it can't serve as antecedent for the pronoun *later*. (E) is also punctuated incorrectly.

34. (A)—The original sentence is the simplest and best version.

35. (C)—In this sentence, the introductory phrase seems to describe *tears*, when it should describe *the actress*. The correct answer has to begin with *the actress*.

36. (E)—This choice eliminates the split infinitive in the original sentence.

37. (A)—The singular verb *was* agrees with *None*. The original sentence is the best of the choices that correctly begin with the verb *was*.

38. (B)—Although it's acceptable to use a participle like *bearing* as the subject of a verb, choice (B) is clearer and more concise than the original sentence.

39. (B)—The sentence contains a dangling modifier: *my volunteer experience* cannot be modified by a clause beginning, "As a student . . ." (B) fixes this problem by recasting the sentence so that *I* is the subject. Of the wrong choices, only (D) correctly uses *I* as the subject, but (D)'s use of the future tense is inconsistent with the rest of the sentence.

40. (E)—(E) corrects the inconsistency in tense and skillfully conveys the sense of contrast between the two clauses with the conjunction *but*. (A) contains a misplaced modifier. The clause, "Working at a hamburger joint," which describes the author, must be followed by *I*, not *it*, and does not convey any idea of contrast. (B), too, contains a misplaced modifier and its use of *until* changes the original meaning of the sentence. (C) is incorrect in context because of its use of *when*. (D) is also incorrect in context because of its use of *when*; moreover, its use of *Despite* is inappropriate.

41. (C)—Although it is clear from the context that the author means that one is motivated by something higher than a mere paycheck, in the sentence as written it sounds as though it is the paycheck, not the motivation, that is *something higher*. (C) is the only choice that clearly conveys the correct meaning. (B), (D), and (E) have the same problem in meaning as the original sentence; moreover, (D)

is unnecessarily wordy and (E) is awkward and grammatically incorrect.

42. (A)—From the context, we know that the author is referring to the students, and replacing *they* with *students* would better convey this.

43. (D)—Sentence 11 simply repeats what the author stated in the first sentence of the essay. There is no real need for this sentence since it is obvious from the context that the author is explaining his opinion of the school board's requirement.

44. (A)—Sentence 12 brings up an entirely new idea at the end of the essay and would therefore be best improved if it expanded on this idea, as (A) suggests. As for (B), there is no need for a definition of *low income*, since this is a commonly used term. Including other criticisms would only introduce more new ideas at the last minute, so (C) is no good. (D) fails because the author gives examples of volunteer opportunities elsewhere in the essay. Finally, (E) is out because student opinion is irrelevant.

45. (C)—The coordinating conjunction *but* relates to the sense of skepticism expressed by the adverb *maybe*. In other words, "*maybe* I'd get something, *but* it wouldn't be anything great." Choice (D) is grammatically awkward.

46. (B)—This choice introduces the idea of a change of opinion, which is articulated and explained in the remainder of the essay.

47. (A)—The sentence preceding sentence 5 claims the author is *unlike* most teenagers. Therefore, choice (A) is best since it presents the actions of the author's peers and contrasts those actions to his apparently more unusual practice of playing piano. Choice (B) does not maintain the tone and meaning of the preceding sentence as clearly.

48. (E)—This choice is consistent in tense with the subsequent sentences. Choices (B) and (C) are grammatically awkward. Choice (A) presents the piano competition as something that already happened.

49. (B)—The phrase *That's why* logically follows

the preceding sentence because sentence 9 refers to the reasons that the author decided to enter the competition. In other words, "I'm always happy to perform, no matter what the circumstances. *That's why* I decided to go ahead and do it."

50. (A)—These sentences are fine as they are. The other choices contain inconsistencies in tense, grammar, and meaning.

51. (D)—The ongoing decline in facade building is happening *simultaneously with* (and as a result of) two other ongoing developments. *Soar* should be in the same tense as *die*, because these two trends coincide. Both verbs should be in the present tense, because although these trends are continuing into the future, they're also happening now.

52. (E)—This sentence contains no error.

53. (A)—*Urge* is the only true subject in this sentence (*as well as* doesn't create a true compound subject). Therefore, *are* should be *is*.

54. (D)—Elements of comparison should be parallel. *Hiking* is not underlined, so we have to change the infinitive to a gerund to match. *Cruising* is correct.

55. (E)—This sentence contains no error.

56. (A)—*Their* should be singular, since its antecedent is *the typical booking agent*, which is singular.

57. (B)—The pronoun in (B) refers to *students*, so it should be the third person plural pronoun *they*.

58. (B)—In idiomatic English, one thing is combined *with* another.

59. (C)—The present infinitive *to introduce* muddles the sequence of events. The sentence should read *to have introduced* in order to show that the introduction occurred prior to the judging.

60. (D)—The subject of the sentence is *concept*, not *parts*, so the verb should be singular.

ANSWER SHEET
FOR PRACTICE TEST 3

1 (A) (B) (C) (D) (E)	16 (A) (B) (C) (D) (E)	31 (A) (B) (C) (D) (E)	46 (A) (B) (C) (D) (E)
2 (A) (B) (C) (D) (E)	17 (A) (B) (C) (D) (E)	32 (A) (B) (C) (D) (E)	47 (A) (B) (C) (D) (E)
3 (A) (B) (C) (D) (E)	18 (A) (B) (C) (D) (E)	33 (A) (B) (C) (D) (E)	48 (A) (B) (C) (D) (E)
4 (A) (B) (C) (D) (E)	19 (A) (B) (C) (D) (E)	34 (A) (B) (C) (D) (E)	49 (A) (B) (C) (D) (E)
5 (A) (B) (C) (D) (E)	20 (A) (B) (C) (D) (E)	35 (A) (B) (C) (D) (E)	50 (A) (B) (C) (D) (E)
6 (A) (B) (C) (D) (E)	21 (A) (B) (C) (D) (E)	36 (A) (B) (C) (D) (E)	51 (A) (B) (C) (D) (E)
7 (A) (B) (C) (D) (E)	22 (A) (B) (C) (D) (E)	37 (A) (B) (C) (D) (E)	52 (A) (B) (C) (D) (E)
8 (A) (B) (C) (D) (E)	23 (A) (B) (C) (D) (E)	38 (A) (B) (C) (D) (E)	53 (A) (B) (C) (D) (E)
9 (A) (B) (C) (D) (E)	24 (A) (B) (C) (D) (E)	39 (A) (B) (C) (D) (E)	54 (A) (B) (C) (D) (E)
10 (A) (B) (C) (D) (E)	25 (A) (B) (C) (D) (E)	40 (A) (B) (C) (D) (E)	55 (A) (B) (C) (D) (E)
11 (A) (B) (C) (D) (E)	26 (A) (B) (C) (D) (E)	41 (A) (B) (C) (D) (E)	56 (A) (B) (C) (D) (E)
12 (A) (B) (C) (D) (E)	27 (A) (B) (C) (D) (E)	42 (A) (B) (C) (D) (E)	57 (A) (B) (C) (D) (E)
13 (A) (B) (C) (D) (E)	28 (A) (B) (C) (D) (E)	43 (A) (B) (C) (D) (E)	58 (A) (B) (C) (D) (E)
14 (A) (B) (C) (D) (E)	29 (A) (B) (C) (D) (E)	44 (A) (B) (C) (D) (E)	59 (A) (B) (C) (D) (E)
15 (A) (B) (C) (D) (E)	30 (A) (B) (C) (D) (E)	45 (A) (B) (C) (D) (E)	60 (A) (B) (C) (D) (E)

right

wrong

Use the answer key following the test to count up the number of questions you got right and the number you got wrong. (Remember not to count omitted questions as wrong.) The "Compute Your Score" section at the back of the book will show you how to find your score.

ANSWER SHEET
FOR PRACTICE TEST 3

Part A (ESSAY). Begin your composition on this side. If you need more space, you may continue on the reverse side.

_____

_____

_____

_____

_____

_____

_____

_____

_____

_____

_____

_____

_____

_____

_____

_____

_____

_____

_____

_____

ANSWER SHEET
FOR PRACTICE TEST 3

Continuation of Part A (ESSAY) from reverse side. Write below if you need more space.

PART A
Time—20 Minutes (1 Question)

Directions: You have 20 minutes to write an essay on the following topic. **DO NOT WRITE AN ESSAY ON ANY OTHER TOPIC. AN ESSAY ON A DIFFERENT TOPIC IS UNACCEPTABLE.**

This essay provides you with an opportunity to demonstrate how well you write. Therefore, you should express your ideas clearly and effectively. How much you write is much less important than how well you write; but to express your thoughts on the topic adequately you may want to write more than a single paragraph. Your essay should be specific.

Your essay must be written in the lines provided on your answer sheet. No other paper will be given to you. There is enough space to write your essay on the answer sheet if you write on every line, avoid wide margins, and keep your handwriting to a reasonable size.

Consider the following statement and assignment. Then write an essay as directed.

> **"The United States recognizes that a person matures at the 'legal' age of 21, but
> I think that the true test of maturity is _____."**

Assignment: Write an essay that completes the statement above. Explain the reasons behind your choice.

WHEN THE PROCTOR ANNOUNCES THAT 20 MINUTES HAVE PASSED, YOU MUST STOP WRITING AND GO ON TO PART B OF THE TEST. IF YOU FINISH YOUR ESSAY BEFORE 20 MINUTES PASS, YOU MAY GO ON TO PART B.

YOU MAY MAKE NOTES ON THIS PAGE AND THE FOLLOWING ONE, BUT YOU MUST WRITE YOUR ESSAY ON THE ANSWER SHEET.

You may use this page to outline your essay or make other notes as you plan your essay. Don't write your essay here, though. Your essay must be written on the lined pages of the answer sheet at the beginning of this answer section.

TURN TO THE NEXT PAGE.

PART B
Time—40 Minutes (60 Questions)

For each of the following questions, choose the best answer from the given choices and darken the corresponding oval on the answer sheet.

Directions: The following sentences contain problems in grammar, usage, diction (choice of words), and idiom.

Some of the sentences are correct.

None of the sentences contains more than one error.

The error, if there is one in the sentence, is underlined and lettered. Parts of the sentence that are not underlined are correct and cannot be changed. In selecting answers, follow the requirements of standard written English.

If there is an error, choose the <u>one underlined part</u> that must be changed to make the sentence correct and fill in the corresponding oval on your answer grid.

If there is no error, fill in oval E.

SAMPLE QUESTION

<u>Even though</u> he <u>had to</u> supervise a large
    A   B

staff, his salary <u>was no greater</u> than <u>a clerk</u>.
                C   D

<u>No error</u>
  E

SAMPLE ANSWER

Ⓐ Ⓑ Ⓒ ● Ⓔ

---

1. The first woman aviator <u>to cross</u> the English
                        A

    Channel, Harriet Quimby <u>flown</u> <u>by monoplane</u>
                    B   C

    from Dover, England, to Hardelot, France, <u>in</u>
                                  D

    1912. <u>No error</u>
          E

2. The French philosopher Jean-Paul Sartre

    <u>is often assumed</u> to have initiated existential
        A

    philosophy, <u>but</u> the Danish philosopher
            B

    Kierkegaard <u>has developed</u> similar ideas
               C

    <u>much earlier</u>. <u>No error</u>
       D   E

TURN TO THE NEXT PAGE.

KAPLAN 265

3. The reproductive behavior of sea horses

   is notable in respect of the male, who,
   ‾‾‾‾‾‾‾‾‾ ‾‾‾‾‾‾‾‾‾‾‾‾ ‾‾‾
   A   B   C
   instead of the female, carries the fertilized
   ‾‾‾‾‾‾‾‾‾
   D

   eggs. No error
        ‾‾‾‾‾‾‾‾
        E

4. German-born architects Walter Gropius and

   Ludwig Mies van der Rohe are thought
                            ‾‾‾‾‾‾‾‾‾‾
                            A
   to have been a major influence on architectural
   ‾‾‾‾‾‾‾‾‾‾‾ ‾‾‾‾‾‾‾‾‾‾‾‾‾‾
   B   C
   training in the United States since the 1930s.
                                 ‾‾‾‾‾
                                 D
   No error
   ‾‾‾‾‾‾‾‾
   E

5. Although Charles Darwin incubated his theory
   ‾‾‾‾‾‾‾‾
   A
   of evolution for twenty years, he wrote
               ‾‾‾‾‾‾‾‾‾‾‾‾‾‾‾‾
               B
   On the Origin of Species relatively rapid once he
                            ‾‾‾‾‾‾‾‾‾‾‾‾‾‾‾
                            C
   began composing. No error
   ‾‾‾‾‾   ‾‾‾‾‾‾‾‾
   D   E

6. An eminent historian who lectured here last
      ‾‾‾‾‾‾‾   ‾‾‾
      A   B
   week lay out an array of causes leading to the
        ‾‾‾   ‾‾‾‾‾‾‾‾‾‾
        C   D
   Civil War. No error
             ‾‾‾‾‾‾‾‾
             E

7. Early experience of racial discrimination made
         ‾‾‾‾‾‾‾‾‾‾‾‾‾   ‾‾‾‾
         A   B
   an indelible impression for the late Supreme
      ‾‾‾‾‾‾‾‾‾ ‾‾‾‾‾‾‾‾‾‾‾
      C   D
   Court Justice Thurgood Marshall. No error
                                   ‾‾‾‾‾‾‾‾
                                   E

8. More journalists as you would suspect are
                   ‾‾
                   A
   secretly writing plays or novels, which they
   ‾‾‾‾‾‾‾‾   ‾‾‾‾‾
   B   C
   hope someday to have published. No error
               ‾‾‾‾‾‾‾‾‾‾‾‾‾‾‾‾‾ ‾‾‾‾‾‾‾‾
               D   E

9. As long ago as the twelfth century, French
   ‾‾‾‾‾‾‾‾‾‾‾
   A
   alchemists have perfected techniques
            ‾‾‾‾
            B
   for refining precious metals from other ores.
   ‾‾‾‾‾‾‾‾‾‾‾‾   ‾‾‾‾
   C   D
   No error
   ‾‾‾‾‾‾‾‾
   E

10. Galileo begged Rome's indulgence for his

    support of a Copernican system in which the
    ‾‾‾‾‾‾‾‾‾   ‾‾‾‾‾‾‾‾
    A   B
    earth circled the sun instead of occupied a
                          ‾‾‾‾‾‾‾‾‾‾ ‾‾‾‾‾‾‾‾
                          C   D
    central position in the universe. No error
                                     ‾‾‾‾‾‾‾‾
                                     E

11. Squandering his inheritance, the prodigal
    ‾‾‾‾‾‾‾‾‾‾‾
    A
    felt no compunction at wasting his father's
    ‾‾‾‾‾‾‾‾‾‾‾‾‾‾‾‾‾ ‾‾   ‾‾‾‾‾‾‾‾
    B   C   D
    hard-earned fortune. No error
                        ‾‾‾‾‾‾‾‾
                        E

12. Although the piano as we know it today did
                     ‾‾‾‾‾‾‾‾‾‾‾‾‾‾‾‾‾
                     A
    not exist in Bach's time, he was writing many
                               ‾‾‾‾‾‾‾‾‾‾‾
                               B
    pieces that are now frequently played
           ‾‾‾‾‾‾‾‾
           C
    on that instrument. No error
    ‾‾‾‾‾‾‾‾‾‾‾‾‾‾‾‾   ‾‾‾‾‾‾‾‾
    D   E

TURN TO THE NEXT PAGE.

13. There are times <u>where</u> we must make <u>decisions</u>
         A   B
    purely <u>on the basis of</u> the financial resources
                    C
    at <u>our</u> disposal. <u>No error</u>
        D   E

14. <u>Like</u> the poetry of Milton, <u>Dryden generally</u>
      A   B
    <u>adheres to</u> classical forms and
        C
    <u>traditional themes.</u> <u>No error</u>
            D   E

15. The work of Byron <u>has been underrated</u> more
                            A
    often by <u>so-called</u> modernists in the field of
                B
    literary criticism <u>than</u> any <u>other</u> Romantic
                          C   D
    poet. <u>No error</u>
              E

16. The chemist Sir Humphrey Davy was a friend

    <u>of the poet</u> William Wordsworth; <u>he</u>
        A   B
    <u>would visit</u> with several other guests <u>at</u> a
        C   D
    tiny cottage in the English Lake District.

    <u>No error</u>
        E

17. The convict escaped <u>with the aid</u> of a <u>recent</u>
                            A   B
    released prisoner, a career criminal <u>who knew</u>
                                            C
    the prison grounds <u>intimately.</u> <u>No error</u>
                            D   E

18. <u>Grading</u> research papers <u>over the years</u>, the
      A   B
    professor became expert <u>at recognizing</u>
                                C
    submissions that <u>have been plagiarized</u> or
                            D
    inadequately documented. <u>No error</u>
                                  E

19. <u>Although</u> he <u>had planned</u> a more pessimistic
      A   B
    ending, Thomas Hardy <u>was persuaded</u> by his
                            C
    readers <u>to close</u> *The Return of the Native* with a
                D
    marriage. <u>No error</u>
                  E

20. During the military coup, the deposed prime

    minister's property was <u>put up</u> for sale
                                A
    <u>without</u> <u>him</u> <u>having</u> any opportunity to object.
        B   C   D
    <u>No error</u>
        E

TURN TO THE NEXT PAGE.

For each of the following questions, choose the best answer from the given choices and darken the corresponding oval on the answer sheet.

Directions: The following sentences test accuracy and effectiveness of expression. In selecting answers, follow the rules of standard written English; in other words, consider grammar, choice of words, sentence construction, and punctuation.

In each of the following sentences, a portion or all of the sentence is underlined. Under each sentence you will find five ways of phrasing the underlined portion. Choice A repeats the original underlined portion; the other four choices provide alternative phrasings.

Select the choice that best expresses the meaning of the original sentence. If the original sentence is better than any of the alternative phrasings, choose A; otherwise select one of the alternatives. Your selection should construct the most effective sentence—clear and precise with no awkwardness or ambiguity.

SAMPLE QUESTION

Wanting to reward her assistant for loyalty,
Sheila gave a bonus to him as large as his paycheck.

(A) Sheila gave a bonus to him as large as his paycheck
(B) given to him by Sheila was a bonus as large as his paycheck
(C) he was given a bonus as large as his paycheck by Sheila
(D) Sheila gave him a bonus as large as his paycheck
(E) Sheila gave him a paycheck to him as large as his bonus

SAMPLE ANSWER

---

21. The Islandian government, under pressure to satisfy the needs of consumers, and loosening its control of the economy.

    (A) and loosening its
    (B) by loosening its
    (C) is loosening their
    (D) but loosening their
    (E) is loosening its

22. The new freshman class being larger than last year's.

    (A) being larger than last year's
    (B) is large, more so than last year
    (C) which is larger than the one last year
    (D) is larger than last year's
    (E) by far larger than the last

TURN TO THE NEXT PAGE.

KAPLAN

23. Night-shift workers lead a strange life, work-ing while the rest of us are sleeping, then sleeping while the rest of us are working.

(A) then sleeping
(B) after which they sleep
(C) then they sleep
(D) until they go to sleep
(E) but soon they are sleeping

24. The difference between the jobs is that one is exciting; the other, boring.

(A) one is exciting; the other, boring
(B) of one being exciting, the other is boring
(C) one is exciting; the other being boring
(D) one is exciting, although the other is boring
(E) of an exciting one and one that is boring

25. The lovers eventually returned to the grassy spot where they had left their sandwiches, strolling hand in hand.

(A) The lovers eventually returned to the grassy spot where they had left their sandwiches, strolling hand in hand.
(B) Eventually, the lovers returned to the grassy spot where they had left their sandwiches, strolling hand in hand.
(C) Strolling hand in hand, the grassy spot where they had left their sandwiches was returned to by the lovers.
(D) The lovers, returning to the grassy spot where they had left their sandwiches, while strolling hand in hand.
(E) Strolling hand in hand, the lovers eventu-ally returned to the grassy spot where they had left their sandwiches.

26. For success in school, it is important not only to be smart but also to do your homework.

(A) to be smart but also to do
(B) being smart but also to do
(C) to be smart but also doing
(D) being smart but also doing
(E) that you be smart but also that you do

27. Amelia Earhart, who was born in Kansas, was the first person to fly from Hawaii to California.

(A) Amelia Earhart, who was born in Kansas, was the first person to fly from Hawaii to California.
(B) Amelia Earhart being the first person to fly from Hawaii to California and was born in Kansas.
(C) Being the first person to fly from Hawaii to California, Amelia Earhart was born in Kansas.
(D) Amelia Earhart was the first person to fly from Hawaii to California and was born in Kansas.
(E) Amelia Earhart was the first person to fly from Hawaii to California and she was born in Kansas.

28. To conserve calories, to promote digestion, or so that they are less vulnerable to predators, wild animals rest during many of their waking hours.

(A) or so that they are less vulnerable to predators
(B) or to remain less visible to predators
(C) or so that their predators cannot see them
(D) or in order that their predators find them less visible
(E) of for the purpose of remaining less visible to predators

TURN TO THE NEXT PAGE.

29. Samuel Johnson's *Dictionary*, published in 1755, <u>was neither the first for English nor the largest</u>, but its quotations illustrating definitions made it the best for many decades.

    (A) was neither the first for English nor the largest
    (B) neither was it the first for English nor the largest
    (C) neither was the first for English nor the largest
    (D) neither was the first for English, and it was not the largest either
    (E) was neither the first for English, nor was it the largest

30. In the Middle Ages, when no one understood most astronomical phenomena, <u>the comets that seemed to portend</u> military conflicts or other social crises.

    (A) the comets that seemed to portend
    (B) the comets seeming to portend
    (C) the comets seemed to portend
    (D) the comets apparently portending
    (E) and when the comets seemed to portend

31. Unusual numbers of playwrights and artists <u>flourishing in the England of Shakespeare's time</u>, and the Italy of Michelangelo's day, when cultural conditions combined to promote creativity.

    (A) flourishing in the England of Shakespeare's time
    (B) by flourishing in the England of Shakespeare's time
    (C) while flourishing in Shakespeare's England
    (D) flourished in the England of Shakespeare's time
    (E) having flourished in Shakespeare's England

32. During World War I, U.S. Army psychologists administered a forerunner of today's I.Q. tests, <u>where it had directions that</u> were given orally in acoustically poor and crowded rooms.

    (A) where it had directions that
    (B) whereby there were directions that
    (C) whose directions
    (D) and for it they had directions which
    (E) and it had directions which

33. A dispute arose between Rimland and Heartland over the eastern provinces from which twenty years before a great many people <u>had emigrated</u>.

    (A) had emigrated
    (B) emigrated
    (C) had immigrated
    (D) immigrated
    (E) migrated

34. Even though the senators on the committee <u>were reluctant to schedule</u> a formal inquiry, they went on record as favoring one.

    (A) were reluctant to schedule
    (B) were reluctant as far as scheduling
    (C) were reluctant in scheduling
    (D) have been reluctant at scheduling
    (E) have had reluctance to schedule

TURN TO THE NEXT PAGE.

35. There is scholarly consensus that, while Walt Whitman often referred to illegitimate children of whom he claimed to be the father, he never had any outside of "dream children."

    (A) of whom he claimed to be the father, he never had any outside of "dream children."
    (B) whom he claimed to have fathered, he had only "dream children."
    (C) who he claimed fatherhood of, he was having only "dream children."
    (D) of whom he said he was the father, "dream children" were his only ones.
    (E) who he claimed to be the father of, he never had anything outside of "dream children."

36. In an effort to sound like an expert, the director's speech which was riddled with esoteric references and specialized terms.

    (A) the director's speech which was riddled with esoteric references
    (B) the director's speech was riddled with esoteric references
    (C) the director delivered a speech riddled with esoteric references
    (D) his speech which was riddled with esoteric references
    (E) the speech of the director was riddled with esoteric references

37. His ambition was not only to study but also mastering the craft of journalism.

    (A) not only to study but also mastering
    (B) not only studying but to try and master
    (C) not studying only, but also mastering
    (D) not only to study but also to master
    (E) to study, and, as well, to master

38. If the construction strike has not occurred, the contractor would have had no problem finishing the restaurant on time.

    (A) If the construction strike has not occurred
    (B) If the construction strike would not have occurred
    (C) Had the construction strike not of occurred
    (D) Had it not been that the construction strike had occurred
    (E) Had it not been for the construction strike

TURN TO THE NEXT PAGE.

Directions: The following passages are first drafts of student essays. Some portions of the essays have to be rewritten.

Read the essays and answer the questions that follow them. Some of the questions concern particular sentences or fragments of sentences and require you to make choices about sentence structure, word choice, and usage. Other questions pertain to the entire essay or pieces of the essay and require you to think about organization, development, and appropriateness of language. Pick the answer that most effectively conveys the meaning and follows the rules of standard written English. Once you have chosen an answer, fill in the corresponding oval on your answer sheet.

Questions 39–44 are based on the following passage, which was written in response to an assignment to write a letter to the editor of a local newspaper.

(1) The school board recently took a controversial vote to allow advertising at Midville High. (2) Many disagree with this decision. (3) I do not. (4) As a member of the student council, it is important to make up for the shortfall in our school budget. (5) And we cannot afford the luxury of worrying about where the money is coming from.

(6) Critics say that by allowing advertising, they are persuading young people to buy certain products, which is unethical. (7) But students are walking advertisements already, what with the corporate logos all over their clothes. (8) Seeing a soft drink ad on the side of a school bus may be unsightly, it can raise thousands of dollars. (9) Isn't it more important to ensure that students have modern textbooks and lab equipment? (10) Advertising has long been found on vending machines in the student lounge. (11) It's already in the schools, so why not use it to help our education? (12) And last month, an opinion poll conducted by the school newspaper found that in general, students do not object to the advertisements or believe they are harmful. (13) "If it's going to help my education, that's great," said one. (14) Faced with the choice of no instruments for the school orchestra or a few fast-food ads hanging over my locker, I know which one I'll take.

39. Which of the following is the best way to revise and combine sentences 2 and 3 (reproduced below)?

    Many disagree with this decision. I do not.

    (A) Many disagreeing with this decision, I am not.
    (B) In contrast to the case with many that are disagreeing with this decision, I do not.
    (C) Although many disagree with this decision, I do not.
    (D) Even though many disagree with this decision, I am agreeing.
    (E) Many disagree with this decision, but not me.

40. In context, which is the best version of the underlined portion of sentence 4 (reproduced below)?

    As a member of the student council, it is important to make up for the shortfall in our school budget.

    (A) (As it is now)
    (B) making up for the shortfall in our school budget is important
    (C) the shortfall in our school budget is the thing that it is important we make up for
    (D) the school budget, especially the shortfall in it, is important to make up for
    (E) I feel that it is important to make up for the shortfall in our school budget

TURN TO THE NEXT PAGE.

41. Which of the following would be the best replacement for the word "*And*" at the beginning of sentence 5?

    (A) Furthermore,
    (B) Nevertheless,
    (C) But,
    (D) Rather,
    (E) However,

42. Which of the following best replaces the word "*they*" in sentence 6?

    (A) critics
    (B) the schools
    (C) young people
    (D) products
    (E) the school board

43. Which of the following versions of sentence 8 (reproduced below) is best?

    Seeing a soft-drink ad on the side of a school bus may be unsightly, it can raise thousands of dollars.

    (A) (As it is now)
    (B) Seeing a soft drink ad on the side of a school bus is unsightly, even though it can raise thousands of dollars.
    (C) Thousands of dollars can be raised by seeing a soft drink ad on the side of a school bus, which is unsightly.
    (D) A soft drink ad on the side of a school bus may be unsightly, but it can raise thousands of dollars.
    (E) The side of a school bus, which a soft drink ad is unsightly on, can raise thousands of dollars.

44. All of the following strategies are used by the writer of the passage EXCEPT

    (A) outlining personal views
    (B) referring to student opinion
    (C) explaining the opposing belief
    (D) asking rhetorical questions
    (E) proposing alternatives to the plan

TURN TO THE NEXT PAGE.

Questions 45–50 are based on the following passage.

(1) Last summer I was fortunate enough to be able to spend a month in France. (2) It was the most exciting time of my life. (3) I stayed with a family in Montpellier, which is in the south of France. (4) It was very different from my life back in the United States. (5) Every morning we bought fresh bread from the bakery and had coffee in a bowl instead of a cup. (6) The milk came in bottles fresh from the dairy.

(7) Back home in Winnetka, Illinois, I wouldn't think anything of taking a ten-minute shower every day, or even twice a day in the summer. (8) In Montpellier, we only showered once every two days and were using far less water. (9) First you turn the water on to get wet, then turn it off and soap yourself up, then you turned it on again to rinse off, so the water is only on for about maybe two minutes. (10) And it was pretty hot there in the summer, I'd never taken showers in cold water before! (11) I couldn't imagine what it was like in the winter. (12) I also noticed that although the family had a car, they hardly ever used it. (13) The father took the bus to work in the morning and the mother rode her bicycle when doing errands. (14) Since the family wasn't poor, they were well off, I realized that gas is much more expensive in France than in the U.S. (15) I realized that as Americans, we can afford to take long showers and drive everywhere because we pay much less for energy. (16) Living in Montpellier and seeing how frugally people lived there, I get angry thinking of the resources wasted in the U.S. (17) When I came home, I was much more energy conscious. (18) I didn't drink coffee out of a bowl anymore, but I started riding my bike to school and turning the thermostat down at night.

45. Which of the following sentences, if added after sentence 6, would best link the first paragraph with the rest of the essay?

(A) These differences were superficial; however I was soon to discover other, more important ones.
(B) How I longed for my familiar existence back in the United States!
(C) I was not prepared for the culture shock I experienced.
(D) But I didn't let such minor inconveniences ruin my overseas experience.
(E) Although it took a while, eventually I got used to the new way of doing things.

46. In context, which of the following versions of sentence 8 (reproduced below) is best?

In Montpellier, we only showered once every two days and were using far less water.

(A) Showering only once every two days, Montpellier was where I used far less water.
(B) Showering only once every two days and using far less water were things we did in Montpellier.
(C) In Montpellier, we showered only once every two days and used far less water.
(D) In Montpellier, where once every two days was when we showered, a lot less water was used.
(E) In Montpellier, we were only showering once every two days and using far less water.

TURN TO THE NEXT PAGE.

47. In context, which of the following is the best way to revise sentence 9 (reproduced below)?

First you turn the water on just to get wet, then turn it off and soap yourself up, then you turned it on again to rinse off, so the water is only on for about maybe two minutes.

(A) First I turn the water on just to get wet, then turn it off and soap myself up, then turn it on again to rinse off, so the water is only on for about maybe two minutes.

(B) First turning the water on just to get wet, then turning it off and soaping yourself off, you turned it on again to rinse off, the water being on for only about maybe two minutes.

(C) First one turns the water on just to get wet, then turns it off and soaps oneself up, then one turns it on again to rinse off, so the water is only on for about maybe two minutes.

(D) First we turned the water on just to get wet, then turned it off and soaped ourselves up, then turned it on again to rinse off, so that the water was only on for about two minutes.

(E) First we turn the water on just to get wet, then turn it off and soap ourselves up, then turn it on again to rinse off, so the water is only on for about two minutes.

48. Which of the following best replaces the word "And" at the beginning of sentence 10?

(A) But
(B) Although
(C) Yet
(D) When
(E) Which

49. In context, which is the best version of the underlined portion of sentence 14 (reproduced below)?

Since the family wasn't poor, they were well off, I realized that gas is much more expensive in France than in the U.S.

(A) The family not being poor, they were well off,
(B) Well off, not poor, being the family,
(C) Since the family was well off, they were not poor,
(D) The family wasn't poor but well off,
(E) Since the family was well off rather than poor,

50. Sentence 16 could best be improved by

(A) including a definition of resources
(B) providing examples
(C) changing it to the past tense
(D) using the first person plural instead of the first person singular
(E) moving it to the end of the essay

TURN TO THE NEXT PAGE.

For each of the following questions, choose the best answer from the given choices and darken the corresponding oval on the answer sheet.

Directions: The following sentences contain problems in grammar, usage, diction (choice of words), and idiom.

Some of the sentences are correct.

None of the sentences contains more than one error.

The error, if there is one in the sentence, is underlined and lettered. Parts of the sentence that are not underlined are correct and cannot be changed. In selecting answers, follow the requirements of standard written English.

If there is an error, choose the <u>one underlined part</u> that must be changed to make the sentence correct and fill in the corresponding oval on your answer grid.

If there is no error, fill in oval E.

SAMPLE QUESTION

<u>Even though</u> he <u>had to</u> supervise a large
   A   B

staff, his salary <u>was no greater</u> than <u>a clerk</u>.
           C   D

<u>No error</u>
  E

SAMPLE ANSWER

Ⓐ Ⓑ Ⓒ ● Ⓔ

---

51. The proposals for insurance reform <u>of</u> the so-
                           A

    called moderate candidate for governor <u>were</u>
                                   B

    as conservative as, or <u>more conservative than</u>,
                            C

    <u>his rival</u>. <u>No error</u>
      D   E

52. <u>It</u> did not occur to the interviewer <u>to ask</u> either
   A   B

    the job applicant <u>nor</u> his reference <u>whether</u> the
                C   D

    applicant had completed the project he initiated.

    <u>No error</u>
      E

53. The Ivorian students <u>considered it</u> more disre-
                    A

    spectful <u>to look</u> <u>directly into</u> an elder's eyes
          B   C

    than to refuse <u>to answer</u> a teacher's question.
               D

    <u>No error</u>
      E

54. <u>Having</u> little concern for others, <u>as well as</u>
    A   B

    <u>a lack of</u> curiosity about the unknown,
      C

    <u>the woman</u> made an ineffectual teacher.
       D

    <u>No error</u>
      E

TURN TO THE NEXT PAGE.

55. There <u>was</u> a huge public outcry <u>over</u> the cruel
        A   B
    methods <u>employed at</u> the animal pound, but in
               C
    the end, nothing came of <u>them</u>. <u>No error</u>
                        D   E

56. A pioneering scholar <u>of</u> anthropology, Ruth
                        A
    Benedict <u>was also</u> a spokesperson <u>against</u>
             B   C
    ethnic bigotry <u>which</u> recognized that cultures
                  D
    influence ideas about gender. <u>No error</u>
                          E

57. <u>Not far from</u> the finest <u>remaining</u> examples of
        A   B
    Federal architecture <u>stands</u> a geometric struc-
                    C
    ture <u>of</u> glass, steel, and chrome. <u>No error</u>
        D   E

58. Alexander Calder <u>first</u> studied
                  A
    <u>mechanical engineering</u>, <u>but later</u> was able
              B   C
    <u>for inventing</u> a new form of sculpture, the
        D
    mobile. <u>No error</u>
             E

59. The political <u>climate of</u> a stable nation can be
                     A
    expected <u>to change</u>, but <u>far more gradually</u>
               B   C
    than trends in art or music <u>do</u>. <u>No error</u>
                         D   E

60. A research paper <u>requires</u> footnotes or end-
                   A
    notes and a bibliography <u>irregardless</u> <u>of which</u>
                          B   C
    references and sources the writer <u>uses</u>.
                             D
    <u>No error</u>
    E

STOP!

END OF TEST. DO NOT TURN THE PAGE UNTIL YOU ARE READY TO CHECK YOUR ANSWERS.

PRACTICE TEST 3 ANSWERS AND EXPLANATIONS

The Essay Section

This section contains sample essays for the essay topic in Practice Test 3. Use these sample essays as benchmarks to help you grade your own essay on the same topic. Does your essay sound more like the grade 6 essay or the grade 3 essay?

Sample Grade 6 Essay

The United States recognizes that a person "matures" when he or she reaches the legal age of 21, but I think the true test of maturity is being able to accept responsibility for one's actions. It's an uncommon trait in today's disposable society, where image is everything, and being rich and famous is more important than being decent and useful. Failing to accept responsibility for one's actions is not only common, it's fashionable. People who commit crimes, but have enough money, hire the best lawyers and get acquitted. Then they go on television or write books about their "ordeal," and make even more money.

But maturity isn't about making a profit; rather, it's about understanding that actions have consequences. If you decide to do something you know is wrong, you have to be prepared to accept the consequences. For example, there's no longer any doubt that driving under the influence of alcohol is morally wrong, not just illegal. Statistics prove it's very dangerous. People who do it aren't prepared to face the consequences, of going to jail or possibly killing themselves or others. They lack maturity.

Facing the consequences means telling the truth, even if it gets you in trouble. This sounds easy but it isn't. It can mean punishment, or at least having to face the anger of the person you're talking to. When he admitted chopping down the cherry tree, George Washington got off easy! When I do something wrong, often my first instinct (and I don't think this is uncommon) is to lie. What I try to remember, though, is that it's always easier in the long run to tell the truth. Maturity means not having guilty secrets.

In fact, reaching legal age is no guaranty of maturity. Many so-called adults are really immature, while some people under 21 are very mature. A teen-ager from a single-parent home who takes care of her younger siblings because her mom is working two jobs, for example, is mature. If she can do this and still go to school every day, then she's really taking responsibility for her actions, and demonstrating a high degree of maturity.

Grader's comments: This is a strong essay, demonstrating superior competence in both organization and command of language. The ideas are clear and well-developed, speak directly to the topic, and flow easily from one paragraph to the next. There are a few minor errors of grammar or spelling (*guaranty* should be *guarantee*, for example); but for a first draft, written in 20 minutes, it's an accomplished piece of work.

Sample Grade 3 Essay

The true test of maturity is self-control. Like Clint Eastwood said in the movie, "a man's got to know his limitations."

Self-control can come in many forms. There's the purely physical, like getting regular exercise and not eating too much of the wrong thing. Many people in this country have a problem with this, that's why there's so many fad diets and so many ads on tv about home exercise machines.

Mental self-control is even tougher. It's about concentration and focus. They don't teach it in school but they should. In Asia, people study mental control for years, doing yoga and the martial arts. Those things are physical too of course, but, the mental control is key. We don't have anything like that in this country, except maybe biofeedback.

And control of the emotions is maybe the toughest thing of all. We think we're just human, but we're human animals, with feelings. Sometimes those feelings get the best of us. It could be murdurous rage, or just feeling discouraged by life. If we give in to those feelings, we get in trouble.

That's why self-control is so necessary. Those who have it are mature whether they are legal age or not. They know what they can and can't do.

Grader's comments: This writer has addressed the topic with a moderate degree of skill. The idea of self-control in its various manifestations is developed in an organized fashion, but the essay itself lacks depth. Moreover, there are numerous flaws in style and grammar.

Sample Grade 2 Essay

The United States recognizes that a person matures at the "legal" age of 21, but I think the true test of maturity is to be your own person. If you can do that, your mature.

Being your own person means making decisions—good ones. Knowing when to say when, staying out of trouble and, being kind. People who give to charity are mature. People who only think about getting more and more money for themselves need to grow up.

Literature are full of examples. Scroog and A Christmas Carol is a good example. He's a greedy miser, until three ghosts come and scare him. He learns the meaning of Christmas and becomes his own person and gets mature.

And by the way. Lots of people think Holden in Catcher In the Rye is cool, but he's really immature. Instead of wining about how phony everybody is, he should learn to face facts, see the world for what it is and get on with his life.

Then he'd be his own person. And that's what maturity means to me.

Grader's comments: This essay suffers from poor organization, as well as frequent errors in grammar, diction, and sentence structure. The writer's equating maturity with "being your own person" is haphazard and unfocused. The examples from literature are promising but undeveloped. Moreover, the use of slang like "when to say when" and "cool" isn't consistent with the rules of standard written English.

The Multiple-Choice Section

This section contains an answer key and explanations for the Multiple-Choice section in Practice Test 3. Use the scoring conversion table in the back of the book to see how you've done on this section. Pay careful attention to the explanations for the multiple-choice questions you got wrong.

Answer Key

1. B	11. E	21. E	31. D	41. A	51. D
2. C	12. B	22. D	32. C	42. B	52. C
3. B	13. A	23. A	33. A	43. D	53. E
4. C	14. B	24. A	34. A	44. E	54. E
5. C	15. C	25. E	35. B	45. A	55. D
6. C	16. B	26. A	36. C	46. C	56. D
7. D	17. B	27. A	37. D	47. D	57. E
8. A	18. D	28. B	38. E	48. B	58. D
9. B	19. E	29. A	39. C	49. E	59. E
10. D	20. C	30. C	40. E	50. C	60. B

Answers and Explanations

1. (B)—The use of the word *flown* isn't right. *Flown*, the past participle form of *fly*, can't be used as a main verb without a form of the verb *have*. What's needed here is the simple past form of *fly*, which is *flew*.

2. (C)—Notice the correct use of the present tense *is assumed* and the perfect infinitive *to have initiated:* the initiating is supposed to have taken place before the assuming. The problem is with the present perfect *has developed*. The present perfect is used to represent a present state as the outcome of recent past events, or to express actions occurring in the past and continuing in the present. The present perfect could represent the actions of a living philosopher, but whether or not you know that Kierkegaard died in 1855, the sentence gives you the time-descriptive phrase, *much earlier*. So whenever Sarte seemed to be initiating existentialism, the sentence tells us that Kierkegaard was developing a protoexistentialism before Sarte. Thus, the past perfect, *had developed*, is needed here.

3. (B)—*In respect of* doesn't sound quite right. Something like *with respect to* would be better.

4. (C)—Here the subject is *Gropius* and *Mies van der Rohe*, and the predicate noun is *major influence*. That doesn't make much sense: *Gropius* and *Mies van der Rohe* were different people, so they should be referred to as *influences*, not *an influence*.

5. (C)—What does *rapid* modify? It modifies *wrote*, a verb; so *rapid* should be changed to *rapidly*.

6. (C)—*Lay* would seem to be the right word here, but this sentence is in the past tense. The past tense of *lay* is *laid*. That's the word that should be used here.

7. (D)—Does something make an *impression for* someone? No, it makes an *impression on* someone.

8. (A)—The correct comparative form is *more . . . than*, not *more . . . as*.

9. **(B)**—This sentence describes events prior to a time in the past, so instead of the present perfect *have perfected*, it should use the past perfect *had perfected*.

10. **(D)**—*Instead of* takes a participle. *Occupied* should be corrected to *occupying*.

11. **(E)**—This sentence contains no error. The verb forms are correct and the preposition *at* is used idiomatically with *compunction*.

12. **(B)**—The past participle—*was writing*—is generally used to describe an ongoing action contemporary with another action. In this case, the simple past tense, *wrote*, would be more appropriate.

13. **(A)**—The word *where* should be used only to refer to a place. To refer to a time, the correct word to use is *when*.

14. **(B)**—This sentence illogically compares Milton's poetry with Dryden himself. The comparison should be between the poetry of Milton and the poetry of Dryden.

15. **(C)**—The things being compared are the work of Byron and the works of other Romantic poets, but the sentence as it's written seems to compare the work of Byron with the other poets themselves. *Than* should be changed to *than that of*.

16. **(B)**—*He* could refer to either *Davy* or *Wordsworth*; this pronoun has no clear antecedent.

17. **(B)**—The phrase *recent released prisoner* doesn't mean *recent and released prisoner*; what's *recent* here is that the *prisoner was released*. *Released* is a participial adjective, and it takes an adverb, *recently*, to modify an adjective.

18. **(D)**—To indicate that plagiarism or documentation came before both the recognition and the becoming expert requires the past perfect tense: *had been plagiarized or inadequately documented*.

19. **(E)**—This sentence contains no error.

20. **(C)**—The gerund, not the pronoun, should be the object of the preposition *without*, and the pronoun *him* should be changed to the possessive *his*.

21. **(E)**—The original sentence doesn't have any verb, because an *-ing* word without a helping verb isn't a verb. Choices (C) and (E) supply verbs, but choice (C) introduces an incorrect pronoun. The pronoun must refer to *government*, which is singular. So, the pronoun must be *its*.

22. **(D)**—Again, the original sentence doesn't have a verb. Choices (B) and (D) supply the missing verb, but (B) makes other changes that introduce new mistakes.

23. **(A)**—The original sentence is best. This sentence describes a two-step process. It's a bit like a very short list. Therefore, both steps must be given parallel forms. The first step is *working* (with no pronoun), so the second step should be simply *sleeping* (with no pronoun).

24. **(A)**—The original sentence is best. The word *although* in (D) changes the logic of the sentence. (B), (C) and (E) don't use parallel wording. (A) contains parallel wording: The comma before *boring* is a stand-in for the verb *is*.

25. **(E)**—*Strolling hand in hand* is a modifying phrase that modifies the noun *lovers*. Only (E) places the modifying phrase next to *lovers*.

26. **(A)**—The original sentence is best. Be wary of choices containing the word *being*. They're often wrong, as are choices (B) and (D) here. (E) is wordy.

27. **(A)**—The original sentence is the clearest.

28. **(B)**—This choice has the right parallel structure. Since the first two elements of the list begin with infinitives, *to conserve . . . to promote*, the third must also. (B) is the only choice that contains an infinitive: *to remain*.

Kaplan Practice Tests

29. (A)—The original sentence is the most clear and concise.

30. (C)—The original sentence has no independent clause. This problem is corrected by getting rid of *that*. Choices (B) and (D) have no independent clauses, either; they contain *-ing* forms of verbs that can't function as main verbs.

31. (D)—Only (D) corrects the problem with the sentence by turning *flourishing* into *flourished*—a main verb in the past tense.

32. (C)—Choice (C) most clearly shows the connection between the first clause of the sentence, which identifies a kind of test, and the second clause, which asserts something about the directions of the test. *Whose directions* compactly states the relation between these clauses.

33. (A)—The original sentence is best. The past perfect tense is correct because it describes an action that occurred prior to the main action of the sentence, which is in the past tense (*arose*). Note that *emigrated*, not *immigrated*, is the correct word here: You *emigrate* from a place, and *immigrate* to a place.

34. (A)—The original sentence is best.

35. (B)—Although the original sentence doesn't contain any actual errors, (B) is preferable because it's considerably more concise. Note that *whom* is the object of the preposition *of*, and is therefore correct; (C) and (E) are wrong to change it to *who*.

36. (C)—Logically, the introductory phrase refers to the *director* himself, not to his *speech*. Therefore, the correct answer has to begin with the *director*.

37. (D)—The idea in the sentence is best expressed with the *not only . . . but also* formula. When this formula is used, the two items connected by it have to be in the same grammatical form. It's most idiomatic to use infinitives to describe his ambitions.

38. (E)—Only (E) formulates the conditional mood correctly.

39. (C)—Although there is nothing grammatically wrong with these sentences, the essay flows better if they are combined into one sentence. (C) does so in the most logical manner. (A) is an incomplete sentence, (B) and (D) are inconsistent in tense, and (E) incorrectly uses *me* rather than *I*.

40. (E)—The sentence contains a dangling modifier and must be recast so that it is clear that the first clause modifies the writer. Only (E) corrects this problem.

41. (A)—Sentence 5 elaborates on the idea expressed in sentence 4: why the writer believes advertising should be allowed in school. Thus the best replacement is *Furthermore*. All of the other choices provide a sense of contrast rather than continuation, and so are inappropriate in context.

42. (B)—There is no clear antecedent for the word *they* in sentence 6, but from context it clearly refers to the schools, so (B) is correct.

43. (D)—Besides being a run-on sentence, sentence 8 is illogical: A soft-drink ad may be *unsightly*, but *seeing* it cannot be. (D) solves the logic problem by removing the word *seeing*, and avoids the run-on problem by adding the conjunction *but*. (B) contains the same logic problem as the original sentence; moreover, (B) changes the meaning of the original somewhat with its use of *even though*. (C) contains a misplaced modifier: It is the ad that is unsightly, not the side of a school bus. In addition to being awkwardly worded, (E) changes the meaning of the original sentence.

44. (E)—The writer provides no alternative means of raising money to close the gap in the school budget, so (E) is correct. (A) is clearly wrong—the entire essay expresses the writer's personal views. Sentences 12 and 13 refer to student opinion, so (B) is out. Sentence 6, explaining the view of critics of the plan, eliminates (C), and sentences 9 and 11, which ask rhetorical questions, rule out (D).

45. (A)—The second paragraph explores differences between French and American lifestyles that are deeper than those outlined in the first paragraph. (Sentence 18 nicely encapsulates the difference between the two paragraphs with its reference to fleeting versus long-lasting changes.) Thus (A), which hints at the "more important" distinctions described in the second paragraph, is the best connection. (B) and (C) come out of nowhere: The writer is merely noting, not lamenting, certain cultural differences. (D) is illogical because the writer describes her time in France as "exciting." (E) isn't bad as a conclusion to the first paragraph, but doesn't work as a tie-in to the second paragraph.

46. (C)—(C) fixes sentence 8's inconsistency in tense by employing the simple past, which is correct in context. (A) contains a misplaced modifier: *Montpellier* cannot be modified by a clause beginning with *showering*. (B) contains an awkward and unnecessary shift to the passive voice. (D) is awkwardly worded and changes the meaning of the original sentence. (E) is consistent in tense but its use of the past continuous (*were . . . showering*) instead of the simple past doesn't work in context.

47. (D)—The sentence is inconsistent in tense, switching back and forth between the past and the present, and the use of *you* is awkward in context. (D) fixes these errors. (A), (C), and (E) fail because of their use of the present tense, and (B) is awkwardly worded and uses *you* when *we* is more appropriate in context.

48. (B)—From context, we know that the writer is trying to say that despite the summer heat, cold-water showers were a new and different experience. (B) makes this clear. (A) and (C), although they seem to provide the requisite sense of contrast, produce ungrammatical sentences. (D) and (E) make no sense and do not form grammatical sentences either.

49. (E)—(E) removes the sentence fragment that is the principal weakness in sentence 14. (A) and (C) create sentence fragments, (B) is awkwardly worded, and (D), by removing the conjunction *Since*, creates a sentence fragment.

50. (C)—Sentence 16's use of the present tense is confusing and awkward, since the writer is clearly referring to the past. Therefore (C) is correct. Contrary to (A), no definition need be provided for *resources*, as context makes it clear what this means. Examples are provided elsewhere in the paragraph, so (B) is out. (D) makes no sense, and (E)'s suggestion would only make matters more confusing by dismantling the logical structure of the essay.

51. (D)—The problem with the comparison is difficult to see, because *proposals* is at the beginning of the sentence, while *rival* is at the end. (D) should read *those of his rival*.

52. (C)—The construction *either . . . or* requires *or*, not *nor*.

53. (E)—This sentence contains no error.

54. (E)—This sentence contains no error.

55. (D)—The pronoun *them* refers to the singular noun *outcry*, so it should be corrected to *it*.

56. (D)—The antecedent of *which* is *Ruth Benedict*. But it's incorrect to use *which* to refer to a person. *Who* is correct here.

57. (E)—This sentence contains no error.

58. (D)—*Able for inventing* isn't correct; *able to invent* is.

59. (E)—This sentence contains no error.

60. (B)—There's no such word as *irregardless*. *Regardless* or *irrespective* is correct here.

ANSWER SHEET
FOR PRACTICE TEST 4

1 Ⓐ Ⓑ Ⓒ Ⓓ Ⓔ	16 Ⓐ Ⓑ Ⓒ Ⓓ Ⓔ	31 Ⓐ Ⓑ Ⓒ Ⓓ Ⓔ	46 Ⓐ Ⓑ Ⓒ Ⓓ Ⓔ
2 Ⓐ Ⓑ Ⓒ Ⓓ Ⓔ	17 Ⓐ Ⓑ Ⓒ Ⓓ Ⓔ	32 Ⓐ Ⓑ Ⓒ Ⓓ Ⓔ	47 Ⓐ Ⓑ Ⓒ Ⓓ Ⓔ
3 Ⓐ Ⓑ Ⓒ Ⓓ Ⓔ	18 Ⓐ Ⓑ Ⓒ Ⓓ Ⓔ	33 Ⓐ Ⓑ Ⓒ Ⓓ Ⓔ	48 Ⓐ Ⓑ Ⓒ Ⓓ Ⓔ
4 Ⓐ Ⓑ Ⓒ Ⓓ Ⓔ	19 Ⓐ Ⓑ Ⓒ Ⓓ Ⓔ	34 Ⓐ Ⓑ Ⓒ Ⓓ Ⓔ	49 Ⓐ Ⓑ Ⓒ Ⓓ Ⓔ
5 Ⓐ Ⓑ Ⓒ Ⓓ Ⓔ	20 Ⓐ Ⓑ Ⓒ Ⓓ Ⓔ	35 Ⓐ Ⓑ Ⓒ Ⓓ Ⓔ	50 Ⓐ Ⓑ Ⓒ Ⓓ Ⓔ
6 Ⓐ Ⓑ Ⓒ Ⓓ Ⓔ	21 Ⓐ Ⓑ Ⓒ Ⓓ Ⓔ	36 Ⓐ Ⓑ Ⓒ Ⓓ Ⓔ	51 Ⓐ Ⓑ Ⓒ Ⓓ Ⓔ
7 Ⓐ Ⓑ Ⓒ Ⓓ Ⓔ	22 Ⓐ Ⓑ Ⓒ Ⓓ Ⓔ	37 Ⓐ Ⓑ Ⓒ Ⓓ Ⓔ	52 Ⓐ Ⓑ Ⓒ Ⓓ Ⓔ
8 Ⓐ Ⓑ Ⓒ Ⓓ Ⓔ	23 Ⓐ Ⓑ Ⓒ Ⓓ Ⓔ	38 Ⓐ Ⓑ Ⓒ Ⓓ Ⓔ	53 Ⓐ Ⓑ Ⓒ Ⓓ Ⓔ
9 Ⓐ Ⓑ Ⓒ Ⓓ Ⓔ	24 Ⓐ Ⓑ Ⓒ Ⓓ Ⓔ	39 Ⓐ Ⓑ Ⓒ Ⓓ Ⓔ	54 Ⓐ Ⓑ Ⓒ Ⓓ Ⓔ
10 Ⓐ Ⓑ Ⓒ Ⓓ Ⓔ	25 Ⓐ Ⓑ Ⓒ Ⓓ Ⓔ	40 Ⓐ Ⓑ Ⓒ Ⓓ Ⓔ	55 Ⓐ Ⓑ Ⓒ Ⓓ Ⓔ
11 Ⓐ Ⓑ Ⓒ Ⓓ Ⓔ	26 Ⓐ Ⓑ Ⓒ Ⓓ Ⓔ	41 Ⓐ Ⓑ Ⓒ Ⓓ Ⓔ	56 Ⓐ Ⓑ Ⓒ Ⓓ Ⓔ
12 Ⓐ Ⓑ Ⓒ Ⓓ Ⓔ	27 Ⓐ Ⓑ Ⓒ Ⓓ Ⓔ	42 Ⓐ Ⓑ Ⓒ Ⓓ Ⓔ	57 Ⓐ Ⓑ Ⓒ Ⓓ Ⓔ
13 Ⓐ Ⓑ Ⓒ Ⓓ Ⓔ	28 Ⓐ Ⓑ Ⓒ Ⓓ Ⓔ	43 Ⓐ Ⓑ Ⓒ Ⓓ Ⓔ	58 Ⓐ Ⓑ Ⓒ Ⓓ Ⓔ
14 Ⓐ Ⓑ Ⓒ Ⓓ Ⓔ	29 Ⓐ Ⓑ Ⓒ Ⓓ Ⓔ	44 Ⓐ Ⓑ Ⓒ Ⓓ Ⓔ	59 Ⓐ Ⓑ Ⓒ Ⓓ Ⓔ
15 Ⓐ Ⓑ Ⓒ Ⓓ Ⓔ	30 Ⓐ Ⓑ Ⓒ Ⓓ Ⓔ	45 Ⓐ Ⓑ Ⓒ Ⓓ Ⓔ	60 Ⓐ Ⓑ Ⓒ Ⓓ Ⓔ

right

wrong

Use the answer key following the test to count up the number of questions you got right and the number you got wrong. (Remember not to count omitted questions as wrong.) The "Compute Your Score" section at the back of the book will show you how to find your score.

ANSWER SHEET
FOR PRACTICE TEST 4

Part A (ESSAY). Begin your composition on this side. If you need more space, you may continue on the reverse side.

_____

_____

_____

_____

_____

_____

_____

_____

_____

_____

_____

_____

_____

_____

_____

_____

_____

_____

_____

_____

_____

_____

ANSWER SHEET
FOR PRACTICE TEST 4

Continuation of Part A (ESSAY) from reverse side. Write below if you need more space.

_____

_____

_____

_____

_____

_____

_____

_____

_____

_____

_____

_____

_____

_____

_____

_____

_____

_____

_____

PART A
Time—20 Minutes (1 Question)

Directions: You have 20 minutes to write an essay on the following topic. **DO NOT WRITE AN ESSAY ON ANY OTHER TOPIC. AN ESSAY ON A DIFFERENT TOPIC IS UNACCEPTABLE.**

This essay provides you with an opportunity to demonstrate how well you write. Therefore, you should express your ideas clearly and effectively. How much you write is much less important than how well you write; but to express your thoughts on the topic adequately you may want to write more than a single paragraph. Your essay should be specific.

Your essay must be written in the lines provided on your answer sheet. No other paper will be given to you. There is enough space to write your essay on the answer sheet if you write on every line, avoid wide margins, and keep your handwriting to a reasonable size.

Consider the following statement and assignment. Then write an essay as directed.

"Thanks to technological advances, the world is getting smaller every day."

Assignment: Write an essay that completes the statement above. Explain the reasons behind your choice.

WHEN THE PROCTOR ANNOUNCES THAT 20 MINUTES HAVE PASSED, YOU MUST STOP WRITING AND GO ON TO PART B OF THE TEST. IF YOU FINISH YOUR ESSAY BEFORE 20 MINUTES PASS, YOU MAY GO ON TO PART B.

YOU MAY MAKE NOTES ON THIS PAGE AND THE FOLLOWING ONE, BUT YOU MUST WRITE YOUR ESSAY ON THE ANSWER SHEET.

You may use this page to outline your essay or make other notes as you plan your essay. Don't write your essay here, though. Your essay must be written on the lined pages of the answer sheet at the beginning of this answer section.

TURN TO THE NEXT PAGE.

PART B

Time—40 Minutes (60 Questions)

For each of the following questions, choose the best answer from the given choices and darken the corresponding oval on the answer sheet.

Directions: The following sentences contain problems in grammar, usage, diction (choice of words), and idiom.

Some of the sentences are correct.

None of the sentences contains more than one error.

The error, if there is one in the sentence, is underlined and lettered. Parts of the sentence that are not underlined are correct and cannot be changed. In selecting answers, follow the requirements of standard written English.

If there is an error, choose the <u>one underlined part</u> that must be changed to make the sentence correct and fill in the corresponding oval on your answer grid.

If there is no error, fill in oval E.

SAMPLE QUESTION

<u>Even though</u> he <u>had to</u> supervise a large
    A   B

staff, his salary <u>was no greater</u> than <u>a clerk</u>.
              C   D

<u>No error</u>
  E

SAMPLE ANSWER

---

1. Since the government <u>was</u> bankrupt, many of
                A

    the soldiers <u>which</u> were sent <u>to quell</u> the riots
                B   C

    had <u>not been</u> paid in months. <u>No error</u>
         D   E

2. Although <u>they had been</u> political rivals on
           A

    <u>more than one</u> occasion, John Quincy Adams
       B

    <u>remained</u> one of Thomas Jefferson's closest
       C

    friends until <u>his</u> death. <u>No error</u>
            D   E

3. Even <u>those who</u> profess <u>to care</u> about "green"
       A   B

    issues often fail to consider <u>how</u> their daily
                       C

    choices <u>effect</u> the environment. <u>No error</u>
          D   E

4. Ants, <u>which</u> have inhabited the earth for at
      A

    least 100 million years, <u>are without doubt</u> the
                      B

    <u>more successful</u> of all the social insects of the
       C

    Hymenoptera, an order <u>that also</u> includes
                   D

    wasps and bees. <u>No error</u>
              E

TURN TO THE NEXT PAGE.

5. For my sister and <u>I</u>, the trip to Paris was the
            A
<u>fulfillment of</u> a lifelong wish we <u>had scarcely</u>
       B   C
<u>dared to express</u>. <u>No error</u>
          D   E

6. The volunteers, <u>upon discovering</u> that
                        A
<u>a large number</u> of the village children <u>were</u>
       B   C
infected by parasites <u>from</u> unclean drinking
                          D
water, decided to make the well-digging

project their highest priority. <u>No error</u>
                                    E

7. Although farmers complained that the

company's new product was expensive,

malodorous, and <u>dangerous to handle</u>,
                      A
<u>there was</u> few who <u>would dispute</u> its
    B   C
effectiveness <u>as</u> an insecticide. <u>No error</u>
                  D   E

8. In the wake <u>of</u> recent thefts, the town's
                  A
wealthier residents <u>have installed</u> gates, alarm
                        B
systems, and even video surveillance

equipment in their neighborhoods, hoping

<u>that it will</u> prevent <u>further</u> burglaries. <u>No error</u>.
    C   D   E

9. <u>To repair</u> the damage <u>that</u> time and the
      A   B
elements <u>had wrought</u> on the ancient fresco,
              C
the restorer used a simple mixture <u>from</u>
                                        D
plaster, pigment, and a little water. <u>No error</u>
                                        E

10. Opponents of the Act <u>argued that</u> the
                              A
legislation <u>was not only</u> vaguely formulated
                  B
and unconstitutional, but also impossible

<u>to enforce</u> in an international <u>and virtually</u>
    C   D
unregulated arena. <u>No error</u>
                        E

11. One reason that a growing number of people

<u>have no</u> family doctor <u>may be that</u> fewer and
    A   B
fewer medical students <u>are choosing to train</u> as
                              C
<u>a general practitioner</u>. <u>No error</u>
          D   E

12. <u>That</u> J. L. Solomon's first novel <u>was selected for</u>
      A   B
several major literary prizes <u>was surprising to</u>
                                  C
no one who had read his <u>previous</u> collections
                              D
of short stories, poems, and essays. <u>No error</u>
                                        E

TURN TO THE NEXT PAGE.

13. Citizens <u>protesting the</u> planned demolition of
                A

    the historic YMCA building claim <u>that without</u>
                                         B

    the YMCA, many young people in the town

    <u>would of</u> grown up <u>with no</u> access to sports
       C   D

    facilities and no place for after-school

    recreation. <u>No error</u>
              E

14. When questioned, <u>a surprising</u> number of
                   A

    fifth-graders said that telling the truth—even

    <u>if it</u> meant <u>being</u> punished—was preferable
     B   C

    <u>than living</u> with a lie. <u>No error</u>
      D   E

15. <u>Though</u> Patricia's résumé was <u>not nearly as</u>
      A   B

    long and impressive as <u>the other applicant,</u>
                   C

    her personal charisma was <u>so great that</u> Mr.
                      D

    Alvarez hired her on the spot. <u>No error</u>
                       E

16. <u>Under</u> the proposed law, which many <u>deem</u>
      A   B

    too harsh, any motorist <u>convicted of</u> drunk
                   C

    driving would spend thirty days in prison and

    lose <u>their license</u> for five years. <u>No error</u>
        D   E

17. When <u>it became apparent</u> to Clive that not one
           A

    of the remaining jurors <u>were going to</u> believe
                      B

    his <u>client's</u> alibi, he began to reconsider the
       C

    District Attorney's <u>offer of</u> a plea bargain.
                 D

    <u>No error</u>
     E

18. <u>If only</u> the factory owners <u>had conducted</u>
      A   B

    regular safety inspections <u>of</u> their equipment,
                    C

    the horrible accident of 1969 <u>may have been</u>
                     D

    averted. <u>No error</u>
           E

19. The symphony <u>had not</u> hardly begun <u>when</u> a
             A   B

    group of schoolchildren, who <u>had been forced</u>
                     C

    to attend, began irritating the rest of the

    audience <u>by talking loudly</u> and kicking the
               D

    seats. <u>No error</u>
         E

20. The gods of Greek mythology, who

    <u>were neither</u> omniscient nor <u>particularly</u>
      A   B

    ethical, amused themselves <u>by taking on</u>
                  C

    disguises and <u>meddling in</u> the affairs of
             D

    mortals. <u>No error</u>
          E

TURN TO THE NEXT PAGE.

For each of the following questions, choose the best answer from the given choices and darken the corresponding oval on the answer sheet.

Directions: The following sentences test accuracy and effectiveness of expression. In selecting answers, follow the rules of standard written English; in other words, consider grammar, choice of words, sentence construction, and punctuation.

In each of the following sentences, a portion or all of the sentence is underlined. Under each sentence you will find five ways of phrasing the underlined portion. Choice A repeats the original underlined portion; the other four choices provide alternative phrasings.

Select the choice that best expresses the meaning of the original sentence. If the original sentence is better than any of the alternative phrasings, choose A; otherwise select one of the alternatives. Your selection should construct the most effective sentence—clear and precise with no awkwardness or ambiguity.

SAMPLE QUESTION

Wanting to reward her assistant for loyalty,
Sheila gave a bonus to him as large as his paycheck.

SAMPLE ANSWER

(A) Sheila gave a bonus to him as large as his paycheck
(B) given to him by Sheila was a bonus as large as his paycheck
(C) he was given a bonus as large as his paycheck by Sheila
(D) Sheila gave him a bonus as large as his paycheck
(E) Sheila gave him a paycheck to him as large as his bonus

---

21. Patients with Alzheimer's disease typically exhibit symptoms such as confusion, memory loss, and their language skills are impaired.

    (A) and their language skills are impaired
    (B) and it also impairs their language skills
    (C) and impaired language skills
    (D) besides their language skills being impaired
    (E) in addition to their language skills being impaired

22. Upon entering the jail, the prisoners' personal belongings are surrendered to the guards.

    (A) Upon entering the jail, the prisoners' personal belongings are surrendered to the guards.
    (B) Upon entering the jail, the prisoners surrender their personal belongings to the guards.
    (C) The prisoners' personal belongings having been surrendered to the guards upon entering the jail.
    (D) Upon entering the jail, the guards are to whom the prisoners surrender their personal belongings.
    (E) Upon entering the jail, the prisoners will have been surrendering their personal belongings to the guards.

TURN TO THE NEXT PAGE.

23. <u>The albatross has a broad wingspan, it is graceful in the air but ungainly on dry land.</u>

   (A) The albatross has a broad wingspan, it is graceful in the air but ungainly on dry land.
   (B) The albatross, with its broad wingspan, is graceful in the air but ungainly on dry land.
   (C) Having a broad wingspan, the albatross is graceful in the air, however it is ungainly on dry land.
   (D) The albatross, which has a broad wingspan, graceful in the air but ungainly on dry land.
   (E) The albatross, although having a broad wingspan, is graceful in the air but ungainly on dry land.

24. King John of England is remembered not so much for his administrative successes <u>but for failing in military engagements</u>.

   (A) but for failing in military engagements
   (B) but more for the fact that he failed in military engagements
   (C) than he was for having failed militarily
   (D) the reason being that he failed in military engagements
   (E) as for his military failures

25. According to older fishermen, cod and haddock were once plentiful in the North Sea, but years of over-fishing and pollution have <u>had a negative overall impact on the fish stocks</u>.

   (A) had a negative overall impact on the fish stocks
   (B) impacted the fish stocks negatively
   (C) the result that the fish stocks are diminished
   (D) depleted the fish stocks
   (E) been depleting the fish stocks overall

26. <u>During the winter months, several feet of snow cover the narrow mountain pass, which is the only route to the monastery.</u>

   (A) During the winter months, several feet of snow cover the narrow mountain pass, which is the only route to the monastery.
   (B) The only route to the monastery, several feet of snow cover the narrow mountain pass during the winter months.
   (C) Several feet of snow cover the narrow mountain pass during the winter months which is the only route to the monastery.
   (D) Several feet of snow cover the narrow mountain pass, which is the only route to the monastery during the winter months.
   (E) During the winter months, covering the narrow mountain pass which is the only route to the monastery is snow.

27. The Townshend Acts, a piece of British legislation enacted on June 29, 1767, <u>were intended for the raising of revenue, to tighten customs enforcement, and assert</u> imperial authority in America.

   (A) were intended for the raising of revenue, to tighten customs enforcement, and assert
   (B) were intended to raise revenue, tighten customs enforcement, and assert
   (C) were with the intention of raising revenue, tightening customs enforcement, and assert
   (D) had for their intention the raising of revenue, tightening of customs enforcement, and asserting
   (E) were intended to raise revenue, also to tighten customs enforcement and assert

TURN TO THE NEXT PAGE.

28. The border crossing proved more unpleasant than the two American reporters had <u>expected, having their cameras seized</u> and their tape recorders smashed by belligerent soldiers.

    (A) expected, having their cameras seized
    (B) expected, their cameras being seized
    (C) expected: their cameras were seized
    (D) expected; when their cameras were seized
    (E) expected and so their cameras had been seized

29. <u>Were it not for the warming effects of the Gulf Stream, England's climate would resemble that of Greenland.</u>

    (A) Were it not for the warming effects of the Gulf Stream, England's climate would resemble that of Greenland.
    (B) Had the Gulf Stream not such warming effects, England's climate would resemble Greenland.
    (C) Without the warming effects of the Gulf Stream, England's climate were resembling Greenland's.
    (D) If not for the warming effects of the Gulf Stream, therefore England's climate would have resembled that of Greenland.
    (E) If the Gulf Stream would not have had its warming effects, England's climate would resemble that of Greenland.

30. Perhaps best known for his portrayal of T. E. Lawrence in the film *Lawrence of Arabia*, <u>Peter O'Toole's distinguished acting career spans nearly five decades.</u>

    (A) Peter O'Toole's distinguished acting career spans nearly five decades
    (B) Peter O'Toole has a distinguished acting career spanning nearly five decades
    (C) Peter O'Toole spans nearly five decades in his distinguished acting career
    (D) Peter O'Toole's distinguished acting career will have spanned nearly five decades
    (E) nearly five decades have been spanned by Peter O'Toole's distinguished acting career

31. In their haste to complete the new stadium before the Olympic games, the contractors disregarded safety <u>codes, thereby they endangered the lives of thousands of spectators.</u>

    (A) codes, thereby they endangered the lives of thousands of spectators
    (B) codes they have endangered the lives of thousands of spectators
    (C) codes and so endangered the lives of thousands of spectators
    (D) codes; thus the lives of thousands of spectators endangered
    (E) codes, they endangered the lives of thousands of spectators as a result

32. When Dr. Park presented an abridged version of his paper at the conference, <u>several tantalizing theories about the origins of life on earth were introduced, but these were not fully developed by him.</u>

    (A) several tantalizing theories about the origins of life on earth were introduced, but these were not fully developed by him
    (B) he introduced several tantalizing theories about the origins of life on earth but they had not been fully developed
    (C) several tantalizing theories about the origins of life were introduced by him and not fully developed
    (D) several tantalizing theories about the origins of life on earth were introduced, but he did not fully develop these
    (E) he introduced, but did not fully develop, several tantalizing theories about the origins of life on earth

TURN TO THE NEXT PAGE.

KAPLAN

33. Many researchers contend that driving while talking on a cellular phone poses essentially the same risks <u>than if you drive</u> while intoxicated.

(A) than if you drive
(B) than to drive
(C) as if one drives
(D) as driving
(E) as it does when driving

34. Before 1988, the corporation's board of directors included one hundred and fifty-three <u>members, none of the members were women</u>.

(A) members, none of the members were women
(B) members; and no women
(C) members, none of them women
(D) members, and of the members not one of them was a woman
(E) members; none of them being women

35. <u>The client was waiting for fifteen minutes when</u> the receptionist suddenly looked up from her work, noticed him, and informed him that his appointment had been canceled.

(A) The client was waiting for fifteen minutes when
(B) The client, having waited for fifteen minutes, when
(C) Already the client was waiting for fifteen minutes when
(D) When the client waited for fifteen minutes,
(E) The client had been waiting for fifteen minutes when

36. A spokesman for the arms dealers boasted that the new weapon was lightweight, effective, <u>and virtually undetectable by the security equipment most commonly used in airports</u>.

(A) and virtually undetectable by the security equipment most commonly used in airports
(B) and the security equipment most commonly used in airports could not detect it
(C) and virtually undetectable for the security equipment most commonly used in airports
(D) and had gone virtually undetected by the security equipment most commonly used in airports
(E) and the security equipment most commonly used in airports virtually unable to detect it

37. <u>Because the polar ice caps are melting, therefore many</u> scientists and environmentalists fear that several small island nations will be completely covered by water in only a few decades.

(A) Because the polar ice caps are melting, therefore many
(B) Because the polar ice caps are melting, many
(C) The polar ice caps are melting, therefore many
(D) Because the polar ice caps are melting; many
(E) The polar ice caps are melting; and many

38. One of the great literary artists of the nineteenth <u>century was Gustave Flaubert known for his obsession with the writer's craft</u>.

(A) century was Gustave Flaubert known for his obsession with the writer's craft
(B) century, Gustave Flaubert's obsession with the writer's craft was well known
(C) century, Gustave Flaubert was known for his obsession with the writer's craft
(D) century, Gustave Flaubert, known for his obsession with the writer's craft
(E) century was Gustave Flaubert: known for his obsession with the writer's craft

TURN TO THE NEXT PAGE.

Directions: The following passages are first drafts of student essays. Some portions of the essays have to be rewritten.

Read the essays and answer the questions that follow them. Some of the questions concern particular sentences or fragments of sentences and require you to make choices about sentence structure, word choice, and usage. Other questions pertain to the entire essay or pieces of the essay and require you to think about organization, development, and appropriateness of language. Pick the answer that most effectively conveys the meaning and follows the rules of standard written English. Once you have chosen an answer, fill in the corresponding oval on your answer sheet.

Questions 39–44 are based on the following essay, which is a response to an assignment to write a letter to a local newspaper protesting cuts in funding for after-school sports programs.

(1) *I disagree with the editor's view that after-school sports programs should be cut in our city government's search for ways to reduce spending. (2) The editor argues that extra-curricular sports play a less important role to academic studies, distracting students from the opportunity to increase their knowledge after school is out. (3) However, I myself believe that playing sports enhances students' academic performance.*

(4) *Why is sports so effective in this regard? (5) The main reason is that sports teaches people to excel. (6) It gives students the chance to strive for greatness. (7) It shows them that it takes courage and discipline to succeed in competition with others. (8) Top athletes such as Michael Jordan become role models for young people everywhere, inspiring them with his brilliant individual performances. (9) In addition to these personal attributes, playing in team sports show young people how to interact with each other, achieving shared goals. (10) Such principles have a direct impact on how students perform in their academic studies. (11) I know that being selected for the school lacrosse team taught me many valuable lessons about working with others. (12) Not only that, friendships which I have made there were carried into the rest of my school life. (13) In summary, I would urge the editor to strongly reconsider his stance on extra-curricular sports. (14) There are doubtless other ways of city government saving the money they require.*

39. Which of the following is the best way to revise the underlined portion of sentence 3 (reproduced below)?

However, I myself believe that playing sports enhances students' academic performance.

(A) However, I myself believe that playing sports should enhance

(B) Playing sports, however, I believe enhances

(C) However, I personally believe that playing sports enhances

(D) I believe, however, that playing sports enhances

(E) However, I myself believe that to play sports is to enhance

---

TURN TO THE NEXT PAGE.

40. Which of the following is the best way to revise and combine sentences 6 and 7 (reproduced below)?

    It gives students the chance to strive for greatness. It shows them that it takes courage and discipline to succeed in competition with others.

    (A) Although it gives students the chance to strive for greatness, it also shows them that it takes courage and discipline to succeed in competition with others.
    (B) While it gives students the chance to strive for greatness, also showing them that it takes courage and discipline to succeed in competition with others.
    (C) It gives students the chance to strive for greatness, showing them that it takes courage and discipline to succeed in competition with others.
    (D) Because it gives students the chance to strive for greatness, they are shown that it takes courage and discipline to succeed in competition with others.
    (E) It gives students the chance to strive for greatness and show them that it takes courage and discipline to succeed in competition with others.

41. In the context of the second paragraph, which of the following is the best version of the underlined portion of sentence 8 (reproduced below)?

    Top athletes such as Michael Jordan become role models for young people everywhere, inspiring them with his brilliant individual performances.

    (A) (As it is now)
    (B) inspiring him with their
    (C) inspiring them with their
    (D) to inspire them with his
    (E) inspiring him with his

42. Which of the following is the best way to revise the underlined portion of sentence 12 (reproduced below)?

    Not only that, friendships which I have made there were carried into the rest of my school life.

    (A) And,
    (B) Moreover,
    (C) Nevertheless,
    (D) Sequentially,
    (E) Finally,

43. Which of the following best describes the author's approach in the passage as a whole?

    (A) defending an unpopular point of view
    (B) criticizing an opponent's opinion
    (C) supporting an argument with evidence
    (D) considering the merits of two competing proposals
    (E) citing statistics to disprove a theory

44. The author could best improve sentence 14 by

    (A) making an analogy to historical events
    (B) taking alternative points of view into account
    (C) including a personal anecdote about her participation in team sports
    (D) speculating about the motivations of those advocating cuts
    (E) providing examples of other areas in which spending could be reduced

TURN TO THE NEXT PAGE.

Questions 45–50 are based on the following passage.

(1) Until recently, I was convinced I had no musical ability whatsoever. (2) In grade school, I could hardly keep my voice in tune with other singers around me. (3) I thought that I would never play a musical instrument or become a rock star. (4) I really enjoyed music, just no one thought I had any talent at all.

(5) When I entered junior high I took music classes with our teacher, Mr. Daniels. (6) At first he seemed really stern and strict. (7) He gave us lots of warnings that even though he had a reputation for being harsh around school, the reality was ten times worse. (8) But after a couple of weeks, he started encouraging us to get into musical ensembles. (9) At first I was disinterested, thinking that I would be ridiculed as to my contribution. (10) Mr. Daniels kept insisted that everyone had to play some kind of instrument, so I chose his handbell choir. (11) Other kids thought handbells were stupid, but I liked the sound they made—it was so much purer than the electric guitar. (12) Mr. Daniels coached us regular after school. (13) Not only did the group actually start to sound good, but also I discovered that I had some rhythmic talents that no one had suspected. (14) Maybe I will be a rock star yet! (15) The whole experience showed me that with encouragement and a sense of adventure you can overcome your limitations. (16) As our former First Lady Eleanor Roosevelt once said, sometimes "you must do that which you think you cannot do."

45. Which of the following versions of sentence 4 (reproduced below) is best?

    I really enjoyed music, just no one thought I had any talent at all.

    (A) (As it is now)
    (B) Even though I really enjoyed music, just no one thought I had any talent at all.
    (C) I really enjoyed music, and therefore no one thought I had any talent at all.
    (D) Although I really enjoyed music, no one thought I had any talent at all.
    (E) The music was enjoyable to me, however no one thought I had any talent at all.

46. Which of the following sentences, if added after sentence 4, would best link the first paragraph with the rest of the essay?

    (A) As a result, I learned that other people's opinions are irrelevant.
    (B) However, I soon met an inspiring person who disproved this assumption.
    (C) This was why no one thought I would become a rock star.
    (D) Nevertheless, I knew all along that I possessed a form of musical genius.
    (E) I have held these beliefs about my musical ability for many years.

TURN TO THE NEXT PAGE.

47. In the context of the second paragraph, which of the following is the best version of the underlined portion of sentence 11 (reproduced below)?

Other kids thought handbells were stupid, but I liked the sound they made—it was so much purer than the electric guitar.

(A) (As it is now)
(B) it was so much more pure than the electric guitar
(C) the sound of it was so much purer than the electric guitar
(D) compared to the electric guitar, its sound was so much purer
(E) it was so much purer than the sound of the electric guitar

48. Which of the following is the best version of the underlined portion of sentence 13 (reproduced below)?

Not only did the group actually start to sound good, but also I discovered that I had some rhythmic talents that no one had suspected.

(A) (As it is now)
(B) The group actually started
(C) While the group actually started
(D) Not only was the group actually starting
(E) Although the group was actually starting

49. In the context of the passage, the word *"encouragement"* in line 15 most likely refers to

(A) the ambition to become a famous musician
(B) Mr. Daniels' efforts to persuade students to try music
(C) the author's decision to pursue a career as a teacher
(D) the attitudes of parents towards the study of music
(E) audience reactions to a satisfying musical performance

50. All of the following strategies are used by the writer of the passage EXCEPT

(A) recounting a series of events
(B) drawing a conclusion based on a discovery
(C) criticizing other people's opinions
(D) introducing a quotation to emphasize a point
(E) describing his own fears and motivations

TURN TO THE NEXT PAGE.

For each of the following questions, choose the best answer from the given choices and darken the corresponding oval on the answer sheet.

Directions: The following sentences contain problems in grammar, usage, diction (choice of words), and idiom.

Some of the sentences are correct.

None of the sentences contains more than one error.

The error, if there is one in the sentence, is underlined and lettered. Parts of the sentence that are not underlined are correct and cannot be changed. In selecting answers, follow the requirements of standard written English.

If there is an error, choose the <u>one underlined part</u> that must be changed to make the sentence correct and fill in the corresponding oval on your answer grid.

If there is no error, fill in oval E.

SAMPLE QUESTION

<u>Even though</u> he <u>had to</u> supervise a large
   A   B
staff, his salary <u>was no greater</u> than <u>a clerk</u>.
            C   D
<u>No error</u>
  E

SAMPLE ANSWER

Ⓐ Ⓑ Ⓒ ● Ⓔ

---

51. <u>Of</u> the four members of the mountain-climbing
   A
team, <u>none were</u> more frightened and
       B
inexperienced <u>than</u> <u>she</u>. <u>No error</u>
          C   D   E

52. Dr. Mfume's team <u>is attempting</u> to cure a
               A
disease that, <u>although</u> harmless <u>to</u> human
         B   C
beings, <u>regularly decimates</u> cattle herds in
        D
Africa and parts of Asia. <u>No error</u>
                E

53. The young scholar's research proposal

<u>consisted in</u> little more than <u>a series of</u> half-
  A   B
formulated ideas, loosely <u>strung</u> together
                C
and <u>poorly</u> documented. <u>No error</u>
     D   E

54. If one wishes <u>to succeed</u> in business,
         A
<u>you should</u> acquire good communication
  B
skills, <u>which</u> corporate leaders agree
     C
<u>are of paramount</u> importance. <u>No error</u>
  D   E

TURN TO THE NEXT PAGE.

55. Analysts were surprised <u>that neither</u> the crises
                              A
facing the nation's public schools <u>nor</u> the
                                     B
decay of urban centers <u>were</u> included in the
                          C
<u>party's</u> official platform. <u>No error</u>
   D   E

56. The twins were indistinguishable <u>from</u> one
                                       A
another in every respect <u>but</u> one: Mary, the
                           B
<u>youngest</u> one, had longer hair than her <u>sister</u>.
   C   D
<u>No error</u>
   E

57. Many physicists believe <u>that</u> interstellar travel
                              A
will never be possible <u>due to</u> the distances
                          B
<u>involved</u> are <u>simply</u> too great. <u>No error</u>
   C   D   E

58. Thomas Becket, <u>who</u> the pope elevated to
                     A
sainthood shortly after 1170, <u>is</u> generally
                                 B
believed <u>to have been</u> murdered <u>on</u> the orders
           C   D
of King Henry II. <u>No error</u>
                     E

59. The university's library, designed during a

period <u>when</u> architects prized function <u>over</u>
         A   B
form, is a drab, utilitarian structure

that <u>clashes</u> with the graceful, Gothic buildings
       C
on either side <u>of it</u>. <u>No error</u>
                  D   E

60. <u>Though</u> some critics deride Warhol's work as
      A
worthless commercial trash, others <u>hail</u> him
                                      B
as <u>the most</u> <u>innovative</u> artist of the modern
      C   D
age. <u>No error</u>
       E

STOP!

END OF TEST. DO NOT TURN THE PAGE UNTIL
YOU ARE READY TO CHECK YOUR ANSWERS.

PRACTICE TEST 4 ANSWERS AND EXPLANATIONS

The Essay Section

This section contains sample essays for the essay topic in Practice Test 4. Use these sample essays as benchmarks to help your own essay on the same topic. Does your essay sound more like the grade 6 essay or the grade 3 essay?

Sample Grade 6 Essay

In the society we live in, we are continually informed about new technology that is being developed to improve our quality of life. Software companies are designing programs to give us access to information on the Internet at the touch of a button. Ordinary citizens can use their credit cards to purchase a limitless variety of goods in countries throughout the world. These are examples of ways in which technology seem to be making the world smaller every day. But not all technological advances lead to an improvement in our quality of life.

The development of nuclear technology, for example, seemed to represent a major advance for the power industry. For centuries, the world had depended on expendable fossil fuels such as coal and wood to generate the power. Not only was dependence on fossil fuels harmful to the environment, scientists also knew the Earth's supply of fossil fuels was limited—at some point it would run out. The development of nuclear technology was greeted as the solution to the Earth's power problems. Because it generated enormous power through a relatively small expenditure of raw materials, nations throughout the Western World made nuclear power the core of their energy policy.

In spite of this initial promise, nuclear technology has proven to involve terrible side-effects that have in fact diminished our quality of life. The safe storage of nuclear waste, for example, is a problem scientists have not yet found a solution to. In the early years of nuclear power, scientists stored these radioactive by-products of nuclear power in lead containers buried under the ground. Such storage methods proved ineffective, and in incidents such as the Love Canal disaster, nuclear waste leaked out, exposing humans to dangerous radioactivity. Another problem with nuclear power has been establishing safe conditions at nuclear power plants. In the infamous Chernobyl disaster, a power plant was allowed to reach a critical "meltdown" state, ultimately blowing up and contaminating hundred of miles of countryside.

In conclusion, I believe that technology generally "makes the world smaller every day" in the sense of improving our quality of life. Nevertheless, like its human inventors, technology has its limits. As the case of nuclear power illustrates, technology that is designed to help us can sometimes do as much harm as good.

Grader's comments: This essay is exceptionally good. If defines the topic nicely, it is well written and it is judicious in its use of supporting evidence. Sentence structure and vocabulary are advanced, and there are few grammatical errors.

Sample Grade 3 Essay

Technology literally does make the world smaller every day. Without television, for example, we wouldn't see documenteries about Africa or those movies with subtitles. if you're just a high school student, which I am, you have only limited possibilities of travelling. I live in Michigan, and though I have been to Florida, California and New York, I have not yet given the chance to travel abroad. This is a pity because I think it's only through travelling and experiencing foreign cultures can you grow as a person.

Technology provides the answer to these problems, however. A teacher at our school had an Internet partnership with a Swedish school last year. Students could dial up other students on the computer, and send them messages. Lots of kids just wrote stupid comment, but I thought it was actually interesting. This way, technology was showing us things about Swedish culture that we would never learn. The CD-ROM game "Safari Hunter" is another example. You're a big game hunter on the African plains, and you have to stop evil poachers from killing endangered species. It's more than just a game, though—it has all this information about each species, so (corny as it sounds) you learn while you're have fun. to me, that's the point of technology, to teach you things and entertain you at the same time.

Grader's comments: This essay demonstrates an adequate competence. The author exhibits a good grasp of the topic, and backs up his argument with several concrete examples. However, these ideas are marred by poor organization and several lapses in grammar and logical coherence.

Sample Grade 1 Essay

I disagree with that statement. Technology can't make the world smaller if people can't afford it. People make a big deal about technology changing people's lives but let me tell you. Not everyone's live is getting changed. What good is a computer system if you're family is struggling for the bear necessitates. Personally, I have a computer, but there are plenty of kids at my school that don't. The ones without fall behind in computer classes, and will be extremely unlikely to get high-paying jobs when they graduate school—if they do at all.

The politicians talk about bringing this into the 20th century. For me, the first step would be getting everyone computers. If everybody was given a computer, they would be that much cheaper. Lots of jobs would be created giving computers to everybody. Also, since the computer industry would be bigger, we'd al know more about them. That's my solution. Until then, I don't think the world is getting smaller at all.

Grader's comments: This essay is flawed. It digresses from the topic and displays very little organizational thought. The author's ideas are not well supported, and word choice is repetitious. There are many errors in grammar, diction and sentence structure.

The Multiple-Choice Section

This section contains an answer key and explanations for the Multiple-Choice section in Practice Test 4. Use the scoring conversion table in the back of the book to see how you've done on this section. Pay careful attention to the explanations for the multiple-choice questions you got wrong.

1. B	11. D	21. C	31. C	41. C	51. B
2. D	12. E	22. B	32. E	42. B	52. E
3. D	13. C	23. B	33. D	43. C	53. A
4. C	14. D	24. E	34. C	44. E	54. B
5. A	15. C	25. D	35. E	45. D	55. C
6. E	16. D	26. A	36. A	46. B	56. C
7. B	17. B	27. B	37. B	47. E	57. B
8. C	18. D	28. C	38. C	48. A	58. A
9. D	19. A	29. A	39. D	49. B	59. E
10. E	20. E	30. B	40. C	50. C	60. E

Answers and Explanations

1. (B)—The relative pronoun *which* refers to the soldiers, but *which* cannot be used to refer to people, only to things. The sentence should use the word *who* instead.

2. (D)—Another pronoun error: in this sentence, it is not clear whether *his* refer to Adams or to Jefferson; hence this sentence contains a vague pronoun reference.

3. (D)—*Affect* and *effect* are commonly confused words. Here, *affect* (meaning "to influence" or "to have an *effect* on") would be the correct word, not *effect*.

4. (C)—Faulty comparison: ants are being compared to all the other social insects in the *Hymenoptera* order. Since this order includes far more than two insect species, the superlative *most successful* should be used instead of the comparative *more successful*.

5. (A)—Take out the words "my sister and," and the error of pronoun case becomes obvious—you wouldn't say "for I." Since this pronoun is the

object of the preposition *for*, it should be in the objective case: for my sister and *me*.

6. (E)—The sentence contains no error.

7. (B)—In the second half of the sentence, the verb *was* does not agree with its subject, *few*. *Few* is a plural noun, so the sentence should read *there were few*. Be careful when the subject follows the verb!

8. (C)—If you look for the antecedent of the pronoun *it* here, you won't find it—this is a case of ambiguous pronoun reference.

9. (D)—Idiom alert! The correct preposition should be *a mixture of*, not *a mixture from*.

10. (E)—The sentence contains no error.

11. (D)—Faulty comparison: since *students* is a plural noun, the second part of the sentence should also be plural: *as general practitioners*.

12. (E)—The sentence contains no error, although the phrasing may have sounded strange to your ear.

13. (C)—Faulty diction: *would of* is not Standard Written English, and it makes no sense. The sentence should read *would have grown up.*

14. (D)—The correct idiom here should be *preferable to,* not *preferable than.*

15. (C)—What is being compared in the sentence? The way it's written, *Patricia's résumé* is being compared to the *other applicant,* which makes no sense. *Patricia's résumé* should be compared to the *other applicant's.*

16. (D)—The pronoun *their* is plural and does not agree in number with its singular antecedent, *motorist.* The sentence should read *his or her license.*

17. (B)—The subject *one* takes a singular verb: *not one of the jurors was* going to believe the alibi.

18. (D)—The context makes it clear that the accident was *not* averted; hence the sentence is describing a situation that is contrary to fact. When you know that something *did* happen (but would likely have been avoided if things had been different), *might* is the correct word to use. *May have* suggests that you are not sure whether a thing happened or not: e.g., "I will try Dr. Miller's office, but she may have left already."

19. (A)—*Not hardly* is a double negative.

20. (E)—The sentence contains no error.

21. (C)—For the sake of parallelism, all three things in this list must be in the same grammatical form. *Confusion* and *memory loss* are both nouns, so *impaired language skills* is the best choice to complete the sentence.

22. (B)—*Upon entering the jail* is an introductory participial phrase that describes the prisoners (they are the ones entering the jail). As the sentence is worded, it sounds as though the prisoners' personal belongings are entering the jail. (B) and (E) are the only two choices that place *the prisoners* right

next to the phrase that describes them. (B) is the best choice; (E) puts the verb in an awkward and incorrect tense.

23. (B)—Choice (B) is the best way to rephrase this run-on sentence; it expresses, in an economical and graceful way, the logical connection between these two pieces of information about the albatross.

24. (E)—*So much* should be followed by the preposition *as.* (E) completes the comparison and conforms to the rules of parallelism; *administrative successes* (an adjective-noun pair) is balanced by *military failures.*

25. (D)—The underlined portion of the sentence is wordy and awkward—it sounds like a badly written business memo. (D) is a concise and correct rephrasing (note that it is also the shortest answer choice).

26. (A)—The sentence contains no error. Choices (B) through (E) are all awkward or grammatically incorrect.

27. (B)—The three items in this list should be in parallel grammatical form. The best way to correct the error is to rephrase all three as infinitive verbs (note, again, that the correct answer is also the shortest and most concise).

28. (C)—The second half of the sentence is an explanation of the first half, and a colon best expresses this logical connection. (A), (B), and (D) all introduce sentence fragments, and (E) uses the wrong verb tense and incorrectly presents the camera seizure as a consequence (not an explanation) of the first half of the sentence.

29. (A)—The sentence contains no error and is not wordy or awkward.

30. (B)—The sentence contains a misplaced modifier: it sounds as though O'Toole's *career* is known for his portrayal of T. E. Lawrence. The introductory phrase describes Peter O'Toole (the man, not his career); hence *Peter O'Toole* should come directly after it. Only choices (B) and (C) begin correctly, and (C) is poorly worded.

31. (C)—The best way to repair this run-on sentence while preserving the logical relationship between the two halves of the sentence is with choice (C), which correctly presents the second half of the sentence as a consequence of the first. (A), (B), and (E) are all run-ons, and (D) makes *spectators* the subject of *endangered*.

32. (E)—The underlined portion of this sentence is passive, wordy, and awkward. A good rephrasing will begin with *he* and will be in the active voice. (B) and (E) are possibilities, but (B) is still somewhat awkward and puts the verb into the past perfect for no apparent reason. (E) is clear and concise.

33. (D)—Idiomatically, *the same* should be followed by the preposition *as*, not *than*. There is also a problem of parallelism here: the two things being compared should be in the same grammatical form. Since *talking* is a gerund, the thing it's being compared to should also be a gerund: *driving*.

34. (C)—This run-on sentence is best corrected by choice (C), which is grammatically correct and doesn't include extra verbiage. (B) and (E) use the semicolon improperly, and (D) is wordy.

35. (E)—The sentence is unclear because it doesn't use the correct sequence of tenses. Since the client had already been waiting for fifteen minutes *before* the moment when the receptionist looked up, the first verb must be in the past perfect: *had been waiting*.

36. (A)—The sentence is correct and conforms to the rules of parallelism: all three items in the list are adjectives describing the weapon.

37. (B)—There is an error of subordination here: To express the causal relationship between melting ice caps and flooding of islands, you need only one conjunction: *because* or *therefore*. To have both is

redundant. (Furthermore, the word *therefore* should be preceded by a semicolon, not a comma.)

38. (C)—This sentence fragment is best corrected by moving the verb *was* and inserting a comma after the introductory phrase describing Flaubert.

39. (D)—The key to this problem is realizing that *I myself* is redundant—if the author has already used *I*, there's no need to add *myself* to clarify. (D) provides the best fix here—notice that it's also the shortest, most straightforward answer. Choice (A) and (E) still include *myself*. (C) substitutes another redundancy—the word *personally*. (B) is unnecessarily convoluted, and is missing a comma following *I believe*.

40. (C)—The context here suggests a strong link between the two sentences—the idea is that sports provide students with the chance to strive for greatness *by* showing them it takes courage etc. Choice (C) is the best answer. (A) introduces an illogical contrast. (B) creates a sentence fragment. (D) uses the passive voice unnecessarily. In (E), the verb *show* doesn't agree with the subject *it*.

41. (C)—The key to this sentence is spotting a subject-verb agreement problem—the subject in the sentence is *top athletes*, not *Michael Jordan*—he's only introduced as an example of a top athlete. So the underlined pronouns should be *them* (to agree with *young people*) and *their* (to agree with *top athletes*).

42. (B)—To fix this ambiguous introductory phrase, you're looking for a conjunction that expresses the idea of listing an *additional benefit* of participation in team sports. (B) *moreover* does this effectively. (A)'s *and* is not an idiomatic conjunction with which to begin a sentence. (C) creates an unnecessary contrast. In (D), *sequentially* means in order, not *consequently*. (E), finally, is wrong because this sentence describes the second item in a list of two.

43. (C)—The author states her opinion outright at the end of paragraph 1, backing it up with evidence in paragraph 2, making (C) the best answer. (A) is wrong because there's no suggestion it's an unpopular point of view. (B) is wrong because the author doesn't waste time criticizing the editor's standpoint. (D)'s out because no space is devoted to considering the editor's proposal—in fact, the passage isn't about a specific proposal at all. Finally, (E)'s wrong because no statistics are mentioned.

44. (E)—Sentence 14 provides a weak ending to the passage because it refers to *other ways of the city government saving money*, without suggesting what these might be. So the best improvement to sentence 14 might be (E) to provide examples of alternative areas for cuts. (A) would be an odd solution—historical events haven't been mentioned thus far in the passage. (B) would weaken the essay just at the point at which the author needs to strengthen it. (C) would be repetitive—the author has already included a personal anecdote. Finally, (D) would simply offer a digression at this point.

45. (D)—The word *just* creates a run-on sentence here that needs fixing. To combine both clauses in a logical manner, you need to remove *just* and add conjunctions that express the idea of *contrast—in spite* of the author's enjoyment of music, everyone thought he was talentless. (D) is the best answer here. (B)'s wrong because it still includes *just*. (C)'s not logical—why would people conclude the author was talentless if he enjoyed music? (E)'s *however* is the wrong conjunction—it expresses contrast, but it doesn't link the two phrases to fix the run-on.

46. (B)—A good setup for paragraph 2 would be a sentence that leads into the author's discovery that he had musical ability, and introduces Mr. Daniels. (B) accomplishes this. (A)'s illogical because Mr. Daniel's opinion soon persuades the author to try playing music. (C) and (E) are *non sequiturs*—they don't lead into paragraph 2 in any way. (D)'s too extreme and a bit premature—the author doesn't discover his talent until mid-paragraph 2.

47. (E)—The key here is realize that sentence 11 contains an illogical comparison. The *sound of the handbell* cannot be purer than the *electric guitar*—it has to be purer than the *sound of the electric guitar*, as (E) suggests. None of the other choices fixes this problem.

48. (A)—There is no error in this sentence—*Not only . . . but also* is a common and perfectly idiomatic expression.

49. (B)—A tricky context question. Since the author is describing the lessons to be drawn from his own experience here, *sense of adventure* must refer to his decision to try handbells, and *encouragement* must refer to his teacher's support—choice (B). There's no evidence for the remaining choices.

50. (C)—Check off each choice against the passage here. (A) is certainly true of the passage. (B) reflects the moral the author draws at the end of the passage. (C)'s *not* mentioned anywhere—the author notes that other students thought handbells were stupid, but doesn't criticize them for it. (D) appears in the last line of the passage. (E) reflects the author's trepidation about trying to play music, and his honesty about realizing he feared ridicule.

51. (B)—The subject *none* is a singular verb (it's a contraction for *no one*) and must take a singular verb: none *was*. The comparison *than she* is correct according to the rules of parallelism, because the verb *was* is understood (no one was more frightened and inexperienced than she was).

52. (E)—The sentence contains no error—the verb *is attempting* describes an action that is currently taking place.

53. (A)—Idiom alert! *Consisted in* is not a correct idiom in standard written English—the proper idiom is *consisted of.*

54. (B)—Pronoun case must be consistent throughout a sentence—since this sentence begins with *one*, *one* must be used rather than *you* later on.

55. (C)—Tricky problem here: *neither . . . nor* constructions *look* like plural nouns, but they're not. The rule about *neither . . . nor* constructions is that the verb must agree with the noun closest to it—so in this case, the verb *to be* must agree with *decay*.

56. (C)—When only two items are being compared, you must use the comparative form, not the superlative. So the sentence should read: *Mary, the younger one.*

57. (B)—A tricky idiom problem here: to coordinate the first and second clauses here, you've got to use *because*, not *due to*. *Due to* cannot function as a conjunction; it can only introduce a noun (for example, "due to circumstances beyond our control").

58. (A)—A pronoun case issue: the subordinate clause should read *whom the people elevated*, not *who*. Reverse the order of the subordinate clause, and it becomes apparent that Becket is the object of it: *The pope elevated him to sainthood*. For the object of the sentence, you must use the *objective* case, e.g., *him, her* or *whom*.

59. (E)—There is no error in this sentence.

60. (E)—There is no error in this sentence.

ANSWER SHEET
FOR PRACTICE TEST 5

1 Ⓐ Ⓑ Ⓒ Ⓓ Ⓔ	16 Ⓐ Ⓑ Ⓒ Ⓓ Ⓔ	31 Ⓐ Ⓑ Ⓒ Ⓓ Ⓔ	46 Ⓐ Ⓑ Ⓒ Ⓓ Ⓔ
2 Ⓐ Ⓑ Ⓒ Ⓓ Ⓔ	17 Ⓐ Ⓑ Ⓒ Ⓓ Ⓔ	32 Ⓐ Ⓑ Ⓒ Ⓓ Ⓔ	47 Ⓐ Ⓑ Ⓒ Ⓓ Ⓔ
3 Ⓐ Ⓑ Ⓒ Ⓓ Ⓔ	18 Ⓐ Ⓑ Ⓒ Ⓓ Ⓔ	33 Ⓐ Ⓑ Ⓒ Ⓓ Ⓔ	48 Ⓐ Ⓑ Ⓒ Ⓓ Ⓔ
4 Ⓐ Ⓑ Ⓒ Ⓓ Ⓔ	19 Ⓐ Ⓑ Ⓒ Ⓓ Ⓔ	34 Ⓐ Ⓑ Ⓒ Ⓓ Ⓔ	49 Ⓐ Ⓑ Ⓒ Ⓓ Ⓔ
5 Ⓐ Ⓑ Ⓒ Ⓓ Ⓔ	20 Ⓐ Ⓑ Ⓒ Ⓓ Ⓔ	35 Ⓐ Ⓑ Ⓒ Ⓓ Ⓔ	50 Ⓐ Ⓑ Ⓒ Ⓓ Ⓔ
6 Ⓐ Ⓑ Ⓒ Ⓓ Ⓔ	21 Ⓐ Ⓑ Ⓒ Ⓓ Ⓔ	36 Ⓐ Ⓑ Ⓒ Ⓓ Ⓔ	51 Ⓐ Ⓑ Ⓒ Ⓓ Ⓔ
7 Ⓐ Ⓑ Ⓒ Ⓓ Ⓔ	22 Ⓐ Ⓑ Ⓒ Ⓓ Ⓔ	37 Ⓐ Ⓑ Ⓒ Ⓓ Ⓔ	52 Ⓐ Ⓑ Ⓒ Ⓓ Ⓔ
8 Ⓐ Ⓑ Ⓒ Ⓓ Ⓔ	23 Ⓐ Ⓑ Ⓒ Ⓓ Ⓔ	38 Ⓐ Ⓑ Ⓒ Ⓓ Ⓔ	53 Ⓐ Ⓑ Ⓒ Ⓓ Ⓔ
9 Ⓐ Ⓑ Ⓒ Ⓓ Ⓔ	24 Ⓐ Ⓑ Ⓒ Ⓓ Ⓔ	39 Ⓐ Ⓑ Ⓒ Ⓓ Ⓔ	54 Ⓐ Ⓑ Ⓒ Ⓓ Ⓔ
10 Ⓐ Ⓑ Ⓒ Ⓓ Ⓔ	25 Ⓐ Ⓑ Ⓒ Ⓓ Ⓔ	40 Ⓐ Ⓑ Ⓒ Ⓓ Ⓔ	55 Ⓐ Ⓑ Ⓒ Ⓓ Ⓔ
11 Ⓐ Ⓑ Ⓒ Ⓓ Ⓔ	26 Ⓐ Ⓑ Ⓒ Ⓓ Ⓔ	41 Ⓐ Ⓑ Ⓒ Ⓓ Ⓔ	56 Ⓐ Ⓑ Ⓒ Ⓓ Ⓔ
12 Ⓐ Ⓑ Ⓒ Ⓓ Ⓔ	27 Ⓐ Ⓑ Ⓒ Ⓓ Ⓔ	42 Ⓐ Ⓑ Ⓒ Ⓓ Ⓔ	57 Ⓐ Ⓑ Ⓒ Ⓓ Ⓔ
13 Ⓐ Ⓑ Ⓒ Ⓓ Ⓔ	28 Ⓐ Ⓑ Ⓒ Ⓓ Ⓔ	43 Ⓐ Ⓑ Ⓒ Ⓓ Ⓔ	58 Ⓐ Ⓑ Ⓒ Ⓓ Ⓔ
14 Ⓐ Ⓑ Ⓒ Ⓓ Ⓔ	29 Ⓐ Ⓑ Ⓒ Ⓓ Ⓔ	44 Ⓐ Ⓑ Ⓒ Ⓓ Ⓔ	59 Ⓐ Ⓑ Ⓒ Ⓓ Ⓔ
15 Ⓐ Ⓑ Ⓒ Ⓓ Ⓔ	30 Ⓐ Ⓑ Ⓒ Ⓓ Ⓔ	45 Ⓐ Ⓑ Ⓒ Ⓓ Ⓔ	60 Ⓐ Ⓑ Ⓒ Ⓓ Ⓔ

right

wrong

Use the answer key following the test to count up the number of questions you got right and the number you got wrong. (Remember not to count omitted questions as wrong.) The "Compute Your Score" section at the back of the book will show you how to find your score.

ANSWER SHEET
FOR PRACTICE TEST 5

Part A (ESSAY). Begin your composition on this side. If you need more space, you may continue on the reverse side.

_____

_____

_____

_____

_____

_____

_____

_____

_____

_____

_____

_____

_____

_____

_____

_____

_____

_____

_____

_____

_____

_____

ANSWER SHEET
FOR PRACTICE TEST 5

Continuation of Part A (ESSAY) from reverse side. Write below if you need more space.

_____

_____

_____

_____

_____

_____

_____

_____

_____

_____

_____

_____

_____

_____

_____

_____

_____

_____

_____

_____

_____

_____

_____

PART A
Time—20 Minutes (1 Question)

Directions: You have 20 minutes to write an essay on the following topic. **DO NOT WRITE AN ESSAY ON ANY OTHER TOPIC. AN ESSAY ON A DIFFERENT TOPIC IS UNACCEPTABLE.**

This essay provides you with an opportunity to demonstrate how well you write. Therefore, you should express your ideas clearly and effectively. How much you write is much less important than how well you write; but to express your thoughts on the topic adequately you may want to write more than a single paragraph. Your essay should be specific.

Your essay must be written in the lines provided on your answer sheet. No other paper will be given to you. There is enough space to write your essay on the answer sheet if you write on every line, avoid wide margins, and keep your handwriting to a reasonable size.

Consider the following statement and assignment. Then write an essay as directed.

> **"There are many things we all take for granted, but one thing I have learned never to take for granted is ___."**

Assignment: Write an essay that completes the statement above. Explain the reasons behind your choice.

WHEN THE PROCTOR ANNOUNCES THAT 20 MINUTES HAVE PASSED, YOU MUST STOP WRITING AND GO ON TO PART B OF THE TEST. IF YOU FINISH YOUR ESSAY BEFORE 20 MINUTES PASS, YOU MAY GO ON TO PART B.

YOU MAY MAKE NOTES ON THIS AND THIS PAGE AND THE FOLLOWING ONE, BUT YOU MUST WRITE YOUR ESSAY ON THE ANSWER SHEET.

You may use this page to outline your essay or make other notes as you plan your essay. Don't write your essay here, though. Your essay must be written on the lined pages of the answer sheet at the beginning of this answer section.

TURN TO THE NEXT PAGE.

PART B
Time—40 Minutes (60 Questions)

For each of the following questions, choose the best answer from the given choices and darken the corresponding oval on the answer sheet.

Directions: The following sentences contain problems in grammar, usage, diction (choice of words), and idiom.

Some of the sentences are correct.

None of the sentences contains more than one error.

The error, if there is one in the sentence, is underlined and lettered. Parts of the sentence that are not underlined are correct and cannot be changed. In selecting answers, follow the requirements of standard written English.

If there is an error, choose the <u>one underlined part</u> that must be changed to make the sentence correct and fill in the corresponding oval on your answer grid.

If there is no error, fill in oval E.

SAMPLE QUESTION

<u>Even though</u> he <u>had to</u> supervise a large
   A   B

staff, his salary <u>was no greater</u> than <u>a clerk</u>.
           C   D

<u>No error</u>
 E

SAMPLE ANSWER

Ⓐ Ⓑ Ⓒ ⬤ Ⓔ

---

1. <u>As</u> a college student, Delaney was hesitant
  A

  <u>to participate</u> <u>in any</u> rallies or demonstrations
     B   C

  because he hoped <u>for having</u> a political career
              D

  someday. <u>No error</u>
        E

2. The castaways' situation was <u>beginning</u> to look
                A

  <u>desperate</u>: They had <u>drank</u> the last of their
    B   C

  water the night <u>before</u>, and there was only one
           D

  flare left in the emergency kit. <u>No error</u>
                   E

3. <u>Among</u> the many factors contributing to the
  A

  revival of the medieval economy <u>was</u> the
                     B

  <u>cessation</u> of Viking raids and the <u>development</u>
    C   D

  of the heavy plow. <u>No error</u>
             E

4. Raoul gave Frederick very little warning before

  <u>striking</u> a match and setting fire <u>to his</u> entire
   A   B

  collection of documents, <u>which</u> had been
               C

  <u>painstakingly</u> compiled over the course of
    D

  several decades. <u>No error</u>
           E

TURN TO THE NEXT PAGE.

5. Native <u>to</u> New Zealand, the kiwi <u>has few</u>
         A   B
natural predators but <u>is</u> currently endangered
                   C
<u>by</u> deforestation and human encroachment.
 D
<u>No error</u>
  E

6. Diabetes can strike anyone, <u>irregardless</u> of age;
                          A
<u>nevertheless</u>, many people <u>still make</u> the
    B   C
mistake <u>of considering</u> it a geriatric disease.
         D
<u>No error</u>
  E

7. The <u>much-publicized</u> study was <u>deemed</u>
        A   B
unscientific because it failed to take <u>into</u>
                           C
account such variables <u>as</u> heredity and income.
             D
<u>No error</u>
  E

8. The early Egyptian monks <u>sought</u> complete
                    A
solitude so <u>that</u> they <u>might</u> pray without
        B   C
distraction, pursue an ideal of perfection, and

<u>to attain</u> a higher level of religious experience.
 D
<u>No error</u>
  E

9. Perhaps the coach was remembered <u>so fondly</u>
                            A
because he was <u>always</u> less interested in
            B
winning than in <u>making sure</u> that all the boys
                 C
participated <u>with</u> the game. <u>No error</u>
         D   E

10. Thirty years ago, one could say that those <u>who</u>
                                  A
the president nominated to <u>serve</u> on the
                    B
Supreme Court were <u>chosen not</u> because of
               C
their political leanings, <u>but because</u> of their
                  D
fine legal minds and their judicial expertise.

<u>No error</u>
  E

11. <u>Even</u> today, there are many who <u>would</u> say
   A   B
that the old tribal practice of <u>paying</u> blood-
                      C
money to families of murder victims <u>are more</u>
                          D
just than our modern system of trial and

punishment. <u>No error</u>
         E

12. In a move <u>that</u> distressed the clergy as much as
          A
<u>it</u> delighted the barons, King Arnulf <u>named</u>
B   C
one of his illegitimate sons <u>as</u> heir and
                   D
successor to the throne. <u>No error</u>
               E

TURN TO THE NEXT PAGE.

13. Hopefully, it is not too late to reverse the
      A   B
    damage that years of neglect and harsh
             C
    weather have wrought on the beautiful old
            D
    mansion. No error
            E

14. Though the young author's most recent play is

    undeniably exciting, well written, and
      A
    memorable, it would be a mistake to place his
            B
    work on a par with David Mamet. No error
      C   D   E

15. Many teachers feel that any parent who fails to
               A   B
    discipline their own child has no right to
          C   D
    complain when the child is punished for

    unruly, disrespectful behavior in school.

    No error
    E

16. The rebels had less guns than their enemies
            A
    and hardly any ammunition; nevertheless,
        B   C
    they were able to overthrow their country's

    military government with the help of a restless
            D
    and sympathetic population. No error
            E

17. A number of immigrants find that loneliness,
      A   B
    along with the challenge of learning a new
            C
    language, hinder their efforts to assimilate into
          D
    a new culture. No error
            E

18. The recent discovery that at least one of
        A
    Jupiter's moons possesses an internal heat
            B
    source has led to speculation that there may be
        C   D
    life elsewhere in our solar system. No error
            E

19. Though Mikhail Gorbachev's policy of glasnost
      A
    ushered in freedoms that would have been
            B
    inconceivable a decade before, many Russians
            C
    still felt that economic and political reform was

    not proceeding quick enough. No error
            D   E

20. When asked whether he was ready to give up
        A
    his quixotic campaign against coeducation,

    Buford replied that he had not scarcely begun
            B   C   D
    to fight. No error
        E

TURN TO THE NEXT PAGE.

For each of the following questions, choose the best answer from the given choices and darken the corresponding oval on the answer sheet.

Directions: The following sentences test accuracy and effectiveness of expression. In selecting answers, follow the rules of standard written English; in other words, consider grammar, choice of words, sentence construction, and punctuation.

In each of the following sentences, a portion or all of the sentence is underlined. Under each sentence you will find five ways of phrasing the underlined portion. Choice A repeats the original underlined portion; the other four choices provide alternative phrasings.

Select the choice that best expresses the meaning of the original sentence. If the original sentence is better than any of the alternative phrasings, choose A; otherwise select one of the alternatives. Your selection should construct the most effective sentence—clear and precise with no awkwardness or ambiguity.

SAMPLE QUESTION   SAMPLE ANSWER

Wanting to reward her assistant for loyalty,
Sheila gave a bonus to him as large as his paycheck.

(A) Sheila gave a bonus to him as large as his paycheck
(B) given to him by Sheila was a bonus as large as his paycheck
(C) he was given a bonus as large as his paycheck by Sheila
(D) Sheila gave him a bonus as large as his paycheck
(E) Sheila gave him a paycheck to him as large as his bonus

---

21. The poet Oscar Wilde was known for his aphoristic wit and brilliant conversation, he wrote a number of memorable literary essays including "The Critic as Artist."

    (A) The poet Oscar Wilde was known for his aphoristic wit and brilliant conversation, he
    (B) The poet Oscar Wilde, known for his aphoristic wit and brilliant conversation; he
    (C) Known for his aphoristic wit and brilliant conversation, the poet Oscar Wilde
    (D) The poet Oscar Wilde was known for his aphoristic wit and brilliant conversation, however he
    (E) Oscar Wilde, the poet, known for his aphoristic wit and brilliant conversation, and he

22. According to Westin's book, the typical Victorian family was more interested in maintaining the appearance of propriety than in securing happiness for its individual members.

    (A) the typical Victorian family was more interested in maintaining the appearance of propriety than in
    (B) the appearance of propriety was more interesting to the typical Victorian family than
    (C) the typical Victorian family, more interested in maintaining the appearance of propriety than it was in
    (D) for a Victorian family it was typical that they would be more interested in maintaining the appearance of propriety than in
    (E) the typical Victorian family was more interested in the appearance of propriety than in

TURN TO THE NEXT PAGE.

23. Once an enclave of privileged white males, the Wodehouse Club's directors have now decided to adopt a more inclusive membership policy.

    (A) Once an enclave of privileged white males, the Wodehouse Club's directors have
    (B) The directors of the Wodehouse Club, which was once an enclave of privileged white males, have
    (C) Though once an enclave of privileged white males, the Wodehouse Club's directors
    (D) Once an enclave of privileged white males, the Wodehouse Club's directors having
    (E) The directors of the enclave of privileged white males, the Wodehouse Club, has

24. Supporters of the Eighteenth Amendment thought that banning alcohol would improve citizens' morals and enhance their quality of life by removing the temptation to drink; national prohibition ushered in thirteen years of bootlegging, speakeasies, and violent gangster crime.

    (A) national prohibition
    (B) in fact, national prohibition
    (C) furthermore, national prohibition
    (D) but national prohibition
    (E) consequently, national prohibition

25. Though multimedia presentations have their place in the school curriculum, it is ridiculous to claim, as some do, that children learn as much from watching a one-hour video as a book.

    (A) that children learn as much from watching a one-hour video as a book
    (B) that children will learn as much from watching a one-hour video as they did from a book
    (C) that children learn as much from watching a one-hour video as they do from reading a book
    (D) that a one-hour video teaches more to children than book-reading
    (E) that children watching a one-hour video learn as much as reading a book

26. Finland's national epic, the *Kalevala*, based on an oral tradition that the Balto-Finnish people preserved for some 2,500 years despite the upheavals of history and the pressures of foreign domination.

    (A) based on an oral tradition that
    (B) being based on an oral tradition that
    (C) is based on an oral tradition; this
    (D) basing itself on an oral tradition which
    (E) is based on an oral tradition that

27. The island of Santa Ynez was once a playground for wealthy American tourists; in recent years, however, civil unrest and a series of natural disasters have made it so that it is not nearly as appealing as a vacation spot.

    (A) have made it so that it is not nearly as appealing
    (B) are causing it to be made less appealing
    (C) greatly reducing its appeal
    (D) have greatly lessened its appeal
    (E) have not nearly made it as appealing

28. In retrospect, one can see the folly of trying to unite a region containing some four hundred distinct ethnic groups, each with its own language, laws, and traditions.

    (A) each with its own language, laws, and traditions
    (B) each of them has its own language, laws, and traditions
    (C) each with their own language, laws, and traditions
    (D) and each of them having its own language, laws, and traditions
    (E) when they each have their own language, laws, and traditions

TURN TO THE NEXT PAGE.

29. Proponents of campaign finance reform point out that people who make large donations to politicians expect to be rewarded with special favors and gaining easy access to the corridors of power.

    (A) and gaining easy access
    (B) and they gain easy access
    (C) and easy access
    (D) as well as gaining easy access
    (E) and to be rewarded with easy access

30. Had Churchill sent planes to defend Coventry from the German air raid, the Nazis would have realized that their secret code had been broken by the Allies.

    (A) Had Churchill sent planes to defend Coventry
    (B) If Churchill would have sent planes to defend Coventry
    (C) Churchill having sent planes to defend Coventry
    (D) If Churchill sent planes to defend Coventry
    (E) Churchill, by sending planes to Coventry to defend it

31. Television shows such as *M*A*S*H* and *All in the Family* took months or even years to build a large audience, most new series today never get that chance.

    (A) Television shows such as *M*A*S*H* and *All in the Family* took
    (B) Although television shows such as *M*A*S*H* and *All in the Family* took
    (C) With television shows such as *M*A*S*H* and *All in the Family* taking
    (D) Such television shows as *M*A*S*H* and *All in the Family* took
    (E) When television shows such as *M*A*S*H* and *All in the Family* took

32. Returning to her home town after a twenty-year absence, the desperate poverty Savka saw there shocked and saddened her.

    (A) the desperate poverty Savka saw there shocked and saddened her
    (B) the desperate poverty Savka saw there was shocking and also sad to her
    (C) Savka, shocked and saddened by the desperate poverty she saw there
    (D) Savka was shocked and saddened by the desperate poverty she saw there
    (E) was a desperate poverty that shocked and saddened Savka

33. The stereotype of the idle, wealthy snob bears little resemblance to real Ivy League students, the majority of them receive financial aid in the form of jobs, loans, and grants.

    (A) of them receive
    (B) of which receive
    (C) which receive
    (D) of them receiving
    (E) of whom receive

34. The brochure for the writing camp promises that by the time you leave the camp, you complete an entire manuscript.

    (A) complete an entire manuscript
    (B) would complete an entire manuscript
    (C) will have completed an entire manuscript
    (D) have complete an entire manuscript
    (E) had completed an entire manuscript

35. The viscount was having such a merry time drinking and carousing and he did not notice the dark stranger who stole into the banquet hall and absconded with his treasured painting.

    (A) and he did not notice
    (B) that he did not notice
    (C) not noticing
    (D) for he did not notice
    (E) and failing to notice

TURN TO THE NEXT PAGE.

36. When the electrochemists Stanley Pons and Martin Fleischmann declared in 1989 that they had achieved <u>cold fusion; scientists around the world tried to duplicate the process, they were not successful.</u>

    (A) cold fusion; scientists around the world tried to duplicate the process, they were not successful

    (B) cold fusion then scientists around the world tried to duplicate the process only without succeeding

    (C) cold fusion, consequently scientists around the world, without success, tried to duplicate the process

    (D) cold fusion, scientists around the world tried without success to duplicate the process

    (E) cold fusion; however, scientists around the world tried to duplicate the process, without success

37. Having read the works of Hemingway, Fitzgerald, and Steinbeck, <u>Hemingway is definitely overrated as a writer.</u>

    (A) Hemingway is definitely overrated as a writer

    (B) Hemingway has definitely been overrated as a writer

    (C) I am convinced that Hemingway is overrated as a writer

    (D) the writing abilities of Hemingway are overrated, I am convinced

    (E) I am convinced as a writer that Hemingway is overrated

38. Her eyes shining with tears, Aunt Helga told us over and over again how much she appreciated <u>us coming to her</u> ninetieth birthday party.

    (A) us coming to her

    (B) our coming to her

    (C) us having come to her

    (D) that we come to her

    (E) us for the fact of our coming to her

TURN TO THE NEXT PAGE.

Directions: The following passages are first drafts of student essays. Some portions of the essays have to be rewritten.

Read the essays and answer the questions that follow them. Some of the questions concern particular sentences or fragments of sentences and require you to make choices about sentence structure, word choice, and usage. Other questions pertain to the entire essay or pieces of the essay and require you to think about organization, development, and appropriateness of language. Pick the answer that most effectively conveys the meaning and follows the rules of standard written English. Once you have chosen an answer, fill in the corresponding oval on your answer sheet.

Questions 39–44 are based on the following essay.

(1) There is no way I expected to enjoy summer camp this year. (2) All of my friends were being sent to fashionable camps in the Berkshires and Vermont. (3) Not only did these camps specialize in sports that I've always wanted to try (tennis, canoing, and white water rafting are examples). (4) Additionally everyone I knew got to go with their best friends.

(5) Was this what my parents did? (6) Instead, Dad decided to send me to this camp in New Hampshire where he'd gone as a kid. (7) Old Deer Head Falls, NH, twenty miles from the nearest signal of human habitation. (8) The camp's main and primary activity was hiking in the rocky, rainy trails of the nearby White Mountains. (9) Thanks a lot, Dad. (10) Regarded as one of the least fit students in my class, this summer had all the hallmarks of a disaster for me. (11) It took a couple of hikes, participation in a handful of camp fire sing-alongs, and bursting many a blister on my feet to change my mind. (12) The scenery in the mountains was a major factor. (13) Another was that (even though I am a self-confessed couch potato) I actually discovered the exercise to be enjoyable. (14) I made new friends, and to my surprise I liked the camp counselors a lot. (15) There were counselors from all over the world. (16) The debates at rest stops got pretty interesting. (17) After a summer above the treeline, I think I returned to school with better stories than my friends who went to "fashionable" resorts!

39. Which of the following is the best way to revise the underlined portions of sentences 3 and 4 (reproduced below) so that the two sentences are combined into one?

Not only did these camps specialize in sports that I've always wanted to <u>try (tennis, canoeing, and white water rafting are examples).</u>

<u>Additionally everyone</u> I knew got to go with their best friends.

(A) try, examples being tennis, canoing, and white water rafting; additionally everyone

(B) try, such as tennis, canoing, and white water rafting, but all the people

(C) try: tennis, canoing, and white water rafting for example, plus they all

(D) try (tennis, canoing, white water rafting, for example), furthermore all the people

(E) try, such as tennis canoing, and white water rafting, and everyone

TURN TO THE NEXT PAGE.

40. Which of the following sentences, if inserted in place of sentence 5, would provide the best transition between the first paragraph and the rest of the essay?

(A) However, my parents chose not to send me to a "fashionable" camp.
(B) Unlike my friends, my parents chose something else altogether.
(C) Rather than being sent to a "fashionable camp," Dad chose otherwise.
(D) Unfortunately, this situation was not the case with my parents.
(E) You might have expected that my parents would have been doing the same.

41. In the context of the second paragraph, which of the following is the best version of the under-lined portion of sentence 10 (reproduced below)?

Regarded as one of the least fit students in my class, this summer had all the hallmarks of a disaster for me.

(A) (As it is now)
(B) I predicted that this summer would be a disaster for me
(C) this summer was beginning to look disastrous for me
(D) and for me, this summer had all the hallmarks of a disaster
(E) so this summer had all the hallmarks of a disaster for me

42. Which of the following versions of the under-lined portion of sentence 11 (reproduced below) is clearest?

It took a couple of hikes, participation in a handful of camp fire sing-alongs, and bursting many a blister on my feet to change my mind.

(A) (As it is now)
(B) a handful of camp fire sing-alongs, and bursting many blisters
(C) the participation in some camp fire sing-alongs, and the bursting of many a blister
(D) a handful of camp fire sing-alongs, and many a burst blister
(E) my participating in a handful of camp fire sing-alongs, and my bursting many a blister

43. In the context of paragraph 2, which of the following is the best way to link sentences 15 and 16 (reproduced below)?

There were counselors from all over the world. The debates at rest stops got pretty interesting.

(A) Even though there were counselors from all over the world, the debates at rest stops still got pretty interesting.
(B) With there being counselors from all over the world, the debates at rest stops got pretty interesting.
(C) Since there were counselors from all over the world, the debates at rest stops got pretty interesting.
(D) There were counselors from all over the world, consequently the debates at rest stops got pretty interesting.
(E) Whereas there were counselors from all over the world, the debates at rest stops got pretty interesting.

44. Which of the following, if added after sentence 17, would be the most logical concluding sentence for the passage?

(A) Everyone should be open to new experi-ences, because they can be unexpectedly rewarding.
(B) I never found stories about "fashionable" resorts particularly interesting, anyway.
(C) I learned that money isn't everything; there's something to be said for hard work, too.
(D) If you start out with a positive attitude, almost anything can be made enjoyable.
(E) Facing challenges alone is often more important than being with friends.

TURN TO THE NEXT PAGE.

<u>Questions 45–50</u> are based on the following essay, which is a response to an assignment to write about the foreign policy of the United States.

(1) Recent events in the Middle East have once again led to calls for the United States to resolve an international conflict. (2) The last great superpower, the nations of the world expect the U.S. to use its military force to restore peace wherever war breaks out. (3) Like some hero in a Clint Eastwood film, the U.S. is in a unique position to dictate global justice and play peacemaker to the world. (4) But should the U.S. continue to play this role?

(5) The arguments for playing the peacemaker role are inextricably linked to our democratic beliefs. (6) Throughout history, the people of the U.S. have struggled against oppression for more fair and democratic society. (7) In the War of Independence, for example, Americans overthrew the tyranny of a British government. (8) In the Civil Rights movement of the 1960s, Black people fought for equal status in American society. (9) We have fought hard for our democratic rights consequently we believe that every country in the world deserves the same. (10) But our beliefs in democracy and equality does not mean we should get involved in every situation. (11) The War of Vietnam showed that even for a country so powerful as the United States, not every battle can be won. (12) After Vietnam, the U.S. has clearly been trying to minimize its use of force to solve international crises. (13) In addition, where military intervention is inevitable, other countries have been involved in diplomatic and military initiatives. (14) In the Gulf War and the War in the former Yugoslavia, the U.S led a group of major countries in the attempt to restore order. (15) This was beneficial because many European countries have been content to take a back seat in such conflicts—even when the bloodshed is occuring very close to them. (16) Rather than playing the lone peacemaker, the U.S. should be a team leader in world affairs—working with other powers in the search for freedom.

45. Which of the following is the best version of sentence 2 (reproduced below)?

    The last great superpower, the nations of the world expect the U.S. to use its military force to restore peace wherever war breaks out.

    (A) (As it is now)
    (B) The last great superpower, the U.S. expects to use its military force to restore peace to the nations of the world wherever war breaks out.
    (C) The last great superpower, the U.S., expected by the nations of the world to use its military force to restore peace wherever war breaks out.
    (D) The nations of the world expect the U.S., the last great superpower, to use its military force to restore peace wherever war breaks out.
    (E) The last great superpower, the U.S. has a military force which is expected by the nations of the world to be used to restore peace wherever war breaks out.

46. Which of the following versions of sentence 4 (reproduced below) provides the most effective transition between the first and second paragraphs?

    But should the U.S. continue to play this role?

    (A) (As it is now.)
    (B) This is just as it should be, for who else would do it?
    (C) I believe that it is time for the U.S. to relinquish this role.
    (D) The arguments for the U.S. taking this role are irrefutable.
    (E) And the U.S is also expected to send aid to less fortunate countries.

TURN TO THE NEXT PAGE.

47. Which of the following is the best revision of sentence 9 (reproduced below)?

We have fought hard for our democratic rights consequently we believe that every country in the world deserves the same.

(A) (As it is now)
(B) Having fought hard for our democratic rights, we consequently believed that every country in the world deserves the same.
(C) We have fought hard for our democratic rights, and we believe that every country in the world also deserves those rights.
(D) We have fought hard for our democratic rights, therefore we believe that every country in the world deserves the same.
(E) Not only have we fought hard for our democratic rights, but we also have the belief that every country in the world deserves to fight for their rights, too.

48. Which of the following would be the most logical place to introduce a paragraph break (ending one paragraph and beginning a new one)?

(A) Between sentences 6 and 7
(B) Between sentences 8 and 9
(C) Between sentences 9 and 10
(D) Between sentences 10 and 11
(E) Between sentences 11 and 12

49. Which of the following is the clearest version of sentence 11, reproduced below?

The War of Vietnam showed that even for a country so powerful as the United States, not every battle can be won.

(A) (As it is now.)
(B) As the War of Vietnam showed, the United States, so powerful as it is, can not win every battle.
(C) The War of Vietnam had shown that even a country so powerful as the United States could not have won every battle.
(D) The Vietnam war showed that not every battle can be won even when the country is as powerful as the United States.
(E) The Vietnam war showed that even a country as powerful as the United States can not win every battle.

50. All of the following strategies are used by the author of the passage EXCEPT

(A) making an analogy
(B) using a rhetorical question
(C) referring to historical examples
(D) analyzing both sides of an issue
(E) quoting the views of politicians

TURN TO THE NEXT PAGE.

For each of the following questions, choose the best answer from the given choices and darken the corresponding oval on the answer sheet.

Directions: The following sentences contain problems in grammar, usage, diction (choice of words), and idiom.

Some of the sentences are correct.

None of the sentences contains more than one error.

The error, if there is one in the sentence, is underlined and lettered. Parts of the sentence that are not underlined are correct and cannot be changed. In selecting answers, follow the requirements of standard written English.

If there is an error, choose the <u>one underlined part</u> that must be changed to make the sentence correct and fill in the corresponding oval on your answer grid.

If there is no error, fill in oval E.

SAMPLE QUESTION

<u>Even though</u> he <u>had to</u> supervise a large
   A   B
staff, his salary <u>was no greater</u> than <u>a clerk.</u>
                C   D
<u>No error</u>
 E

SAMPLE ANSWER

Ⓐ Ⓑ Ⓒ ● Ⓔ

---

51. As <u>soon</u> as the employees realized <u>that</u>
     A   B
    management would never accede <u>with</u> their
                                C
    demands for a shorter work week, a strike

    became <u>inevitable.</u> <u>No error</u>
              D   E

52. <u>Lacking</u> an objective standard <u>by which</u> to
     A   B
    judge the contestants, the sponsors of the

    pageant <u>finally</u> resorted <u>to drawing a</u> name
            C   D
    at random from a hat. <u>No error</u>
                     E

53. The aurora borealis is a dazzling <u>phenomena</u>
                                      A
    that <u>occurs when the</u> earth's magnetic field
               B
    interacts <u>with</u> the solar wind, <u>producing</u>
             C   D
    ionized atoms and molecules. <u>No error</u>
                              E

54. So <u>great was</u> John Lennon's fame <u>as</u> he
      A   B
    <u>could scarcely</u> walk out his door without <u>being</u>
        C   D
    accosted by fans and photographers. <u>No error</u>
                                    E

TURN TO THE NEXT PAGE.

55. Cecil came <u>to</u> dread these weekly visits to his
          A

    <u>father</u>, since they always culminated <u>in</u> an
    B   C

    argument over <u>his</u> plans to sell the family
                   D

    business. <u>No error</u>
             E

56. <u>At</u> the counseling center, <u>a person</u> should feel
    A   B

    <u>free to</u> express their true emotions without fear
    C

    <u>of</u> ridicule or reprisal. <u>No error</u>
    D   E

57. <u>Conspicuously</u> absent <u>from</u> the vice-presiden-
       A   B

    tial debates <u>was</u> any mention of arms
             C

    reduction or the <u>so-called</u> peace dividend.
                  D

    <u>No error</u>
    E

58. As she turned the corner, Anne <u>quickened</u> her
                             A

    pace and reflected that if she <u>was</u> a man, she
                        B

    <u>would</u> not need to feel frightened when
    C

    <u>walking</u> alone at night. <u>No error</u>
    D   E

59. Blind Willy Blynde was <u>at least</u> as <u>famous for</u>
                        A   B

    his flamboyant personality and <u>scandalous</u>
                             C

    behavior <u>than</u> he was for his blues guitar.
            D

    <u>No error</u>
    E

60. The positivist view, <u>which</u> sees history as an
                  A

    <u>inexorable march</u> of progress <u>from</u> barbarism
           B   C

    to enlightenment, could <u>hardly</u> have survived
                      D

    the horrors and devastation of a World War I.

    <u>No error</u>
    E

STOP!

END OF TEST. DO NOT TURN THE PAGE UNTIL YOU ARE READY TO CHECK YOUR ANSWERS.

Practice Test 5 Answers and Explanations

The Essay Section

This section contains sample essays for the essay topic in Practice Test 5. Use these sample essays as benchmarks to help you grade your own essay on the same topic. Does your essay sound more like the grade 5 essay or the grade 3 essay?

Sample Grade 5 Essay

Running for the bus was one of those things that seem like a good idea at the time. Our school is located on the edge of town, five miles from my house. Miss the school bus, and you have a long wait ahead of you. And so when I saw that the rear of that yellow vehicle disappearing past the gymnasium, I automatically burst into a sprint across the car park to try and catch it. This seemed like a very good idea until Carl Lewis tripped and turned into the human torpedo, pitching headlong into the concrete and breaking his right arm in the process.

There are many things I will continue to take for granted in life, but the use of my right arm is not one of them. As a junior, many exams were looming in front of me which I needed to be able to write for. Not only did I have classes that I wanted to do well in. I had the PSAT coming up, and I couldn't even scrawl my name. At least, not in a form that people could read. Teachers were kind enough to let me borrow notes from other students, but I was definitely concerned about keeping up.

Of course, academic studies weren't the only area of my life effected by my broken arm. I had all these commitments to sports teams (football, basketball, etc.) that now had to play on without me. Boy was I concerned about that! There were some benefits to this however—I still wanted to stay involved while I got better, so I travelled with the teams and helped out organizationally. I was impatient to play again, but I realized that there is more to sport than putting on the number 19 jersey.

Breaking my arm definitely helped me value the use of my right arm, and my health in general. As the old saying goes, you don't know what you've got until you lose it. Next time I have a bright idea like running for the bus, I'll have another think coming!

Grader's comments: This essay fulfills the writing assignment with a high degree of competence. It shows an original approach to the topic and a solid grasp of structure. The writer picks good examples to support the argument, and occasional grammatical flaws and digressions do not detract from its overall effectiveness.

Sample Grade 3 Essay

One thing I will never take for granted is my favorite bands. Music has a major impact on people's lives. Almost everyone listens to it—for pleasure, relaxation and to be entertained. And yet, music is more than just popcorn for the ears. You can learn things from it. Some of the best bands have lyrics that are pretty intelligent—they tell a story or make a political statement. At its best, they can be almost as good as poetry.

My favorite example of a good songwriter is Sting, formerly in the Police. For years, Sting was an English teacher. Then he realized his dream to be a pop star with one of the biggest groups of the 1980s. His music was not like all the other groups—he didn't only write fluffy songs about falling in love. He had lyrics about the Cold War, unemployment and the rainforest. Additionally to the lyrics, he always used musicians of the highest calibber. Some of the best jazz musicians in New York ended up in his solo band producing sophisticated music indeed.

A lot of adults and learned people think that only classical music, opera and jaz are "art." I don't necessarily agree. I think that Sting's music shows that "pop" music can just as complicated and meaningful than so-called "art" forms. While many people take things for granted in life, I think music contributes heavily to our understanding of the world. For this reason, I'll never take pop music for granted.

Grader's comments: This essay demonstrates limited competence. In the first paragraph, the author's argument lacks some coherence. The author chooses good examples to illustrate points in paragraphs 2 and 3, but there are many lapses in grammar and logic.

Sample Grade 1 Essay

I definitely take a lot of things for granted. Movies, computer games and TV dinners are examples that spring to mind. Plenty of people globally don't have access to these. And we take them for granted—just like that! How would it be if someone came to our neighborhood and took all our convenience away? People would be in a sorry state, let me tell you. Immigrants show you that you can't take stuff for granted for a minute they come over here and work all hours of the day feeding their families. I think that plenty of people forgot that they where in the same position. That's the problem with the country today—too many people sitting on they're butts and not enough action. If I was elected mayor, this would be the first thing I'd fix and fast.

Grader's comments: This essay is deficient. Firstly, it fails to answer the basic question posed in the topic: "One thing I have learned never to take for granted is ___." Secondly, the author's ideas are not adequately developed. Thirdly, there are many errors in usage and syntax.

The Multiple-Choice Section

This section contains an answer key and explanations for the Multiple-Choice section in Practice Test 5. Use the scoring conversion table in the back of the book to see how you've done on this section. Pay careful attention to the explanations for the multiple-choice questions you got wrong.

1. D	11. D	21. C	31. B	41. B	51. C
2. C	12. E	22. A	32. D	42. D	52. E
3. B	13. A	23. B	33. E	43. C	53. A
4. B	14. D	24. B	34. C	44. A	54. B
5. E	15. C	25. C	35. B	45. D	55. D
6. A	16. A	26. E	36. D	46. A	56. B
7. E	17. D	27. D	37. C	47. C	57. E
8. D	18. E	28. A	38. B	48. C	58. B
9. D	19. D	29. C	39. B	49. E	59. D
10. A	20. C	30. A	40. A	50. E	60. E

Answers and Explanations

1. (D)—An idiom error—watch out for those little connecting words on test day. The sentence should read *he hoped to have*, not *he hoped for having*.

2. (C)—The past participle of *drink* is *drunk*, so the sentence should read *they had drunk* the last of the water. *Drank* is the simple past tense: "they drank the water."

3. (B)—A tricky one, since the subject follows the verb: *the cessation . . . and the development* is a compound subject requiring the plural verb *were*.

4. (B)—Whose collection of documents was it? It is not clear from the sentence whether *his* refers to Raoul or to Frederick; hence this is a case of vague pronoun reference.

5. (E)—The sentence contains no error.

6. (A)—There is no such word as *irregardless*. People who make this mistake are probably conflating *irrespective* and *regardless*, either of which would be correct here.

7. (E)—The sentence contains no error.

8. (D)—Because the third verb in this list of monastic goals is in a different form from the other two verbs, it ruins the parallelism of the sentence. The sentence should read *so that they might pray . . . pursue . . . and attain*.

9. (D)—Another idiom problem here. *Participate* takes the preposition *in*, not *with*.

10. (A)—The pronoun should be *whom* rather than *who*, because it is the object of the verb *nominated*. (*Who* should only be used when the pronoun is the verb's subject.) If in doubt about whether to use *who* or *whom*, try reversing the sentence: you'd say the president nominated *him*, not the president nominated *he*.

11. (D)—If a verb is underlined, always check that it agrees with the subject. Here, the second verb should be *is* to agree with its singular subject, *practice*.

12. (E)—The sentence contains no error.

13. (A)—In standard written English, it is unacceptable to use *hopefully* as a shorthand substitute for "I hope," even though we frequently use it this way in casual conversation. *Hopefully* should only be used as an adverb (e.g., "She smiled hopefully").

14. (D)—The sentence sets up an illogical comparison: One cannot compare one person's *work* to another *person*, only to that person's work. Therefore, the sentence should end with David Mamet's (in other words, with *David Mamet*'s work).

15. (C)—The antecedent of the possessive pronoun *their* is *any parent*. Since *parent* is singular, the pronoun should be *his or her*.

16. (A)—When speaking of things that can be numbered, such as guns, you should use *fewer* rather than *less*. For instance, you would say "fewer items" but "less money," because money has no plural (you'd never say *two moneys*).

17. (D)—False compound subject: the verb should be *hinders* (singular) to agree with *loneliness*, which is the real subject of this sentence. Remember that *x along with y* constructions are never compound subjects.

18. (E)—The sentence contains no error.

19. (D)—The adjective *quick* should be replaced with the adverb *quickly*, because it modifies the verb *was . . . proceeding*.

20. (C)—*Not scarcely* is a double negative.

21. (C)—(C) is the only choice which corrects this run-on sentence in a logical way: *Known for his aphoristic wit and brilliant conversation* introduces Oscar Wilde; the rest of the sentence provides additional information about him. (B) contains a fragment, (D) is a run-on which presents an illogical contrast between Wilde's wit and his writing, and (E) is extremely garbled.

22. (A)—The sentence is correct: *Maintaining* and *securing* are in the proper parallel form (both gerunds). (B) is convoluted and slightly alters the meaning of the sentence. (C) is a fragment. (D) is

verbose and tangled. (E) has sacrificed correct parallel structure for the sake of brevity, comparing *the appearance* (a noun) to *securing* (a gerund).

23. (B)—The sentence contains a misplaced modifier: *Once an enclave of privileged white males* refers to *the Wodehouse Club*, not to its *directors*. Choice (B) correctly places the modifying phrase right next to the thing it's describing. (C) and (D) do not correct the misplaced modifier, and (D) is a fragment. (E) is poorly worded, and the verb has does not agree with the subject, *directors*.

24. (B)—What actually occurred when alcohol was banned turned out to be the opposite of what the prohobitionists had envisioned. Drinking continued (illegally) and crime actually increased. Therefore, you're looking for words that will express this ironic contrast between the idea and the reality. *In fact* is the best choice. (D) is wrong because although *but* expresses a contrast, it also creates a fragment (*but* must follow a comma, not a semicolon). (A), (C), and (E) fail to express the logical contrast between the two halves of the sentence.

25. (C)—What is being compared here? You can't compare an action (*watching* a video) to an object (*a book*)—it's not logical and it violates the rules of parallelism. (C) corrects the sentence by putting the two activities in parallel form. (B) fails to fix the parallelism problem, and it introduces strange and unnecessary changes in verb tense. (D) is awkwardly phrased (would you say "book-reading"?), and (E) also fails to fix the parallelism problem, creating a somewhat confusing comparison.

26. (E)—To correct this sentence fragment, all you need to do is insert the helping verb *is* before the participle based. *Based, being based,* and *basing* are all verb forms that cannot stand on their own as a sentence's main verb.

27. (D)—The underlined portion of the sentence is wordy and awkward. (D) expresses the same thought in a clearer, more concise way. (B) and (E) are just as convoluted as the original sentence, and (C) is a fragment.

28. (A)—The sentence is fine as it is. (B) is a run-on. (C) and (E) contain plural pronouns that don't agree with their singular antecedents, and (D) makes no sense grammatically.

29. (C)—The donors expect to be rewarded with two things: *special favors* and *easy access*. For the sake of parallelism, both these things should be expressed in the same grammatial form: adjective + noun. The other choices are wordy and lack parallel structure; (E) is also redundant.

30. (A)—The first clause of the sentence correctly sets up a condition which was not fulfilled: Churchill did not send planes to defend Coventry, and hence the Nazis did not realize the allies had broken their code. (A) is another way of saying *If Churchill had sent planes to defend Coventry*. (B) is gramatically unsound: "if he would have" is a very common error. Watch out for it! (C) and (E) are fragments, and (D) uses a wrong verb tense (*sent* for the past perfect *had sent*).

31. (B)—The conjunction *although* correctly expresses the contrast that is implied here: television shows were formerly given time to build up an audience, but now they are not. (A) and (D) are run-on sentences, and (C) and (E) are illogical.

32. (D)—The opening phrase describes Savka, but the way the sentence is phrased, it sounds as though *the desperate poverty* is returning home after a 20-year absence. You know the correct answer will begin with *Savka* to correct the misplaced modifier. (C) is a sentence fragment, so (D) is the correct answer.

33. (E)—Only (E) correctly subordinates the second clause to the first. (A) is a run-on, (B) incorrectly uses *which* to refer to people, (C) and (D) create nonsensical sentences.

34. (C)—The phrase *by the time you leave* is the clue to the sentence's meaning. Some time in the future you will leave the camp, but before that happens, you will complete a manuscript. To express this sequence of events clearly, you need to use the future perfect tense: *you will have completed*.

35. (B)—A thought that is introduced by *such* must be completed by *that*. (Just remember that *such . . . . that* is one of those expressions consisting of words that always go together, like *neither . . . nor*.)

36. (D)—The sentence as it stands contains a fragment before the semicolon and a run-on after it. Choices (B), (C), and (E) are all awkward and ungrammatical.

37. (C)—*Having read the works* describes the speaker, so you know that the correct answer will have *I* as the first word (the way the sentence is written, it sounds as though *Hemingway* read the works, because his name is placed directly after the modifying phrase). Only (C) and (E) begin with *I*, but (E) introduces yet another misplaced modifier (it says the speaker is a writer, not Hemingway).

38. (B)—The key to this question is realizing what Aunt Helga appreciates: it's not *us*, but our act of coming to her birthday party. *Our coming* correctly phrases this idea; *coming* is a gerund (a verb form that acts as a noun), and *our* is a possessive pronoun. *Us coming* is a common mistake; it's wrong because the pronoun *us* is not in the possessive form.

39. (B)—Remember that the phrase *not only* needs to be followed by *but* or *but also*. (B) completes the thought begun with the *not only* clause, and it also uses *such as* to introduce the examples, which is less wordy and more graceful than the phrasing of the original sentence. The other answer choices are wordy and awkward, and they do not introduce the second clause with the required *but*. (Note, too, that *everyone* has been changed to a plural noun to agree with the plural pronoun *their*.)

40. (A)—You're looking for a sentence that sums up the actions of other kids' parents (i.e., sending their kids to fashionable resorts) to set up a contrast with the author's father's decision. Choice (A) expresses this idea. Choice (B) sets up an illogical comparison—between the choices of friends and the choices of parents. Choice (C) has a misplaced modifier—Dad wasn't being sent to a camp. (D) has a vague linking phrase—it's not clear from the preceding sentence what "this situation" might refer to. (E) is also too vague a transition (*do the same as what?*). Since the previous sentence refers to students, you need a linking sentence that focuses on parents' decisions, as (A) does.

41. (B)—*Regarded as one of the least fit students in my class* describes the author, not the summer. All the other choices contain misplaced modifiers, and (D) and (E) are not complete sentences.

42. (D)—You have a list of three things, all of which should be in parallel grammatical form. The first item in the list (which you can't change) sets the pattern that the other two must follow: *a [quantity] of [plural noun]*. Only choice (D) puts the other two list items in this form: *a handful of camp fire sing-alongs, and many a·burst blister*. It is also concise rather than wordy (notice that it's the shortest answer choice).

43. (C)—Since the author clearly means to say that the interesting conversations were a result of the counselors' being from all over the world, you need a word that expresses cause and effect. *Since* is the only option that does this in a grammatical way. (D)'s *consequently* presents cause-and-effect, but without a semicolon it creates a run-on sentence. (A) and (E) are illogical (you aren't looking for a contrast here), and (B) is awkward and wordy.

44. (A)—Choice (A) sums up the author's main point: though he dreaded the rigors of this remote camp, he found, to his surprise, that he enjoyed his summer there. (B) contradicts the passage, because the author indicates at the beginning of the passage that he *had been* interested in fashionable

resorts. (C) and (E) take elements of the passage and distort them—money's not mentioned, and the author didn't face challenges alone in New Hampshire. Finally, (D) contradicts the passage, because we know that the author did NOT start camp with a positive attitude.

45. (D)—The sentence contains a misplaced modifier, which (D) corrects by placing *the last great superpower* next to the noun it describes: the U.S. (B) is a distortion of what the author is trying to say. (C) is a sentence fragment. (E) is passive, wordy, and terribly convoluted—rule out such choices on test day!

46. (A)—The question is an effective rhetorical device here. In effect, the rest of the essay is spent trying to answer it. The author goes on to examine both sides of the issue, presenting the pros and cons of designating the United States as the world's peacekeeper, and finally decides on a qualified "no" answer. (B) is inconsistent with the author's logic in the second half of the essay. (C) does not provide an effective transition; it's too much of a jarring contrast to the next few sentences, in which the author enumerates the reasons for America's traditional role as peacekeeper. (D) is inconsistent with the author's logic (the author does, in fact, refute these arguments). And (E) strays far from the topic of the essay, bringing in extraneous and irrelevant information.

47. (C)—The sentence as it stands is a run-on, and if you look closely you'll notice that it's also slightly illogical. It's saying that *because* we fought for our rights, we believe that every country deserves the same—to fight for its rights! The two ideas are closely related, but the second is not a direct result of the first. Rather, both things (one, that we fought for our democratic rights, and two, that we think other people deserve democratic rights) are a consequence of our general belief that equality is a good thing. Therefore, *and* is a better connecting word here—choice (C). (D) merely reproduces the original error (run-on), (B) retains the ambiguity of the original sentence, and (E) is illogical, wordy, and awkward.

48. (C)—In the first half of paragraph 2, the author presents the arguments for America's playing a peacemaker role. With sentence 10, the author shifts gears and begins presenting the counter-argument. The rest of the passage builds a case *against* America's playing the sole peacekeeper and intervening in every situation. Therefore, this would be the most logical place for a paragraph break: whenever you introduce a new idea, topic, or line of reasoning, you should begin a new paragraph. You might have been tempted to pick (D), placing the transition sentence at the end of paragraph 2 rather than at the beginning of paragraph 3. This choice, however, would leave the final paragraph without a topic sentence, and readers would think that sentence 10 was introducing a paragraph about Vietnam.

49. (E)—The original sentence has a couple of problems—the *so . . . as* construction violates the common pair *as . . . as*, and the final phrase *not every battle can be won* is passive. Choice (E) is the most direct and concise rewording of the sentence. The other choices are wordy and awkward. Notice that (B) *has cannot* written as two words, which is incorrect, and (C) uses inappropriate verb tenses.

50. (E)—Though the passage is about foreign policy, the author doesn't quote the views of specific politicians anywhere in the passage—so (E)'s the answer here. Let's check off the remaining choices. The author uses (A) an analogy (comparing the United States to the hero in a Clint Eastwood movie) as well as a (B) rhetorical question (sentence 4). The entire essay consists of an analysis of two sides of an issue (C), and there are plenty of examples drawn from U.S. history (D).

51. (C)—Another idiom error: the sentence should read *accede to* (meaning "agree to"), not *accede with*.

52. (E)—The sentence contains no error.

53. (A)—*Phenomena* is the plural form of *phenomenon*, which would be the correct word here. Other plural nouns commonly mistaken for singulars include *alumni* (plural of *alumnus*), *media* (plural of *medium*), and *criteria* (plural of *criterion*).

54. (B)—So *great* should be followed by *that*, not *as*.

55. (D)—A case of ambiguous pronoun reference. From the sentence, it's not clear whether Cecil or his father is planning to *sell the family business*.

56. (B)—The subject should be the plural noun *people* in order to agree in number with the pronoun *their*.

57. (E)—The sentence contains no error. The verb *was* agrees with its subject, *mention*.

58. (B)—It's clear from the sentence that Anne is not a man; therefore, the *if* clause is setting up a condition that is contrary to fact. In a conditional sentence, when the *if* clause is contrary-to-fact, you must use *if she were* rather than *if she was*. (This is called the "subjunctive mood" of the verb, but you don't have to know that terminology. The subjunctive mood is also what you see in sentences like "It is important that all employees *be* on time." Fortunately, its use in English is pretty rare.)

59. (D)—Idiomatically, the comparison should be *as famous . . . as* (not *than*).

60. (E)—The sentence contains no error.

COMPUTE YOUR SCORE

Your SAT II: Writing Test score report will reflect three different scores: an essay subscore, a multiple-choice subscore, and an overall score, the most important of the three. Here are step-by-step instructions for calculating subscores and overall scores for the practice tests in this book.

Don't take these scores too literally. Practice test conditions cannot precisely mirror real test conditions. Your actual SAT II: Writing scores will almost certainly vary from your practice test scores. Your score on the practice tests will give you a rough idea of your range on the actual exam.

Step 1: Calculate your essay subscore.

Read through your essay carefully and use the Essay Grading Criteria to assign a 1–6 score to it. Better still, have a parent, older sibling, or trusted teacher read the essay and assign a score. Then, double the 1–6 score to get your raw essay score. (You'll use this raw essay score to calculate your overall 200–800 score in Step 3.) Use the table called "Find Your Essay Subscore" to convert this raw score into a 20–80 scaled score. (The essay subscore is a stand-alone score.)

Essay Grading Criteria

⑥ **Outstanding Essay**—convincingly and insightfully fulfills the writing assignment; ideas are well developed, clearly presented, and logically organized; superior command of vocabulary, grammar, style, and accepted conventions of writing; a few minor flaws may occur.

⑤ **Solid Essay**—convincingly fulfills the writing assignment; ideas are adequately developed, clearly presented, and logically organized; strong command of vocabulary, grammar, style, and accepted conventions of writing; some minor flaws may occur.

④ **Adequate Essay**—fulfills the writing assignment; ideas are adequately developed, presented, and organized; satisfactory command of vocabulary, grammar, style, and accepted conventions of writing; some flaws may occur.

③ **Limited Essay**—doesn't adequately fulfill the writing assignment; ideas aren't adequately developed, clearly presented, or logically organized; unsatisfactory command of vocabulary, grammar, style, and accepted conventions of writing; contains many flaws.

② **Flawed Essay**—doesn't fulfill the writing assignment; ideas are vague, poorly presented, and not logically organized; poor command of vocabulary, grammar, style, and accepted conventions of writing; contains numerous serious flaws.

① **Deficient Essay**—doesn't fulfill the writing assignment; ideas are extremely vague, very poorly presented, and not logically organized; extremely poor command of vocabulary, grammar, style, and accepted conventions of writing; is so seriously flawed that basic meaning is obscured.

	ESSAY SCORE	RAW ESSAY SCORE	ESSAY SUBSCORE
TEST 1:	☐ x 2	= ☐	☐
TEST 2:	☐ x 2	= ☐	☐
TEST 3:	☐ x 2	= ☐	☐
TEST 4:	☐ x 2	= ☐	☐
TEST 5:	☐ x 2	= ☐	☐

Find Your Essay Subscore

Raw Essay Score	Essay Subscore
12	72
11	66
10	61
9	55
8	49
7	43
6	38
5	34
4	31
3	27
2	24
0	21

Step 2: Find your multiple-choice subscore.

Refer to your practice test answer sheet for the number of questions you answered right and the number you answered wrong. You can use the chart on the next page to calculate your raw score: Multiply the number wrong by .25, and subtract the result from the number right. Round your raw score to the nearest whole number. Use the table on the next page to find your multiple-choice subscore based on your raw score.

	NUMBER CORRECT	NUMBER WRONG	RAW MULTIPLE-CHOICE SCORE	MULTIPLE-CHOICE SUBSCORE
TEST 1:	☐	– (.25 x ☐)	= ☐ (ROUNDED)	☐
TEST 2:	☐	– (.25 x ☐)	= ☐ (ROUNDED)	☐
TEST 3:	☐	– (.25 x ☐)	= ☐ (ROUNDED)	☐
TEST 4:	☐	– (.25 x ☐)	= ☐ (ROUNDED)	☐
TEST 5:	☐	– (.25 x ☐)	= ☐ (ROUNDED)	☐

Find Your Multiple-Choice Subscore

Raw Score	Subscore	Raw Score	Subscore
60	80	25	43
59	78	24	43
58	78	23	43
57	75	22	42
56	74	21	41
55	72	20	40
54	72	19	39
53	71	18	38
52	70	17	38
51	68	16	37
50	66	15	37
49	65	14	36
48	63	13	36
47	62	12	35
46	61	11	34
45	61	10	33
44	60	9	32
43	59	8	31
42	58	7	31
41	57	6	30
40	56	5	29
39	55	4	28
38	54	3	27
37	53	2	26
36	52	1	25
35	51	0	24
34	50	–1	23
33	49	–2	22
32	48	–3	21
31	48	–4	20
30	47	–5	20
29	46	–6	20
28	45	–7	20
27	44		
26	44		

Step 3: Find your overall score.

Multiply your raw essay score (from Step 1) by 3. Then add this number to your raw multiple-choice score from Step 2. The total of these two numbers is called the raw composite score. Use the following table to find your overall score based on your raw composite score.

	RAW ESSAY SCORE	RAW MULTIPLE-CHOICE SCORE	RAW COMPOSITE SCORE	OVERALL SCORE
TEST 1:	(☐ X 3)	+ ☐	= ☐	☐
TEST 2:	(☐ X 3)	+ ☐	= ☐	☐
TEST 3:	(☐ X 3)	+ ☐	= ☐	☐
TEST 4:	(☐ X 3)	+ ☐	= ☐	☐
TEST 5:	(☐ X 3)	+ ☐	= ☐	☐

Find Your Overall Score

Raw Composite Score	Overall Score	Raw Composite Score	Overall Score	Raw Composite Score	Overall Score	Raw Composite Score	Overall Score
96	800	71	610	46	440	21	290
95	800	70	600	45	430	20	280
94	790	69	590	44	430	19	280
93	790	68	590	43	420	18	270
92	780	67	580	42	420	17	260
91	780	66	570	41	410	16	260
90	770	65	560	40	410	15	250
89	770	64	560	39	400	14	240
88	760	63	550	38	390	13	230
87	750	62	540	37	380	12	230
86	740	61	530	36	370	11	220
85	740	60	530	35	360	10	210
84	730	59	520	34	350	9	210
83	720	58	520	33	350	8	200
82	710	57	510	32	340	7	200
81	700	56	500	31	340	6	200
80	690	55	500	30	330	5	200
79	680	54	490	29	330	4	200
78	670	53	480	28	320	3	200
77	660	52	480	27	320	2	200
76	650	51	470	26	310	1	200
75	640	50	460	25	310	−1	200
74	630	49	450	24	300	−2	200
73	620	48	450	23	300	−3	200
72	620	47	440	22	290	−4	200

NOTES

NOTES

NOTES

NOTES

How Did We Do? Grade Us.

Thank you for choosing a Kaplan book. Your comments and suggestions are very useful to us. Please answer the following questions to assist us in our continued development of high-quality resources to meet your needs. Or go online and complete our interactive survey form at **kaplansurveys.com/books**.

The title of the Kaplan book I read was: _____

My name is: _____

My address is: _____

_____

My e-mail address is: _____

What overall grade would you give this book?   (A)   (B)   (C)   (D)   (F)

How relevant was the information to your goals?   (A)   (B)   (C)   (D)   (F)

How comprehensive was the information in this book?   (A)   (B)   (C)   (D)   (F)

How accurate was the information in this book?   (A)   (B)   (C)   (D)   (F)

How easy was the book to use?   (A)   (B)   (C)   (D)   (F)

How appealing was the book's design?   (A)   (B)   (C)   (D)   (F)

What were the book's strong points? _____

How could this book be improved? _____

Is there anything that we left out that you wanted to know more about?

Would you recommend this book to others?   ☐ YES   ☐ NO

Other comments: _____

_____

_____

Do we have permission to quote you?   ☐ YES   ☐ NO

Thank you for your help.
Please tear out this page and mail it to:

Managing Editor
Kaplan, Inc.
1440 Broadway, 8th floor
New York, NY 10018

KAPLAN

Thanks!

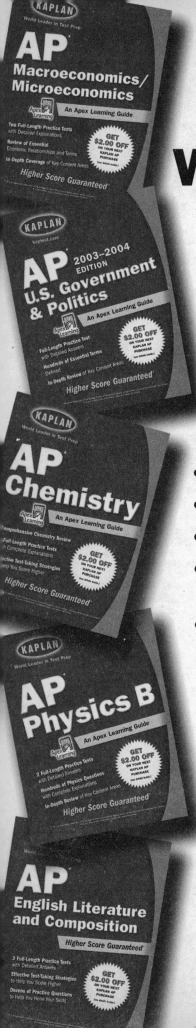
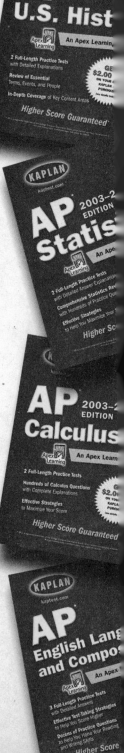